# Sex, Marriage and Society

# Sex, Marriage and Society

*Advisory Editors*

Charles Rosenberg

Carroll Smith-Rosenberg

# MARRIAGE

# AND

# PARENTAGE

Henry C. Wright

ARNO PRESS
A New York Times Company
New York — 1974

HQ
31
.W95
1974

Reprint Edition 1974 by Arno Press Inc.

SEX, MARRIAGE AND SOCIETY
ISBN for complete set: 0-405-05790-3
See last pages of this volume for titles.

Manufactured in the United States of America

**Library of Congress Cataloging in Publication Data**

Wright, Henry Clarke, 1797-1870.
  Marriage and parentage.

  (Sex, marriage, and society)
  Reprint of the 2d. ed. published in 1855 by B. Marsh,
Boston under title: Marriage and parentage; or, The
reproductive element in man as a mens to his elevation
and happiness.
  1. Sexual ethics.  2. Hygiene, Sexual.  I. Title.
II. Series.  [DNLM:  HQ W949m 1855]
HQ31.W95     1974     301.42     73-20651
ISBN 0-405-05823-3

# MARRIAGE AND PARENTAGE

"My Wee Darling."

# MARRIAGE AND PARENTAGE:

OR,

# The Reproductive Element in Man,

AS A MEANS TO HIS

# ELEVATION AND HAPPINESS.

By HENRY C. WRIGHT.

Second Edition,

---

THE PRESENT IS THE CHILD OF THE PAST, —
THE PARENT OF THE FUTURE.

---

BOSTON:
PUBLISHED BY BELA MARSH,
No. 9 FRANKLIN STREET.
1855.

Entered according to Act of Congress, in the year eighteen hundred and fifty four,

BY HENRY C. WRIGHT,

in the Clerk's office of the District Court of the District of Massachusetts.

# PREFACE.

Man has power to understand and appreciate whatever is essential to his welfare. The Reproductive Element is that to which the author of the following pages looks as the Heaven-appointed means, not only to perpetuate, but to refine, to elevate and perfect the race. To ascertain the nature of that element, its action on the body and soul, when retained in the system; the only natural and justifiable object of its expenditure; the natural laws that are designed to govern it; how it can be made most conducive to the improvement of the organization, character and destiny of man, and most helpful to his individual progress; — these are subjects which must ere long command the attention and respect of every true man and woman.

The author has considered this element, not as a means of sensual enjoyment, but solely as an instrumentality through which Human Nature may be redeemed from its diseases and its miseries. To those who regard and use it as a means of mere sensual pleasure, he can only say, they have their reward. Nature will be true to herself, and, in due time, vindicate her violated laws. There is no peace to those who disregard her behests; there can be none. But to those who seek to know her laws, especially in regard to the government of their sexual nature, and who conscientiously aim to obey them, she will manifest her richest favors and her purest delights.

To create a conscience in men and women, as to the use of their sexual nature and relations, is the great end at which the ensuing work aims. This is *the* want, in every class of society. Men and women have tender consciences about the use of other organs and elements of their natures. In the family, in the school, and from the pulpit, the appeal is ever being made to the child, the youth and the man, to bring them under the control of reason and conscience. But what is done by these sources of instruction to bring the sexual element under the government of an enlightened reason and a tender conscience? No other element in our nature has so much to do in deciding our birthright conditions of soul and body, and in forming our character and shaping our destiny; yet in regard to no one are children and youth, and men and women, left in such bewildering ignorance as in reference to this, or so much at the mercy of blind, reckless, animal passion.

In the first part of the following work, the author has endeavored to give the scientific facts in regard to the function of Reproduction in the human being, and to show that parents, alone, are responsible for the existence, the organization and constitutional tendencies of the bodies and souls of their children.

The second part — the Correspondence between

a Husband and a Wife—considers the laws by which the sexual element should be governed in the marriage relation, and how it may be made subservient to life, health and happiness, or productive of disease and wretchedness, to parents and children.

This work must speak for itself. So far as it belongs to the Present, it will be found on the tables, in the hands and in the hearts of all who are able to appreciate and to obtain it; so far as it belongs to the ages of the Future, it will be found on the tables, in the hands and in the hearts of those who, in the "good time coming," shall be able rightly to value and use it. Calmly it goes forth, earnestly to do its work, without anxiety as to its ultimate effect.

HENRY C. WRIGHT.

# CONTENTS.

## PART I.

LETTER I. INTRODUCTION .......................... 9

LETTER II. DISTINCTION OF SEX. In what it consists — Its extent — Its object............................ 21

LETTER III. THE REPRODUCTIVE SYSTEM. Office of the Male — Office of the Female — Spermatic Secretion — Spermatozoa — Ovaries — Periodical function of the Female; its relation to her health and happiness........ 28

LETTER IV. DEVELOPMENT OF THE FETUS. Nutrition before Birth — Fetal Circulation — Connection between Nutrition and Reproduction ....................... 40

LETTER V. THE HUMAN SOUL. Its origin, nature, and relations to the body — Science of Society — Communion of Soul with Soul.................................. 54

LETTER VI. TRANSMISSION OF DISEASE. Hereditary conditions — Acquired conditions — Conditions of the Mother during Gestation and Lactation — Illustrative Facts... 66

LETTER VII. THE WELCOME CHILD. Parentage the result of conscientious Forethought, not of reckless Passion.. 90

LETTER VIII. THE UNWELCOME CHILD. Questions to be asked and answered in the Future of this World — Results of Sexual Abuse to Parents and Children........101

LETTER IX. EXISTENCE OF CHILDREN. To whose agency is it to be attributed? — Who is responsible for it? — A fatal popular Error............................115

## PART II.

CORRESPONDENCE BETWEEN A HUSBAND AND WIFE.

| | | | |
|---|---|---|---:|
| LETTER | I. | FIDELITY TO OUR NATURE............... | 137 |
| LETTER | II. | THE MISSION OF THE SEXES............. | 142 |
| LETTER | III. | WHAT IS MARRIAGE?................... | 165 |
| LETTER | IV. | PERPETUITY OF MARRIAGE............... | 175 |
| LETTER | V. | VARIETY IN LOVE, OR POLYGAMY......... | 182 |
| LETTER | VI. | DIVORCE............................. | 188 |
| LETTER | VII. | THE TRANSIENT AND PERMANENT IN MARRIAGE | 204 |
| LETTER | VIII. | HARMONY OF DEVELOPMENT.............. | 211 |
| LETTER | IX. | LOVE AND PASSION..................... | 219 |

LETTER X. THE REPRODUCTIVE ELEMENT. Its Expenditure governed by fixed laws...................... 225

LETTER XI. THE REPRODUCTIVE ELEMENT. Its Expenditure governed by Mutual Love..................... 234

LETTER XII. THE REPRODUCTIVE ELEMENT. Its Expenditure to be governed by the conditions of the Wife... 242

LETTER XIII. THE REPRODUCTIVE ELEMENT. Is Offspring the only justifiable end of its Expenditure?......... 256

LETTER XIV. GESTATION AND LACTATION. Treatment of the Wife by the Husband during these periods....... 275

LETTER XV. HOME AND ITS INFLUENCE............... 289

## APPENDIX.

THE SEXUAL ELEMENT. Its natural use — Its abuse...... 321

# PART I.

## INTRODUCTORY LETTER.

Lenawee, June, 1852.

Dear Friend:

Of all men, my spirit turns to you, when I would deliberate and act for the improvement of mankind. We have so long acted in harmony, in our practical efforts to remove the evils that afflict the race, by the introduction of truer and more elevated views of human beings, and their relations and ultimate destiny, that I feel impelled to address the following series of letters to you. I arrange my thoughts in the form of letters to a living friend, because I can express myself more freely when I am thus speaking, than when I am speaking to mankind in general.

What shall we do to be saved? The past has given one answer to this question; the future will give another. I will endeavor to anticipate the answer which the future of this world will give to this important question. What can *we* do to raise the entire human being to the highest point of perfection which it is capable of attaining? Man has certain capabilities. He is designed to be, and should be, as wise, good, beautiful and happy, as he is capable of being. What can we do to make him what he was designed to be? — to enable him to work out for himself perfect salvation?

I speak not of happiness in the next state, but in this. When we enter the next state, then it will be our business to inquire into the conditions of life, health and happiness there, and to comply with them. But while we are here, our sole business is to acquaint ourselves with the laws or conditions of present life and health, and to comply with them. Then shall we be, now, all we are capable of being. Fidelity to ourselves, in this world, is the only true preparation for the next. A religion that promises all things in the future, but does nothing to improve and elevate our nature and condition in the present, is not adapted to our present necessities. To know the fixed, natural conditions of present life and health, to our whole nature, and to be true to them, is "the chief end of man," while in this state. Our prayer to the great Father should be, "Thy kingdom come," — *now*, not in the indefinite future; "Thy will be done," — *on earth*, not in some unknown future state. This prayer is truly answered only in those who understand and obey the laws of being under which they now exist. The kingdom of heaven is within those, and only those, who understand and comply with the conditions of present life and health to body and soul. This is salvation; nothing else is.

To save our bodies from being victimized by disease, it is thought to be essential that doctors should have a certain knowledge of the human physical organism, and of the laws and conditions of its life and health. So, to save the soul, it is deemed important that priests should have a certain amount of knowledge of the laws and conditions of life and health under which it exists. Whatever knowledge is necessary to enable a man to be a doctor or a priest, is necessary for each and every human being, to enable them to be healthy and true men and women. If a man needs a certain amount of knowledge concerning the physical organism, to enable him to *cure* disease, much more does each one need that same knowledge, to enable him to *prevent* disease. Whatever it is necessary for priests to know to *cure* crime, each one should know to enable him to *prevent* it. The prevention of disease and crime is more important to human welfare than their cure. Violations of Nature's laws constitute man's only source of disease to body and soul. Where there is no violation of *natural* law, there is no disease, no sin. It is, therefore, as necessary that each human being should have a perfect knowledge of the anatomy and physiology of the human system, and all the laws and conditions of physical life and health, as it is that a few should have it, to enable them to be doctors. It is as necessary that each one should perfectly understand the laws and conditions of health and happiness to the soul, as it is that a few should understand them, to qualify them to be priests. Those who attain to a knowledge of the laws of life and health to body and soul, and live accordingly, have become reconciled to themselves, have found the true comforter, and entered into rest. THEY ARE SAVED.

We live for the race, in all coming time. We cannot live only for ourselves, or for the present state, nation, or age. The principles we adopt, and the practices we pursue, must bear on the race, for good or evil, while man exists. There is no isolation for an individual man or woman. Our nature identifies our existence and happiness with that of the human family. Whatever principle or maxim of life it would benefit the race to adopt and carry out, it is the duty of each individual to adopt and carry out, as soon as he understands it. Whatever would be injurious to the race, if all were to adopt and practice it, it is the duty of each to shun. Would it be for the security and happiness of the whole human family, if all were Non-Resistants in spirit and practice? Then is each one bound, at once, to cease from all violence, to put away wrath, revenge, and all deadly weapons, and to be gentle and kind, loving and forgiving, and learn war no more. Would it be better for the race, if Alcohol, as a beverage, were never more to be used? Then should each and every one abstain, at once and for ever, from its use. Would it have been better for the human family had there never been a slave? Then is it the duty of each and every one to be Abolitionists, and to seek the immediate overthrow of slavery, and of whatever, in Church or State, sanctions or sustains it. In all things, the true man will regard himself as the representative of the race, and will be sternly just and true to himself, because only in so doing can he be just and true to all of human kind.

It is certain that all human improvement must result from human effort. This maxim is recognised and acted on by all, in reference to our outward surroundings; but as to internal, organic soundness and vigor, men think but little of it. Practically, it is denied that man has any control over his constitutional tendencies of body or soul, and affirmed that these are determined by a power with which he has no strength to contend, and which is beyond the reach of all human agency.

Man recognises his power to beautify, strengthen and improve the nature and quality of all animated and vegetable beings and things beneath himself. There is not a grass, a flower, or a fruit, whose nature he cannot elevate, when he attempts to do so. There is not a domestic animal whose nature and qualities he does not successfully attempt to improve. Man, alone, is neglected. Human nature, it is thought, can be regenerated by God alone. Human efforts are thought to be unavailing, when directed to develop and strengthen the tendencies of the human body and soul to perfection of health and happiness, and to assimilate the human to the divine.

It is admitted that the conduct, character and destiny of the human being depend on his organization and development. A healthy organization may be placed in a situation in which it cannot be perfectly developed. A diseased organization, on the contrary, may be placed in circumstances in which the organic or constitutional imperfection may be, in a measure, remedied by circumstantial influences. But how can this world ever be peopled by true and perfect men and women, so long as the organization and the development are both wrong?

A perfect organization and a perfect development are the right of every child. This is what future generations have a right to demand of the present. This right of the child, of all other natural rights of their children, parents are bound most sacredly to respect. This demand of the future, the present is bound to heed, as the most sacred and imperative.

What can we do to secure to future generations a more perfect organization and a more perfect development? All systems of philosophy, morals and religion, thus far, have given essentially the same answer to this question. They have directed man to a power outside of himself. They have failed to acquaint man with the laws of life and health, and to induce him to obey them. Another, and a more appropriate and potent remedy, must be had. It is the work of the present age to discover and apply it.

My appeal is to those who are born, in behalf of the unborn. Those who now exist are beyond the reach of the power to which I would call attention, as the means through which the human being is to be redeemed. They have their birthright inheritance, be it for weal or wo. So far as it can be directly influenced by the conditions of the parents, their organization is accomplished. All that can be done further for them, is to give them as fair a chance for healthful growth as may be, and to do what can be done to remedy the evils of a bad organization by a healthful development. But the present can do much for the future; the living, for those who are to live. There are many ways in which they can do it. Every generation is more or less affected by the external conditions entailed upon it by its predecessors. The sun, the atmosphere, the earth, water and electricity, are the common inheritance of each successive age; but in skill to apply these to the use of man, generations differ. Great improvements have been made, in making these physical elements conducive to human welfare. We shall bequeath to those who succeed us, all our improvements in the use of water, in the shape of steam, to propel machinery in the manufacture of food and clothing, and in transporting ourselves and goods on railways and steamships. Our improvements in erecting houses, and in education, in short, all that gives us control over the elements in and on which we live, we shall transmit to the future. In this respect, our relation to posterity is very important, inasmuch as human happiness, in every respect, is so materially affected by outward surroundings. Every improvement of each age, in agriculture, in mechanics, in manufactures, in the arts, in facilities for procuring the necessaries, comforts and elegancies of life, is so much gain to the next age.

But the present sustains a more direct and powerful relation to the future than that which is felt through these external arrangements. Children inherit not only the farms, the roads, the houses and barns, the orchards and gardens, the flowers and fruits, the social, political and religious maxims and institutions of their parents, but also their *bodies* and *souls*. It is certainly for this generation to say what kind of outward conditions the next shall receive from them. It is as certain that this age must determine what conditions of body and soul are to be the birthright portion of the next. To improve the human being — to beautify and ennoble the nature we bear, and present a more perfect and exalted type of manhood and womanhood — is the one great object at which philanthropy and all true religion will aim. Exterior surroundings are useless, except as they conduce to this end. What power have parents over the organization of their child? What influence have organization and constitutional tendencies on the character and destiny? In proportion as character and destiny are affected by organization, and in proportion as organization is affected by parental conditions, so is the control of parents over the destiny of their child, so is the power of the present over the happiness of the future. This power, and the responsibility involved in its use, cannot be over-estimated. It is direct, it is intimate, it is absolute, and all but omnipotent.

This direct and intimate connection between the conditions of the bodies and souls of the father and mother, and the health, character and destiny of their child, in all its future being, is little understood, and, of course, not appreciated. The child is born, and if its conditions of body and soul are deformed and unnatural, the parents have no thought of looking to themselves as the cause, but attribute it to some mysterious providence, or agency beyond their control. I would take up these deformed, suffering specimens of Humanity, lay them in the arms of their parents, and say to them, "Behold, this is your work! These deformities, and the sufferings that must ensue, are all to be traced to you." The cry of anguish comes up from the future of this world, earnestly appealing to the present, saying, "Give us healthy, vigorous bodies and souls; give us perfect, harmonious organizations and constitutional tendencies, and we will take care of all external arrangements."

What kind of bodies shall the present give to the future?—healthy or diseased, symmetrical or deformed, harmonious or discordant? What kind of souls shall the present give to the future?—true or false, loving or hating, forgiving or revengeful, noble or ignoble? In a word, shall their organization be healthful or diseased? It seems impossible that this question can be overlooked, or merged in those of minor importance. But it often is; and it is more frequently asked by parents, What property, what social position, what title or station shall I leave to my children? This, too, when they know, by the experience of every day and hour, how utterly worthless are these to give beauty to deformity, health to the diseased body, or purity and elevation to an impure and grovelling soul.

But the practical question is, By what agency is this advancement to be effected? It is certain, no medical prescriptions can give to the body health for disease, strength for weakness, beauty for deformity; nor can theological prescriptions give to the soul high and holy thoughts, and noble aims, for thoughts that are low and vicious, and aims that are ignoble. These means have been tried long and faithfully. Humanity has been drugged to repletion with medical, political and religious prescriptions. What has been the result? As the ages pass, is the nature we bear becoming more free from disease? As exterior surroundings are improved, as the means of physical comfort and luxury are multiplied, as the sources of intellectual and social enjoyment become more abundant and accessible, and as political, educational and religious institutions become more perfect, do the bodies of men and women become more beautiful, more healthful, and more vigorous and active, and their souls more pure and noble? The result has demonstrated that no system of *arbitrary* arrangements, by whatever name called, can avail to eradicate the diseases which transgression of the fixed laws of life and health has introduced. The human body and soul have been but little improved under this regimen. Means more natural, and more efficient and available, are at hand.

To the LAW OF REPRODUCTION will human beings, in the future of this world, look as the one great means to expel disease from the body and soul. It needs no direct communication from Heaven to inform us that human nature is fearfully diseased. The fact is stamped on nearly every human being that lives and moves around us. We see it in the countenance, in the gait, in the whole body; we hear it in the voice; in every form in which human nature can express itself, its diseases are made manifest. To relieve human nature, as represented in individual man, of its deformities, to regenerate and exalt it, will be the object of all who respect themselves or wish well to the race.

Much is said about a reörganization of society. It is well; too much cannot be thought and said about it, provided a due regard be had for individual man. It should ever be kept in mind, by all who would reörganize society, that Man is above society, and that the former should never be sacrificed to the latter. All forms of social combination are transient; the individual alone lives, and must live, for ever. No social institution based on the assumption that the physical, intellectual, or spiritual life and health of one individual, however poor, ignorant, depraved and outcast, may be sacrificed on the altar of society, can permanently benefit the race, or those who create and sustain it; for all such social arrangements tend to depreciate Man, as MAN. In all human combinations, the purity, vigor and happiness of society depend on the purity, energy and happiness of the individuals composing it. Society cannot be healthful, physically or spiritually, while it is composed of diseased individuals. The only natural and true end of society is, to perfect and ennoble individual man. A society that tends to destroy respect for the rights of individuals, has in it the element of destruction, and sooner or later must be destroyed. All such churches, states and kingdoms must be dashed in pieces and consumed for ever. A social disease can never be cured, so long as it exists in individuals. It is with man as it is with minerals. A mass of gold or silver will be pure in proportion to the purity of the particles of which it is composed. So society will be pure, intelligent, energetic and noble, in proportion to the purity, intelligence, energy and nobleness of the men and women who compose it. To sacrifice an individual man, woman or child to the good of society, is to tear down a house to save the windows, or to kill a child to save its toys. MAN cannot forfeit his rights to society, for his rights, as an individual, are above the rights of social combinations. Remove disease from the bodies and souls of individuals, and the evils of society will cease. Elevate man, and society is necessarily elevated.

Society must express the individuals that compose it. It can rise no higher, and sink no lower. Social manifestations are but the manifestations of its individual members. The reörganization of man and woman must precede the reörganization of society. A new type of Manhood and Womanhood must precede the new type of Society. How can health, beauty and strength of body be substituted for disease, feebleness and deformity? How can the Love-nature be substituted for the Wrath-nature, nobleness for meanness, truth for falsehood, in the human soul? I will proceed to give what seems to me the true answer.

HENRY C. WRIGHT.

## LETTER II.

## Distinction of Sex:

IN WHAT IT CONSISTS—ITS EXTENT—ITS OBJECT.

LENAWEE, June, 1852.

MY FRIEND:

To secure to man a more perfect organization is the first direct object to be sought; to secure to that organization a more natural and healthful development is the second. The former stands connected with marriage and parentage, and all that pertains to those relations; the latter, with all the outward physical, social, literary, governmental and religious surroundings that bear upon human life and happiness.

My object now is, to consider organization, and those functions and relations of human beings that bear most directly upon it. This must lead to a consideration of the distinction of sex, and of the rights, privileges, relations and duties that are based upon it. To no one who knows how directly they bear on human character and destiny, is an apology needed. I shall make none to any one, except to say to all readers of these pages, distinctly understand and appreciate the one great object which the writer has in view, and then judge his thoughts and words in the light of that object, and I have no fear of being greatly misunderstood, or that any reader will be greatly shocked.

DISTINCTION OF SEX. In what does it consist? It is not pertinent to my purpose to go into a detail of all the particulars. It is sufficient to notice the one great distinctive feature. The human family is divided into two parts. What constitutes the dividing line? What makes a man a man, and a woman a woman? In the number, nature and uses of the bones, muscles, veins, arteries and nerves, they are alike. In the number, nature and use of the intellectual, social and moral powers, they are alike. Both are qualified to perform each its respective part in the perpetuation and perfection of the race. But they differ essentially in the part each is to perform. The distinctive characteristic of a man is that which qualifies him to be a *father;* that of woman, the qualification to be a *mother*. The male organism, including body and soul, is adapted to elaborate, secrete and impart the primary element, or germ, of a new being; the female is adapted to receive, nourish and develop that germ into a living human form. In the masculine organism, the life-germ is formed; in the feminine, it must be nourished. The office of each is distinct, yet both are essential. Neither can reproduce without the other; and the physical, social, intellectual and passional organization of each, perfectly fits them for the parts they are to perform in the economy of human life. Though perfectly distinct, neither can be perfected without the other. In the continuance and elevation of the race, one is just as necessary as the other. They differ, yet one has no superiority over the other; and the part assigned by Nature to one is no more important than that which she assigns to the other. Man is just as dependent on woman as woman is on man. Man, by himself, is powerless; so is woman; but, united, both are perfected, and alike potent.

*Universality of this Distinction.* It extends to the animal and vegetable kingdoms. Every animal and every vegetable that reproduces is marked by it, having two elements, which correspond to the male and female principles in the human species. Every flower, fruit, grain, tree, weed and grass, as well as every animated existence, is produced by the commingling of the male and female elements. Take away the fecundating power of the one, or the nutritive power of the other, in any species of animal or vegetable, and that species must perish.

Two great principles pervade universal being, so far as it is subject to human scrutiny—the MASCULINE and the FEMININE. The blending of these two elements constitutes the creative power of the universe. This sexual or reproductive power is embodied in every species of animal and vegetable life, according to its kind. In each species, there are fixed natural laws to regulate the blending of these two elements, in order to produce healthy and perfect offspring. These laws must be known and observed, or man strives in vain to perfect any species of flower, grass, fruit, grain, or animal. This fact is recognised, in all attempts to improve any animal or vegetable existence beneath man. The first inquiry is, By what laws must the blending of the masculine and feminine elements be governed, in order to produce a more beautiful, healthy and noble type of any particular species of plant or animal? Universal nature returns one answer,—LIKE BEGETS LIKE. Whatever conditions belong to the elements before they are united, must reäppear in the offspring of such union. This law is fixed and known, and acted upon by all who would improve any species of existence.

The distinction, as it seems to me, exists not merely in the body, but also in the soul; and the bodily forms are but organs, through which the souls of each sex express their sexual peculiarities. This distinction extends also to the great primeval Intelligence, or Life-Principle of the universe. In God, the union of the two is complete. He is feminine as well as masculine. It is as true and natural to pray to the God-Mother as to the God-Father; to say "Our Mother," as well as "Our Father, which art in heaven." A woman is the female element of the Divine Being manifested in human form; a man is the masculine element of the same being, thus manifested. The perfect combination of these two makes the true God visible and tangible, so far as he can be. The more perfect the oneness of the husband and wife, the more like God. That which constitutes the distinction between male and female, and divides all animals and vegetables into two classes, is also the bond that binds all things together, that gives to every being a companion, leaving nothing to solitude and isolation. It is the harmonizing principle of the universe, to bring each man and woman into harmony with self and with God. If the relation in which we originate be unnatural and inharmonious, the offspring must be at war with itself and with all around. Discord would be its birthright inheritance.

*The objects of the Distinction.* They are two: the *continuation of the race*, and its *perfection*. That the perpetuation of the race is one great object, needs no argument to prove. Blot out the distinction, and the human race ceases. So of every other species of animal and vegetable existence. Or, blot out either sex, and the same result follows. Neither can reproduce by itself. The union of the two elements, alone, constitutes the creative power. Or, let both sexes exist, if there were no sexual union between them, the extinction of the race would follow. That the perfection of the race is another great object, will be made apparent in the following pages.

So far as the human race is concerned, the object of the sexual distinction is to reproduce *human* beings, with all the physical, intellectual, social and moral attributes natural to that class of existences. Whatever qualities and conditions are natural to men and women were designed to be perpetuated. It is a violation of the law of sex to perpetuate any others. How it may be made to conduce to the perfection of our nature or to its degradation, will in due time be fully considered. To this I shall call *special* attention.

The question naturally arises, What is it that makes man a man, and woman a woman? Can any one attribute be pointed out that constitutes the dividing line? Whatever it be, it is that which gives to man a power over woman, and to woman a power over man, which neither has over their own sex. Man is attracted to woman as he is not to man, and woman is attracted to man as she is not to woman. The fact exists, as every man and woman knows by experience. The feeling is different; its effects are different, on the entire being; and this difference extends to every department of life. Wherever, and under whatever circumstances, the sexes meet, a different spirit pervades the heart of each, and a different tone and air are manifest in their deportment, from that which is felt and witnessed when man meets man, or woman meets woman. This difference cannot be the result of an educational process, for it appears in all classes and conditions of society. The world over, where men are associated, and the female element is entirely excluded, there a degenerating process goes on; roughness and brutality of manner ensue, and depravity of heart. Men degenerate in every particular, when left for a long time without the refining and elevating influence of females. If the character of the latter be such as to make their influence bad, the degradation becomes complete. A woman, whether her influence be for good or evil, always has more control over men than man has. So with man in regard to woman. The reciprocal influence of the sexes must be direct and powerful, and one of life unto life or of death unto death to each.

That which marks the distinction of sex is not only the secret of the great power each has over the other, but it is, also, the unseen, yet ever-present bond which binds them together. It constitutes the attractive force of each over the other; the power by which each attracts and is attracted to the other. Man, as the embodiment of the masculine element, has no significance to man; nor has woman to woman, as the incarnation of the feminine element. The sexuality of each has significance only to the other. Each needs the influence and aid of the other, not only to reproduce, but also to prepare in each such healthful conditions of body and soul as they may rightly and proudly transmit to their offspring. Take away this sexual element, and a woman is no more drawn to man than she is to woman. In the general economy of human existence, this reciprocal tendency of the sexes each to the other, is the basis of our most perfect and exalted relations, without which, complete isolation might be tolerable. Now, it is neither tolerable nor possible, without certain ruin. A man and woman may be happy together, and completely satisfy each other's social wants. Isolated *pairs* may exist and be perfected in happiness; but individuals cannot be; neither can pairs of the same sex be.

Parentage, then, and a preparation for parentage, constitute the great object of the sexual distinction. This element is not only essential to parentage, but it is as essential to qualify men and women for this high relation. This alone can bring them into that state of oneness, which is essential rightly to give existence to new beings in human likeness.

H. C. W.

## LETTER III.

## The Reproductive System:

OFFICE OF THE MALE — OFFICE OF THE FEMALE — SPERMATIC SECRETION, SPERMATOZOA, OVARIES, &c.

LENAWEE, June, 1852.

MY FRIEND:

I HAVE remarked, that, in the economy of Nature in the distinction of sex, the organism of each is adapted to perform the part assigned to it in the continuance and perfection of the race. To prepare the germ of a new man or woman, is the noblest function of the male; to provide it sustenance and develop it into a human form, is the most perfect work of the female.

As I shall have frequent occasion to refer to "*Principles of Human Physiology*, by WILLIAM B. CARPENTER," I shall, as I quote him, only refer to the *section*, without quoting the title at each time.

The life-germ of the human being is, with other ingredients, contained in what is called the spermatic fluid. This is secreted in the appropriate organs. Thence it is transmitted to the female. Of the process of reproduction, Carpenter thus speaks:—

"The mysterious process of reproduction evidently consists, in flowering plants, of nothing else than the implantation of a cell-germ, prepared by *male* organs, in a nidus, or receptacle, adapted to aid its early development; which nidus constitutes the essential part of the *female* system.

## THE REPRODUCTIVE SYSTEM. 29

"There is now good reason to believe, that, in no animals, is the reproductive apparatus less simple than it is in the higher plants; — that is to say, in every instance, two sets of organs, a *germ-preparing* and a *germ-nourishing*, are present. These organs differ much in form and complexity of structure in the various tribes of animals; but their essential function is the same in all. Those which are termed male organs, prepare and set free certain bodies, which, having an inherent power of motion, have been supposed to be independent animalcules, and have been termed Spermatozoa; there is but little reason, however, to regard them in this light, since ciliated, epithelium-cells may exhibit as much activity; and there is no evidence that their function is any higher than that of the pollen-tube of plants, which conveys into the Ovulum the germ of the first cells of the embryo. This view of the character of the Spermatozoa rests alike upon the nature of their movements, and the mode of their production. Dr. Barry's observations on the history of the Ovum, and on the nature of the act of fecundation, have left scarcely any doubt that this act consists in the introduction of some new element into the Ovule, through the medium of the Spermatozoa; the arrival of which at the surface of the Ovary had been more than once previously seen, and the penetration of which to the Ovum there was good reason to suspect; and these have been confirmed by the observations of Dr. A. Farre on the Ovum of the earth-worm, which he has distinctly seen to be penetrated by Spermatozoa. The act of fecundation is evidently analogous, therefore, in animals, to the process which is described as taking place in flowering plants." (Secs. 899, 900.)

Thus, the origin of the human being, as the offspring of human beings, is similar to that of all other existences. The reproductive system consists of two sets of organs, whose functions are essentially distinct, each performing its office entirely independent of the other. Fully to understand how the organization and consequent character and destiny of the child are to be affected by the conditions of the parents, it is important to know what part each performs in the act of reproduction. Is the part performed by each such, that the condition of the different organisms must, of necessity, affect the child for good or evil?

*Office of the Male Organism.* It is to prepare, from the various substances taken into it, the life-germ of a new creation in human form. On the "action of the male" in reproduction, Carpenter says:—

"The spermatic fluid secreted by the testes of the male, differs from all other secretions, in containing a large number of very minute bodies, only discernible with a high power of microscope, and these, in ordinary cases, remain in active motion for some time after they have quitted the living body. The human Spermatozoon consists of a little oval flattened body, from the $1.600^{th}$ to $1.800^{th}$ of a line in length, from which proceeds a long filiform tail, gradually tapering to the finest point, of one-fiftieth, or, at most, one-fortieth of a line in length. The whole is perfectly transparent, and nothing that can be termed structure can be satisfactorily distinguished within it. The movements are principally executed by the tail, which has a kind of vibratile, undulating motion. . . . Their presence may be readily detected by a microscope of sufficient power, even when they have long ceased to move, and are broken into fragments. . . . That the Spermatozoa are the essential elements of the spermatic fluid, has been reasonably inferred from several circumstances, such as their absence or imperfect development in hybrid animals, which are nearly or entirely sterile; and the fact that fecundation essentially consists in the direct communication of one of them with a certain point in the Ovum, appears too well established to admit of further doubt. Regarding the uses of the other constituents of the Semen, no sufficient account can be given." (Secs. 901, 902.)

*At what time of life does he begin to prepare and secrete the Spermatozoa, or life-germ of human beings?* The period during which his nature is capable of this office is limited. His system may secrete an element that is called the spermatic fluid; but the living germs, the Spermatozoa, may be wanting. As to the time when the human male begins to be capable of reproduction, and when he loses that power, by a natural process, Carpenter says:—

"The power of procreation does not usually exist in the human male until the age of from fourteen to sixteen years; and it may be considered probable that no Spermatozoa are produced until that period, although a fluid is secreted, by the testes. At this epoch, which is ordinarily designated as that of puberty, a considerable change takes place in the bodily constitution. . . . . Instances, however, are by no means rare, in which these changes take place at a much earlier period; the full development of the generative organs, with manifestations of the sexual passion, having been observed in children of but a few years old.\* The procreative power may last, if not abused, during a very prolonged period. Undoubted instances of virility at the age of more than one hundred years are on record; but in these cases, the general bodily vigor was preserved in a very remarkable degree. The ordinary rule seems to be, that sexual power is not retained by the male, in any considerable degree, after the age of 60 or 65 years." (Sec. 903.)

*Office of the Human Female in continuing and perfecting the race.* My sole object being to show how, and to what extent, the organization and subsequent character and destiny of the child are directly

---

\* This is ever a certain indication of a diseased state, and that the child's nature has been outraged by its parents, before birth, or afterwards.— H. C. W.

influenced by the mother, it would not be pertinent to notice her connection with the germ, till it comes into the position in which its existence and growth depend on nourishment derived through her system. This period commences when the Spermatozoon enters the germ-receiving cell, or vessel. The male, having prepared and imparted the living germ, can have no more direct influence over it, for good or evil, till it is developed into the living child and born. A knowledge of two or three organs seems to be important, and connected with my purpose. I quote from those whose profession leads them into such researches. I would remark, however, that every man and woman should have this knowledge, as well as the physician or physiologist. EMBRYOLOGY, and the science of Reproduction, should be known to every human being. The entire process by which the germ is prepared and imparted by the male, and by which it is received and nourished and developed by the female, and all the organs, and their functions, in this most responsible of human acts, should be perfectly understood by every human being, as far as possible. This knowledge belongs not merely to the surgeon, the doctor, or the midwife, but to all who take part in the perpetuation and progress of the human race. Without it, they cannot comprehend and appreciate the power which the conditions of the parents exercise over the character and destiny of their children. I say to every man and woman entering into marriage relations, by all that is pure and noble in Manhood and Womanhood, let nothing deter you from a familiar knowledge of all the organs and facts connected with reproduction.

## THE REPRODUCTIVE SYSTEM.

"OVARIES. These are two oval-shaped bodies, about the size of an almond nut, placed on each side, nearly in the groin. They contain a number of small, round grains, or granules, called *Ovæ*, or eggs; which are the germs of future human beings, as the eggs of birds are of their particular kind. They are connected with the Uterus by two short arms, or prolongations, and are enclosed in the folds of the broad ligaments."

"FALLOPIAN TUBES. These are two tubes, one on each side, beneath the Ovaries, and extending further. Each of them has a small passage, which opens into the Uterus at one end, and opposite the Ovaries at the other. Their use is to convey the impregnating principle to the Ovaries at the time of conception, and to convey the Ovæ, when impregnated, to the interior of the Womb."

"THE UTERUS, or WOMB. This is a hollow organ, placed between the bladder, which is in front, and the rectum, which is behind. It is connected with the Vagina, and opens into it by the small orifice, called the mouth of the Womb. The Uterus is the organ which receives the impregnated Ovum, and in which it is developed into the human being. It is connected with the Ovaries by the Fallopian Tubes, and with the Vagina by the Os Tincæ, and is retained in its situation partly by its connections with other organs, and partly by the round and broad ligaments." — *Hollick*.

Carpenter says: —

"The essential part of the female generative system is that in which the Ova are prepared; the other organs are merely accessory, and are not to be found in a large proportion of the animal kingdom. . . . In the lower animals, the Ovarium consists of a loose tissue, containing many cells, in which the Ova are formed, and from which they escape by the rupture of the cell walls; in the higher animals, as in the human female, the tissue of the Ovarium is more compact, forming what is known as the *Stroma*, and the Ova, except when they are approaching maturity, can only be distinguished in the interstices of this by the aid of a high magnifying power." (Sec. 905.) "According to the most valuable inquiries of Dr. Ritchie, it appears that even during the period of childhood, there is a continual rupture of Ovisacs, and discharge of Ova, at the surface of the Ovarium. . . . At the period of puberty, the stroma (or tissue) of the Ovarium is crowded with Ovisacs, which are still so minute that in the ox, (according to Dr. Barry's computation,) a cubic inch would contain two hundred millions of them." (Sec. 907.)

*Reproductive period of the Female.* This commences at about the age of fourteen years, and extends to the forty-fifth year, but it is sometimes extended ten or fifteen years longer; but the cases are rare in which women above fifty years of age have borne children. Carpenter says:—

" In the human female, the period of puberty, or of commencing aptitude for procreation, is usually between the 13th and 16th years; it is earlier in warm climates than in cold; and in densely populated manufacturing towns, than in thinly peopled agricultural districts. The mental and bodily habits of the individual have also a considerable influence upon the time of its occurrence; girls brought up in the midst of luxury or sensual indulgence, undergoing this change earlier than those reared in hardihood and self-denial. The changes in which puberty consists are for the most part connected with the reproductive system. The external and internal organs of generation undergo considerable increase of size; the mammary glands enlarge; and a deposition of fat takes place in the mammæ and on the pubes, as well as over the whole surface of the body,—giving to the person that roundness and fullness which are so attractive to the opposite sex, at the period of commencing Womanhood." (Sec. 908.)

As to the conditions of the female organism, during its periodical functions, Carpenter says:—

" The state of the female generative system, during its continuance," is such that " there is good reason to believe that, in women, the sexual feeling becomes stronger at that epoch ; and it is quite certain that there is a greater aptitude for conception, immediately before and after menstruation, than there is at any intermediate period. Observations to this effect were made by Hippocrates, and were confirmed by Boerhaave and Haller; indeed, coitus immediately after menstruation, appears to have been frequently recommended as a cure for sterility, and to have proved successful." (Sec. 909.)

It is to this *periodical* function of her system, — which, by some strange hallucination, females often regard with shame, or sadness, — that woman owes health, life, and all that can make her attractive, as woman, to the opposite sex. It cannot be that it was designed to be a period of suffering. It is as essential a function of her organism as is breathing. On the regular, healthful recurrence of no function of her nature do her beauty, her energy, her health and happiness more essentially depend. Yet, feebly organized and developed as women, in civilized life, now are, it is generally a period of physical and mental prostration, and often of deepest suffering to the body and anguish to the soul. It is then her nature calls for the tenderest love and sympathy from the opposite sex; but it is the very time when, often, even from him who holds to her the relation of husband, she gets the least. But, if men were taught in early life to understand this function of the female system, and its relations to her beauty, health and happiness, and to all the dearest relations of life, they would accord to her, during this period, their purest, tenderest, and manliest sympathy. Do men consider that this is essential to qualify woman for the relations of wife and mother? Do they know how her health, her character, her joys, her very life, as a wife, a mother, a sister and daughter, from the fourteenth to the forty-fifth year of her life, depend on the healthful, regular recurrence of this period? Every husband, father, son, brother and lover should know it; and if they did, I believe that women would seldom, at such times, be without the tenderest, holiest and most efficient sympathy of those of the opposite sex who stand in intimate relations to them. Such knowledge would save woman from great suffering; it would add grace and dignity to Manhood and Womanhood; it would ennoble the intercourse between the sexes; it would bind man to woman in a tenderer and holier union; it would consecrate woman in the estimation of man, and endear man to woman as a truer, nobler being, in all relations. Every one should, therefore, be early taught to honor and respect this function of the female organism, in all its causes and purposes, as far as possible. *Let there be light!* There will then be LIFE.

*Function of the Female in the Reproductive act.* Of this, Carpenter says:—

"The function of the female, during coitus, is entirely of a passive character. . . . . . It is a fact well established, that fruitful intercourse may take place, when the female is in a state of narcotism, of somnambulism, or even of profound ordinary sleep. . . . . . The introduction of a small quantity of the fluid just within the Vagina, appears to be all that is absolutely necessary for conception. . . . . . That the Spermatozoa make their way towards the Ovarium, and fecundate the Ovum either before it entirely quits the Ovisac or very shortly afterwards, appears to be the general rule in regard to the mammalia." (Sec. 911.)

The following extract from Carpenter, (Sec. 946,) gives his views of the distinct function of the male and female in reproduction, and also, of the influence of the kind of nourishment taken by the mother, and of the mental condition of the mother, during pregnancy, on the health and character of the child. He says: —

"The most important of all the facts that have come under our review, is that which has been stated as in the highest degree probable, if not yet absolutely proved, in regard to the relative offices of the male and female in this hitherto mysterious process. According to the view here given, the male furnishes the *germ*, and the female supplies it with nutriment, during the whole period of its early development. There is no difficulty in reconciling such a doctrine with the well-known fact, that the offspring commonly bears a resemblance to both parents (of which the production of a hybrid between distinct species is the most striking example); since numerous phenomena prove that, in this earliest and simplest condition of the organism, the form it will ultimately assume very much depends upon circumstances external to it; among which circumstances, the kind of nutriment supplied will be one of the most important. Upon the same principle, we may account for the influence of the mental condition of the mother upon her offspring, during a later period of pregnancy. That such influence may occur, there can be no reasonable doubt. 'We have demonstrative evidence,' says Dr. A. Combe, 'that a fit of passion in a nurse vitiates the quality of the milk to such a degree, as to cause colic and indigestion [or even death] in the suckling infant. If, in the child already born, and in so far independent of its parent, the relation between the two is thus strong, is it unreasonable to suppose that it should be yet stronger, when the infant lies in its mother's womb, is nourished indirectly by its mother's blood, and is, to all intents and purposes, a part of her own body? If a sudden and powerful emotion of her own mind exerts such an influence upon her stomach as to excite immediate vomiting, and upon her heart as almost to arrest its motion and induce fainting, can we believe that it will have no effect on her womb and the fragile being contained within it? Facts and reason, then, alike demonstrate the reality of the influence : and much practical advantage would result to both parent and child, were the conditions and extent of its operations better understood.' Among facts of this class, there is, perhaps, none more striking than that quoted by the same author from Baron Percy, as having occurred after the siege of Landau, in 1793. In addition to a violent cannonading, which kept the women for some time in a constant state of alarm, the arsenal blew up with a terrific explosion, which few could hear with unshaken nerves. Out of 92 children born in that district within a few months afterwards, Baron Percy states that 16 died at the instant of birth ; 33 languished for from 8 to 10 months, and then died ; 8 became idiotic, and died before the age of five years ; and 2 came into the world with numerous fractures of the bones of the limbs, caused by the cannonading and explosion. Here, then, is a total of 59 children out of 92, or within a trifle of 2 out of every 3, actually killed through the medium of the mother's alarm and the natural consequences upon her own organization, — an experiment (for such it is to the Physiologist) upon too large a scale for its results to be set down as mere ' coincidences.' No soundly-judging Physiologist of the present day is likely to fall into the popular error, of supposing that marks upon the infant are to be referred to some *transient* though strong impression upon the imagination of the mother ; but there appears to be a sufficient number of facts on record, to prove that *habitual* mental conditions on the part of the mother *may* have influence enough, at an early period of gestation, to produce evident bodily deformity, or peculiar tendencies of the mind. But whatever be the nature and degree of the influence thus transmitted, it must be such as can act by modifying the character of the nutritive materials supplied by the mother to the fetus ; since there is no other channel by which any influence can be propagated. The absurdity of the vulgar notion just alluded to, is sufficiently evident from this fact alone ; as it is impossible to suppose that a sudden fright, speedily forgotten, can exert such a continued influence on the nutrition of the embryo, as to occasion any personal peculiarity. The view here stated is one which ought to have great weight, in making manifest the importance of careful management of the health of the mother, both corporeal and mental, during the period of pregnancy ; since the constitution of the offspring so much depends upon the impressions then made upon its most impressible structure."

Of all knowledge, that which pertains to the nature and functions of the reproductive organs, to the diseases to which they are liable, to what constitutes an abuse of them, to their relations to the general physical system, and how they are affected by the general health, is the most important, but yet, the least regarded. Indeed, a thorough knowledge, among the people, of the scientific facts connected with the origin, fetal-development, and birth of children, it is generally supposed, would be dangerous to their morals. Especially is it thought that it would be dangerous to communicate this knowledge to youth and children. Hence parents and teachers suppress all inquiries on this subject; and school-books on Physiology carefully avoid all allusions to it. This is a mistake, alike fatal to the physical and spiritual development of sons and daughters. Ignorance on no subject has caused so much pollution, crime and wretchedness, as on this. The children of the present are to be the fathers and mothers of the children of the future. How can they nobly fill the office to which they are born, if ignorant of its nature and duties ? Again I say, LET THERE BE LIGHT !

H. C. W.

## LETTER IV.

### Development of the Fetus:

NUTRITION BEFORE BIRTH — FETAL CIRCULATION — CONNECTION BEWEEN NUTRITION AND REPRODUCTION.

LENAWEE, June, 1852.

MY FRIEND:

To the facts and statements in the following letter, I would call particular attention, as they are closely connected with all rational hopes of improving the organization of the human being. *The Present is the offspring of the Past, and the parent of the Future.*

The impregnated Ovum, being transmitted into the Womb, is there placed in its natural position for development. There, being nourished by appropriate means, it is, within the space of nine months, developed into a human being, with all the organs, physical and mental, in an embryo state, of a man or a woman. With a good degree of accuracy, the appearance, size and weight of the fetus can be determined, at various stages of its growth.

The following description of the process of fetal development is taken from "*Midwifery Illustrated*, by J. G. MAYGRIER, M. D.," — a French work, "translated by A. SYDNEY DOANE, A. M., M. D."

"DEVELOPMENT OF THE FETUS.

"We see nothing in the Uterus, previous to the seventh day, to indicate the existence of a new being.

## DEVELOPMENT OF THE FETUS. 41

"At the eighth day, there is a mucilaginous film, and some transparent filaments.

"At the tenth day, a grayish semi-transparent floccula, the form of which cannot be determined.

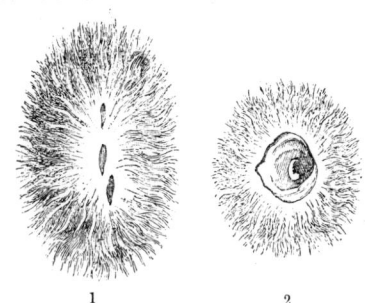

"From the twelfth to the thirteenth day, there is a vesicle as large as a pea, containing a thick fluid, in the midst of which swims an opaque point (*punctum saliens*.) It is thought that the heart alone exists at this period, and this also is the first lineament of the child, which is now termed the embryo. It is enveloped by the chorion and the amnios. Its weight is estimated at one grain. (*See Figs.* 1, 2.)

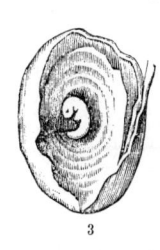

"At the twenty-first day, the embryo appears in the form of a large ant (*Aristotle*,) of a grain of wheat (*Burton*,) of the malleus (*Beaudeloque:*) it weighs from three to four grains, and is from four to five lines long. At this time, the different portions of the embryo are rather more consistent: and those parts which afterwards become bones, now pass to the state of cartilage. (*See Fig.* 3.)

"At the thirtieth day, the embryo resembles a worm which is curled up. We observe at this period some very faint traces of the principal organs, and of the situation of the upper extremities. It weighs from nine to ten grains, and its length is from ten to twelve lines.

"At the forty-fifth day, the form of the child is very distinct, and it is now termed a fetus. The clavicles and the scapulæ, hitherto cartilaginous, now begin to ossify: the limbs appear in the form of tubercles, resembling the sprouts of vegetables.

The body lengthens, but preserves its oval figure: the head, which is larger, constitutes one of its extremities: the base of the trunk, which is pointed and elongated, forms the other. The eyes, mouth and nose, are marked by blackish points and lines. Similar and parallel points correspond to the places of the vertebræ. Its weight is one drachm, its length two inches. (*See Fig.* 4.)

"At two months. All the parts of the fetus are present: the dark points which represent the eyes, enlarge; the eyelids may be traced, and appear very transparent: the nose begins to be prominent: the mouth enlarges and opens: the brain is soft and pulpy: the neck shows itself: the heart is very much developed, and opaque lines are seen to proceed from it, which are the first traces of the large vessels. The fingers and toes are distinct. Its weight is five drachms, and its length four inches. (*See Fig.* 5.)

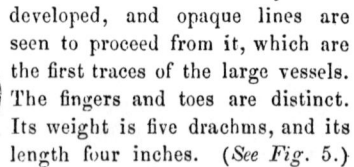

"At ninety days (three months.) All the essential parts of the fetus are perfectly formed and developed. The eyelids, although enlarged, are exactly closed: a small hole shows the place of the external ear: the back and the alæ of the nose are prominent: the lips are very distinct, and are in close contact, and the mouth is shut. The genital organs of both sexes, also, are now very much increased in size: the penis is very long, the scrotum empty; sometimes, however, it is filled and distended with a little water. The vulva is very apparent, and the clitoris is prominent. The brain, although still pulpy, is very much developed, as is also the spinal marrow. The heart pulsates strongly, and the principal vessels carry red blood. The lungs are empty, and hardly visible: the liver is very large, but soft and pulpy; it secretes but little bile. The whole of the upper and lower extremities are developed: the long bones of these limbs are evidently ossified, as are also the ribs and the flat bones of the skull: finally, the muscular system begins to be marked. Weight, two and a half

## DEVELOPMENT OF THE FETUS. 43

ounces; length, six inches. Intellectual functions undeveloped. (*See Fig.* 6.)

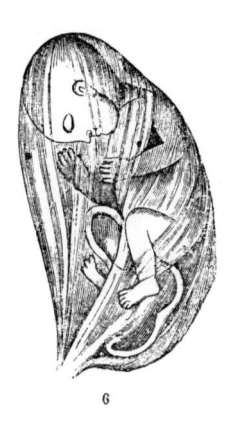

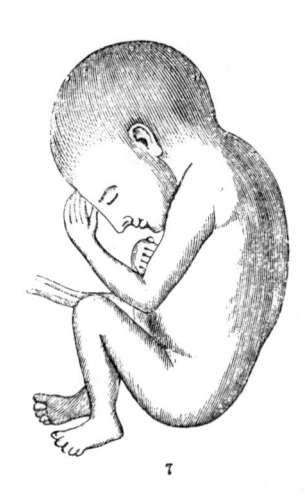

"At one hundred and twenty days (four months.) This period is remarkable for the great development, and the marked character of all the parts of the fetus. The head and the liver alone increase no longer, and constantly become less and less in proportion to the other parts. The brain and the spinal marrow become more consistent: a little meconium collects in the commencement of the intestinal canal: the muscular system is distinct, and the fetus moves slightly, but almost imperceptibly. We here and there find some cellular tissue. Length, eight inches; weight, from seven to eight ounces. Intellectual functions undeveloped. (*See Fig.* 7.)

"At one hundred and fifty days (five months.) The development of all the parts of the fetus is not only greater, but, at this period, individual differences appear: the muscular system is very well marked, and the motions of the child are no longer equivocal: the lungs increase, and are capable of being dilated to a certain extent. The envelope of skin, although existing

44     MARRIAGE AND PARENTAGE.

for a long time, becomes, especially at this period, very consistent: the epidermis is stronger and thicker: the meconium is more abundant, and descends in the intestinal canal: the places for the nails are marked out. Length, ten inches; weight, one pound. Intellectual functions, none. (*See Fig.* 8.)

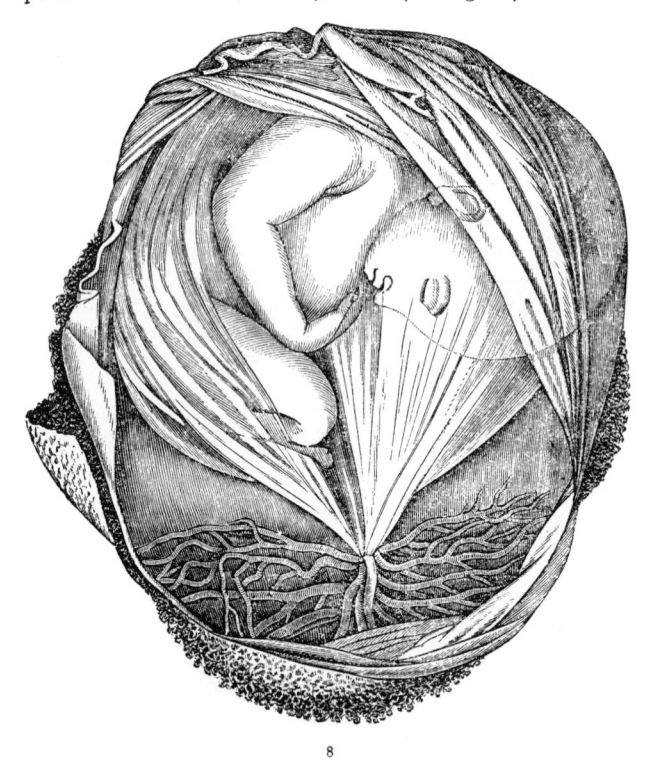

8

"At one hundred and eighty days (six months.) At this period, the child may be strictly said to be in a measure viable: the nails may be distinguished: a little of down, the first indication of the hair, is seen on the head; the thymus gland

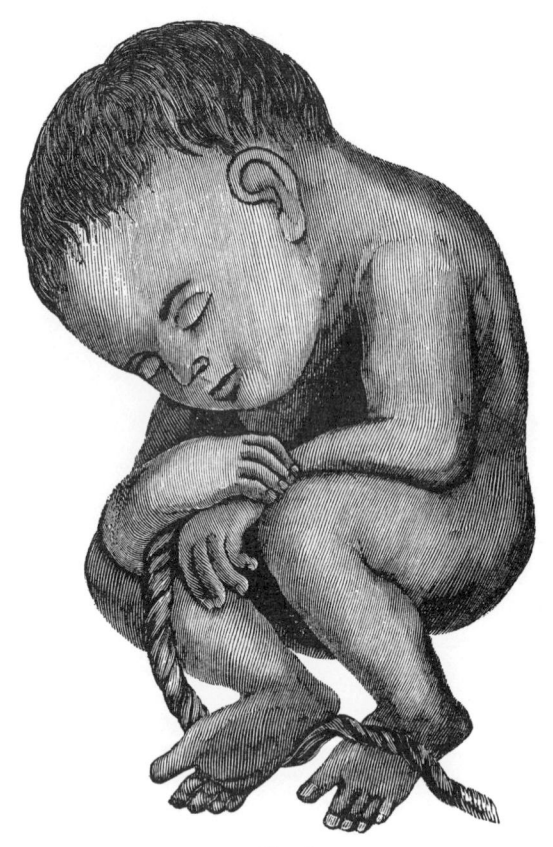

Fig. 9.

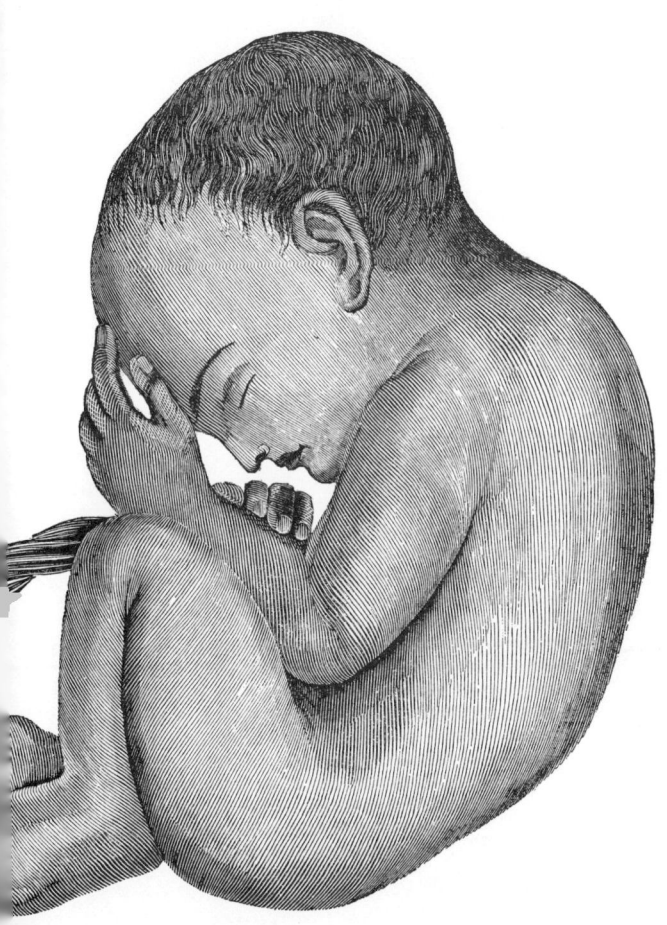

Fig. 10.

exists, the meconium passes through a great portion of the intestinal canal, the testicles appear in the abdomen, and begin to move towards the inguinal ring: the cellular tissue is abundant, and a little adipose tissue is deposited in its cellules: the form of the whole child is distinct. Length, twelve inches; weight, two pounds. Intellectual functions undeveloped.

"At two hundred and ten days (seven months.) Every part of the fetus is enlarged: the child is perfectly viable: the nails are formed: the hairs of the head appear: the testicles descend into the scrotum. The child, if born at this period, can breathe, cry, and suck. The meconium descends into the large intestine, and the whole osseous system of the skull, the ribs, and the limbs, is complete; the extremities of the long bones alone remain as epiphyses: the arterial canal enlarges: the pulmonary arteries, on the contrary, remain small. Length, fourteen inches; weight, three pounds. Intellectual functions undeveloped: the senses are alone susceptible of some impressions. (*See Fig*. 9.)

"At two hundred and forty days (eight months.) Viability, growth of the fetus nearly terminated; each part assuming separately its strength and volume: the muscular system is very well marked. Length, sixteen inches; weight, four pounds. Intellectual functions undeveloped: the senses susceptible of impressions.

"At two hundred and seventy days (nine months.) The common and natural period of the birth of the child: the organs have then acquired all that is necessary to support life. (*See Fig*. 10.)

"The whole osseous system rapidly gains that degree of solidity proper for the functions which devolve upon it. The muscular system is very well marked, and the motions of the child are lively and quick: the heart pulsates rapidly, the circulation is very active, the blood is abundant and rich in nutritious principles, the nervous system is very apparent: the lungs perform their functions, and respiration is established: great changes take place in the manner of the circulation: the whole alimentary canal, which hitherto had no special action, can immediately become active: the intestinal canal contracts upon the meconium, which tends to escape through the anus: the urine is excreted, the arterial capillaries of the skin become very active, the skin is colored, and transpiration is established. Length, eighteen to twenty inches; weight, five to six pounds. Intellectual functions are undeveloped, but the senses (particularly the taste) are very much developed. The child is sensible to pain, it cries from hunger and cold, it is appeased by warmth and nursing, and gentle rocking puts it to sleep."

Thus, the embryo man or woman, which, when twelve days old, weighed only one grain, is, within the space of nine months, increased in weight more than twenty-eight thousand times. In this organization and development, there are no privileged classes. So far as the mere physical nature is concerned, all come into being by exactly the same process.

There is, however, as great a difference in the condition of the maternal organisms in which we are developed, as there is in the soil in which the seed is cast. Some are developed in a healthy organism; others suffer, and must ever suffer, in this life, the horrors of a living martyrdom, as the unhappy victims of an unhealthy maternal organism. When suffering from inherited disease, their bitter reflection is upon the parents, in whose diseased systems they originated, and who, recklessly and wantonly, it may be, disqualified themselves to bestow on their child the blessing of a healthy constitution. How will such parents feel, when their children shall come to understand this matter, and sternly upbraid them for sacrificing the happiness of the entire lives of their offspring to their vanity, their ambition, their ignorance, their love of pleasure, or their unnatural and excessive toil?

Of all man's birthright treasures, to be born of healthy parents is the richest. An heir to a perfect organization of body and soul is richer in all that makes life a blessing, than the heir of millions of gold and silver.

*Whence does the fetus derive its nourishment?* A constant and regular succession of new materials, from a source without itself, is essential to its development. Accordingly, the living germ, from the moment it arrives in the Womb, has the power of attracting and assimilating to itself, from the substances surrounding it, those particles of matter which are adapted and essential to its healthful development. But the fetus is surrounded by, and enclosed within, the organism of another being, and all that reaches it, as nourishment, must come through that organism, and must, of necessity, partake of the conditions of the medium through which it comes, be they healthful or diseased. Speaking of the nutrition of the fetus, Maygrier says:—

"NUTRITION. It is an incontestable fact, that the fetus is nourished by the fluids derived from the mother; but it is not equally easy to demonstrate by what mode it is nourished, and in what manner these fluids come to it. Physicians differ much upon this great physiological question. In fact, some assert, that the infant is nourished by sucking the waters in which it is enclosed, and that these fluids, on entering the stomach, are subjected to the common laws of digestion, and thus become the elements of the nutrition of the fetus. But experiments made on the waters of the amnios have demonstrated that they contain but little, or rather, no nutritious substance; that at the end of pregnancy, particularly, they are often turbid, blackish, purulent, &c.: it has also been observed, that the membranes are sometimes ruptured for several days, a month, even, before the commencement of real labor, which would necessarily cause the premature discharge of the waters of the amnios, long before that of the child: finally, it is certain that some children have been born with the mouth imperforate, and consequently, it was physically impossible for them to receive any of the amniotic fluid.

"The reasons adduced in support of the opinion we have mentioned, also deserve to be answered. It is asserted, that the child, by sucking the waters of the amnios, prepares for the more complex and more difficult operation of sucking the mother. We must admit, that this propensity of the new-born child, and the power of exercising it at birth, are phenomena as astonishing as they are inexplicable; but how is it that the young duck, when hatched out by a hen, as soon as it emerges from the shell, plunges into the water, regardless of the cries of its mother, while the chicken of the same brood avoids this element? Besides, there is nothing on the inside of the amnios resembling the nipple, which might be sucked by the fetus, and therefore its propensity at the moment of birth is innate, and not an acquired faculty.

"On the other hand, the opinion that the fetus is nourished by intussusception, or by absorption, cannot be admitted. The cutaneous system of the fetus is inactive so long as it continues in the Uterus, and the waters have neither the properties nor the qualities proper for absorption.

"Those physiologists who have attempted to explain the nutrition of the fetus, may have erred by confounding this nutrition with proper digestion, wishing to establish an analogy between this imaginary digestion of the fetus and that of the adult; they have maintained that the nutritious juices should follow the same course, and pass through the same passages in both; not thinking that one lives in a light, elastic, aëriform fluid, that it fully enjoys an active respiration, and all the advantages of a rich and abundant circulation, while the other

## DEVELOPMENT OF THE FETUS.

rests in the midst of the Uterus, surrounded by a thick and incompressible liquid, has no respiration, and only as it were a vegetative life and an imperfect existence. All these reasons, and as many more, which are superfluous, should lead us to reject both the theory of deglutition, and that of absorption, as the only modes in which the fetus is nourished. The fetus, then, must be considered, during the whole of pregnancy, as a new part, added for a time to the female, which part is nourished through the common and known medium of the circulation. The child then receives the fluids necessary for its growth through the umbilical cord, and does not subsist upon the waters of the amnios."

FETAL CIRCULATION. Materials for nutrition are carried to every part of the system in the blood. Every particle of nourishment received by the child, which goes to make its growth, from the moment the germ enters the Womb, till the time of birth, must be conveyed to it through the blood of the mother. The manner in which the maternal blood reaches the fetus, conveying to it the means of growth, and how the nutrition is distributed to various parts of the fetus, is thus described by Maygrier:—

"CIRCULATION OF THE FETUS. If the circulation in the fetus were the same as in the adult, we should omit it; but it differs in several respects, and therefore requires a particular description.

"As the fetus has no organs to perform the hematosis, since the lungs are inactive till the moment of birth, it is necessary for the mother to furnish, already prepared, the fluids, which, as soon even as they are carried into the circulation, become the elements of its nutrition. This function belongs to the umbilical vein.

"This vein arises in the placenta, goes towards the umbilicus of the child, and, without communicating with the umbilical arteries, penetrates into the abdomen. Being sustained by a fold of the peritoneum, it is directed from before backward, and from below upward, toward the upper part of the great fissure of the liver. There it gives off a large and short twig, a kind of sinus destined for the liver, into which it penetrates, after dividing into two branches, one for the right lobe, the other for the left.

"The umbilical vein then becomes very small, and goes, under the name of the *venous canal*, towards the right auricle of the heart, into which it penetrates, blending with the ascending vena-cava. The blood which comes to the heart through this latter is separated by the Eustachian valve from the current formed by the descending vena-cava. Being sent forth in a different direction, it strikes against the septum of the auricles, passes through the foramen ovale or the foramen of Botal, and raises its valve, which, being on the side of the left auricle, does not permit the blood to repass into the right auricle.

"Arrived in the left auricle, the blood is transmitted into the left ventricle, and from thence into the ascending aorta, at least, in great part: after passing through the head and the thoracic extremities, it is carried by the descending vena-cava into the right auricle, which sends it into the right ventricle, and from thence it passes into the trunk of the pulmonary artery. A small portion of the blood which is transmitted through this artery goes to the lungs, which, being collapsed and inactive, cannot receive more of it. Most of it passes into the descending aorta, by the arterial canal, and after proceeding through the whole extent of this latter, returns to the mother through the umbilical arteries."

*The connection between Nutrition and Reproduction.* This connection is most intimate. Nothing is more certain than the fact, that the kind and quantity of the food on which the mother lives, during gestation, deeply affect the organic condition of the child's body and soul, and of course its future character and destiny. The materials which are conveyed to the fetus, through the maternal blood, and which must be attracted and assimilated to it to produce its growth, must be affected, not only by the physical diseases of the mother, but also, by her mental conditions. Any powerful excitement of anger, revenge, or of any unpleasant emotion, must injuriously affect the materials that are passing through her blood to nourish her child. Carpenter gives the following account of the connection between nutrition and reproduction: —

"The process of reproduction, like that of nutrition, has been, until recently, involved in great obscurity; and although it cannot be said to be yet fully elucidated, it has been brought, by late investigations, far more within our comprehension, than was formerly deemed possible. The close connection between the reproductive and nutritive operations, both as regards their respective characters, and their dependence upon one another, has long been recognised; and it is now rendered still more evident. Nutrition has been not unaptly designated 'a perpetual reproduction;' and the expression is strictly correct. In the fully-formed organism, the supply of alimentary material to every part of the fabric, enables it to produce a tissue resembling itself; thus, we only find true bone produced in continuity with bone, nerve with nerve, muscle with muscle, and so on. Hence it would appear that, when a group of cells has once taken on a particular *kind* of development, it continues to reproduce itself on the same plan. But in the reproductive process, it is different. A single cell is generated by certain preliminary actions, — from which single cell, all those which subsequently compose the embryonic structures take their origin; and it is not until a later period that any distinction of parts can be traced, in the mass of vesicles which spring from it. Hence, the essential character of the process of reproduction consists in the formation of a cell, which can give origin to others, from which again others spring; — and, in the capability of these last to undergo *several* kinds of transformation, so as ultimately to produce a fabric, in which the number of different parts is equal to that of the functions to be performed, every separate part having a purpose distinct from that of the rest. Such a fabric is considered as a very *heterogeneous* one ; and is eminently distinguished from those homogeneous organisms, in which every part is but a repetition of the rest. Of all animals, man possesses, as already shown, the greatest variety of endowments, — the greatest number of distinct organs ; and yet man, in common with the simplest animal or plant, takes his origin in a single cell. It is in the almost homogeneous fabrics of the cellular plants, that we find the closest connection between the function of nutrition and that of reproduction ; for every one of the vesicles which compose their fabric is endowed with the power of generating others similar to itself ; and these may either extend the parent structure, or separate into new and distinct organisms. Hence it is scarcely possible to draw a line, in these cases, between the nutrition of the individual and the reproduction of the species.

" But, it will be inquired, how and where in the human body (and in the higher animals in general) is this embryonic vesicle produced, and what are the relative offices of the two sexes in its formation ? This is a question which must still be answered with some degree of doubt ; and yet, observed phenomena, if explained by the aid of analogy, seem to lead to a very direct conclusion. The embryonic vesicle itself, like other cells, must arise from a germ ; and reasons will be hereafter given for the belief that the germ is supplied by the male parent, and that the female supplies only the materials for its development. Here, as in the nutritive processes, we find that the operations immediately concerned in this function, — namely, the act of fecundation and the development of the ovum, — are not directly influenced in any way by the nervous system ; and that the functions of animal life are called into play, only in the preliminary and concluding steps of the process. In many of the

## DEVELOPMENT OF THE FETUS.

lower animals, there is no sexual congress, even where the concurrence of two sets of organs (as in the phanerogamic plants) is necessary for the process; the ova are liberated by one, and the spermatozoa by the other; and the accidental meeting of the two produces the desired result. In many animals higher in the scale, the impulse which brings the sexes together is of a purely instinctive kind. But in man, it is of a very compound nature. The instinctive propensity, unless unduly strong, is controlled and guided by the will, and serves (like the feelings of hunger and thirst) as a stimulus to the reasoning processes, by which the means of gratifying it are obtained; and a moral sentiment or affection of a much higher kind is closely connected with it, which acts as an additional incitement. Those movements, however, which are most closely connected with the essential parts of the process, are, like those of deglutition, respiration, &c., simply reflex and involuntary in their character; and thus we have another proof of the constancy of the principle, that, where the action of the apparatus of animal life is brought into near connection with the organic functions, it is not such as requires the operation of the purely animal powers, — sensation and volition. Thus, then, as it has been lucidly remarked, 'the nervous system lives and grows within an animal, as a parasitic plant does in a vegetable; with its life and growth, certain sensations and mental acts, varying in the different classes of animals, are connected by nature in a manner altogether inscrutable to man; but the objects of the existence of animals require that these mental acts should exert a powerful controlling influence over all the textures and organs of which they are composed.'" (Secs. 281, 282.)

H. C. W.

## LETTER V.

### The Human Soul:

ITS ORIGIN, NATURE, AND RELATIONS TO THE BODY — SCIENCE OF SOCIETY — COMMUNION OF SOUL WITH SOUL.

LENAWEE, June, 1852.

DEAR FRIEND:

FULLY to understand the influence of parents over the organization and destiny of the child, it is important to show whence the soul, as well as the body, originates. It is well understood that the latter is derived directly from the mother. The germ, — whatever that mysterious essence or substance may be, — has, in itself, a power to attract and assimilate to itself the particles of matter conveyed from the maternal blood to the fetus, necessary for its physical development into a human body. The process by which the body is formed seems very plain and simple. The operation is one which, to a good extent, can be made visible, and the connection of the parent with this process is direct and certain. But, whence is the soul, the vital force, or life-principle? Does the germ, before it is received into the female organism, contain the elements of a human soul, as well as of a human body? Is the soul, or vital force, derived from the parents, as is the body? What part does the father take in forming the soul, and what part does the mother take? Is the soul, in its nature and constitutional tendencies, directly or indirectly under the control of the will of either parent, or of both?

These questions cannot be satisfactorily answered, at present. The Science of Reproduction is, as yet, in an imperfect state; especially as it relates to the nature and origin of the Life-Principle. The following seems the most rational and philosophical account of the origin of the soul of the child.

The soul is a *substance*, as well as the body, so refined as to be susceptible of thought and feeling, and all the phenomena of mind. If our sense of seeing were sufficiently refined, might not electricity, air, or magnetism, be visible? So, to the eye of the soul, might not the soul be visible, as iron now is to the eye of the body? This vital force, or soul-substance, is under the same law of attraction that governs all other substances.

It seems most rational to conclude, that all the mineral, vegetable and animal existences that are on this globe originate in forces that are innate in the earth and its surroundings. There is, inherent in the earth and its surroundings, a *soul-substance*, — a substance of which souls are made, as well as a substance of which rocks, earth, trees, flowers, fruits and human bodies are made. It matters not what name is given to that substance; whether it be soul-substance, life-principle, or vital force. Let it be understood that it is this essence, or substance, that goes to form the living, thinking, feeling, motive power of human existence.

In the germ, there is a power to attract and assimilate to itself, not only the substance necessary to make a body, but also, a soul. Whence that substance is derived, we know not, as we know not whence comes the substance that forms the body. We know there is a substance connected with the earth, of which the body is made. May we not know, as certainly, that there is a substance or element connected with this planet, from which the Life-Principle of all animated beings on it is derived, and from which the human soul originates? To conclude that there is, seems natural and reasonable. From the moment the germ is received into the Womb, this process of absorption and assimilation of the materials necessary to form the human soul, as well as the human body, begins, and goes on, till the child is prepared to commence an existence independent of the mother. The substance necessary to form the soul of the child must come to it through the blood and life of the mother, as well as the material necessary to form the body.

The arguments adduced to prove that the body of the child originates with the parents, prove, also, that the soul does. The intellectual, social and spiritual conditions of the parents descend to the children, as well as the physical. Functional derangements of souls, as well as of bodies, are transmitted. It is true of the soul, as well as of the body, that parents reproduce in their own likeness.

If these facts be so, it follows that souls are formed by nutrition, by absorption and assimilation, as well as bodies. That the soul will exist after the dissolution of the body, I do not doubt. As little do I doubt that, as a thinking, feeling, conscious being or substance, in human form, its existence will be eternal. And this idea of the soul's immortality, with all its present attributes of will, thought, feeling, volition, &c., seems consistent with the fact, that it is derived from forces in and around the earth, operating through the parental organisms.

It may not be amiss to quote the remarks of Carpenter on the vital forces and functions. They go to show that there is a power, a vital force or soul, in man, whose existence depends not on any such physical or chemical forces as are observed in the body. They also show, that all acts of the mind depend upon material changes in the nervous system; that the action of the soul is essentially and necessarily affected by the bodily conditions; that every physical derangement produces a corresponding derangement in the soul, or vital force. He says, (Sec. 254,) "The idea of *Life*, in its simplest and most correct acceptation, is that of *Vital Action*, and obviously, therefore, involves that of *change*. We do not consider any being as *alive*, which is not undergoing some continued alteration, that may be rendered perceptible to the senses." Carpenter thus continues: —

"There can be no doubt whatever, that, of the many changes which take place during the *life*, or state of *vital activity*, of an organized being, and which intervene between its first development and its final decay, a large proportion are effected by the direct agency of those forces which operate in the inorganic world; and there is no necessity whatever for the supposition, that these forces have any other operation *in* the living body, than they would have *out* of it, under similar circumstances. But, after every possible allowance has been made for the operation of physical and chemical forces in the living organism, there still remain a large number of phenomena, which cannot be in the least explained by them; and which we can only investigate with success, when we regard them as resulting from the agency of forces as distinct from those of Physics and Chemistry, as *these* are from each other. It is to such phenomena that the name of *Vital* is properly restricted; the forces from whose operation we assume them to result are termed *vital forces;* and the properties, which we must attribute to the substances exerting those forces, are termed *vital properties.* Thus, we say that the contraction of Muscle is a Vital phenomenon; because its character and conditions appear to be totally distinct from those of Chemical or Physical phenomena. The act is the manifestation of a certain Force, the possession of which is peculiar to the muscular structure, and which is named the Contractile force. Further, that force may remain dormant (as it were) in the muscular structure; not manifesting itself for a great length of time, and yet resting capable of being called into operation at any moment. This dormant force is termed a Property; thus we regard it as the essential peculiarity of living muscular tissue, that it possesses the vital property of Contractility. Or, to reverse the order, the Muscle is said to possess the property of Contractility; the property, called into operation by the appropriate stimulus, gives rise to the Contractile force; and the force produces, if its operation be unopposed, the act of Contraction.

"These distinctions, though apparently verbal only, are of importance in leading us to the correct method of investigating Vital Phenomena, and of comparing them with those of the Inorganic world. It is now almost universally admitted by intelligent Physiologists, that we gain nothing by the assumption of some general controlling agency, or Vital Principle, distinct from the organized structure itself; and that the Laws of Life are nothing else than general expressions of the conditions under which Vital operations take place,— expressions analogous to those which constitute the laws of Physics or Chemistry, and to be arrived at in the same manner, namely, by the collection and comparison of phenomena. The difficulty of thus generalising in Physiology results merely from the complex nature of the phenomena, and the consequent difficulty of precisely determining their conditions. We have as much ground for believing in the fixity and constancy of Physiological phenomena, when the causes and conditions are the same, as we have in those of any other department of science; and the apparent uncertainty of the actions of the living body, results merely from the influence of differences in those conditions, so trivial in appearance as frequently to elude observation, and yet sufficiently powerful in reality to produce an entire change in the result.

"All Vital phenomena are dependent upon at least two sets of conditions; — an Organized structure, possessed of peculiar properties; and certain Stimuli, by which these properties are called into action. Thus, to revert to the example just cited, the Contraction of a Muscle is due to the inherent Contractility of the Muscular tissue, called into operation by the stimulus of innervation; — other conditions, as a certain elevated temperature, a supply of oxygen, &c., being at the same time requisite. The Microscopical and Chemical researches of recent years have given increased stability to the position, that the peculiar properties, which we term Vital, are dependent upon those peculiar modes of combination and aggregation of the elementary particles, which are characteristic of Organized structures. We have no evidence of the existence of Vital properties in any other form of matter than that which we term Organized; whilst, on the other hand, we have no reason to believe that Organized matter can possess its normal constitution, and be placed in the requisite conditions, without exhibiting Vital Actions. The advance of Pathological science renders it every day more probable, (indeed, the probability may now be said to amount almost to positive certainty,) that derangement in *function*, — in other words, an imperfect or irregular *action*, — always results, either from some change of structure or composition in the tissue itself, or from some corresponding change in the external conditions under which the properties of the organ are called into action." (Secs. 256, 257, 258.)

Then again, he says: —

" By the study of the various forms of Elementary Tissue, of which the Human fabric (or any other of similar complexity) is made up, we are led to the very same conclusion with that which we should derive from the observation of the simplest forms of organized being, or from the scrutiny into the earliest condition of the most complex; namely, that *the simple Cell may be regarded as the type of Organization; and that its actions constitute the simplest idea of Life.*" (Sec. 259.)

It is easy to see why a constant and liberal supply of nutriment should be required for the development of the human being, before and after birth, till full growth is attained; for, during that period, a process of integration, as well as of disintegration, is ever going on; the human organism is constantly receiving accessions, that continue as permanent parts of it. It receives more than it throws off. But after the full growth is attained, why is so large an amount of food still necessary? What necessity for the continued activity of the organic functions in obtaining and taking food into the system, and in converting it into blood, and distributing it to every part of the body? To this question, Carpenter answers: —

" The answer to this question lies in the fact, that *the exercise of the Animal functions is essentially destructive of their instruments;* every operation of the Nervous and Muscular systems requiring, as its necessary condition, a disintegration of a certain part of their tissues, probably by their elements being caused to unite with oxygen. The duration of the existence of those tissues varies inversely to the use that is made of them ; being less as their functional activity is greater. Hence, w en an Animal is very inactive, it requires but little nutrition if in moderate activity, there is a moderate demand for food; but if its Nervous and Muscular energy be frequently and powerfully aroused, the supply must be increased, in order to maintain the vigor of the system. In like manner, the amount of certain products of excretion, which result from the disintegration of the Nervous and Muscular tissues, increases with their activity, and diminishes in proportion to their freedom from exertion. We are not to measure the activity of the Nervous system, however, like that of the Muscular, only by the amount of *movement* to which it gives origin. For there is equal evidence, that the demand for blood in the brain, the amount of nutrition it receives, and the degree of disintegration it undergoes, are proportional likewise to the energy of the purely *psychical* operations ; so that the vigorous exercise of the intellectual powers, or a long-continued state of agitation of the feelings, produces as great a *waste* of Nervous matter, as is occasioned by active bodily exercise. From this and other considerations, we are almost irresistibly led to the belief, that every act of Mind is inseparably connected, in our present state of being, with material changes in the Nervous System ; a doctrine not in the least inconsistent with the belief in the separate immaterial existence of the Mind itself, nor with the expectation of a future state, in which the communion of Mind with Mind shall be more direct and unfettered." (Sec. 263.)

As to the comparative influence of Organic life and Animal life in the economy of human existence and happiness; as to the dependence of the soul on the Nervous condition for its intellectual and affectional action; and as to the manner in which soul generally communicates with soul in the present state, and probably in the future, Carpenter says:—

"So far from his organic life exhibiting a predominance, it appears entirely subordinate to his animal functions, and seems destined only to afford the conditions for their performance. If we could imagine his nervous and muscular systems to be isolated from the remainder of his corporeal structure, and endowed in themselves with the power of retaining their integrity and activity, we should have all that is essential to our idea of Man. But, as at present constituted, these organs are dependent, for the maintenance of their integrity and functional activity, upon the nutritive apparatus; and the whole object of the latter appears to be the supply of those conditions which are necessary to the exercise of the peculiarly *animal* functions. That his mental activity should be thus made dependent upon the due supply of his bodily wants, is a part of the general scheme of his probationary existence; and the first excitement of his intellectual powers is in a great degree dependent upon this arrangement.

"The ministration of the Nervous system to purely Animal life, obviously consists in its rendering the mind cognizant of that which is taking place around, and in enabling it to act upon the material world, by the instruments with which the body is provided for the purpose. It is important to observe, that every method at present known, by which Mind can act upon Mind, requires muscular contraction as its medium, and sensation as its recipient. This is the case, for example, not only in that communication which takes place by language, whether written or spoken, *but in the look, the touch, the gesture, which are so frequently more expressive than any words can be;* and thus we trace the limitation, which, even in communication that appears so far removed from the material world, constantly bounds the operations of the most powerful intellect, and the highest flights of the imagination. That in a future state of being, the communion of mind with mind will be more intimate, and that Man will be admitted into more immediate converse with his Maker, appears to be alike the teaching of the most comprehensive philosophical inquiries, and of the most direct Revelation of the Divinity." (Secs. 284, 285.)

THE SCIENCE OF SOCIETY, of the action of soul upon soul, is, as yet, but little understood. Does this require "muscular contraction as its medium, and sensation as its recipient"? May not mind act upon mind, intellectually, affectionally, and sympathetically, by direct contact, and independent of the bodily senses, muscles or nerves? The facts of clairvoyance seem to show that it can and does. Words, written and spoken, do, indeed, transfer the action of mind to mind, in this state. But this action, especially the affectional, when transmitted from soul to soul by the *look*, the *touch*, the *gesture*, is much more expressive, vitalizing, endearing and controlling, in the more intimate relations of life, than when communicated in words. But may not soul commune with soul without any of these means? Facts demonstrate that each human being gives out himself into the atmosphere, and stamps his own individuality on the material objects around him. May not that essence or substance, thus emanating from him, as it comes in contact with the nervous system of others, transmit to their souls a consciousness of his presence and identity? There is reason to think it may and does; and that the individual Aura by which each human being is surrounded, will ere long form a direct medium of the most intimate communion of soul with soul. To some extent, it is already actualized; it will be far more so, when the human being shall have become more perfectly and harmoniously organized and developed.

In what sense are the social and moral feelings, the intellectual powers, volition, love, sympathy, &c., *functions* of the Nervous system? Has the soul itself any existence, independent of the material organism? The question is often proposed and earnestly discussed; but that it has, seems as self-evident a truth as conscious existence. Immortality seems as fixed and natural a want or necessity of the soul, as air or food is of the body. The soul itself, it seems most rational to conclude, is a material organism, so refined in its texture as to be susceptible of the phenomena of thought and feeling; its present action, to some extent, dependent on the grosser material organism of the body, yet distinct from and independent of it, and destined to live and be susceptible of unending improvement and enjoyment. Referring to this, Carpenter says:—

"It is well to explain, that though the Physiologist speaks of the intellectual powers, moral feelings, &c., as *functions* of the Nervous System, they are not so in the sense in which the term is employed in regard to other operations of the bodily frame. In general, by the *function* of an organ, we understand some change which may be made evident to the senses; as well in our own system, as in the body of another. Sensation, Thought, Emotion, and Volition, however, are changes imperceptible to our senses, by any means of observation we at present possess. We are cognizant of them in ourselves, without the intervention of those processes by which we observe material changes external to our minds; but we judge of them in others, only by inferences founded on the actions to which they give rise, when compared with our own. When we speak of sensation, thought, emotion, or volition, therefore, as functions of the Nervous System, we mean only, that this system furnishes the conditions under which they take place in the living body; and we leave the question entirely open, whether the soul has or has not an existence independent of that of the material organism, by which it operates in Man, as he is at present constituted." (Sec. 308.)

The fact is obvious, that the manifestations of the soul are, in this state, dependent on the conditions of the nervous system. As are those conditions, so will the demonstrations of the soul be perfect or imperfect. Whatever tends to derange that system, must necessarily tend to distort the soul in all its operations. The soul cannot manifest itself purely and truthfully through a diseased medium. True and loving souls would fain give to one another a true and loving utterance; but they cannot, by reason of the distorted conditions of the nerves through which they must speak.

Who controls the organization and development of the nervous system, previous to birth? The parents, absolutely; the mother, directly, the father, indirectly. The manifestations of the soul and the nervous conditions must correspond. Religions, which, ignoring this fact, seek to beautify and adorn the soul, have proved, and must prove, failures. The first business of all religions should be to secure to the human being healthy nervous conditions. This can never be done while existing abuses of the sexual nature remain, and till men and women better understand, and more perfectly obey, the laws which should govern the sexual relations.

H. C. W.

## LETTER VI.

### Transmission of Disease:

HEREDITARY CONDITIONS — ACQUIRED CONDITIONS — TRANSIENT CONDITIONS — CONDITIONS OF MOTHER DURING GESTATION AND LACTATION — ILLUSTRATIVE FACTS.

LENAWEE, June, 1852.

DEAR FRIEND:

IN the preceding Letters, I have endeavored to give the leading scientific facts respecting the process of reproduction, the part performed by each parent in this mysterious act, and the relations of each to the organization, character and destiny of the child. It is conceded, that the influence of parents is great after birth. If it is so direct and potent after, how much more so before? In preparing the germ, the physical, intellectual and moral conditions of the father must necessarily affect more or less its conditions in similar directions; and in nourishing and developing that germ, the mother must, necessarily, impart to it her conditions. A healthy mother might, before birth, impart to a diseased and deformed germ of a weak and sickly father, some degree of health, strength and beauty; or a weakly and sickly mother may impart disease and deformity to a healthy germ of a healthy father.

Man may easily trace his history back to the period of his birth. With considerable accuracy, he may trace himself to the period when, in the germ state, he was received into the womb of his mother. Still further, he may trace himself, a living substance, secreted, as a Spermatozoon, in the paternal organ. Further, he finds no distinct trace of his existence; yet he knows that the life-germ of his body and soul, in some form, had an existence before it was secreted there. He knows it was elaborated in the paternal system, from substances taken into it from without, in the form of food, air, and other elements. But the great question we are most concerned to solve is, Does the father, in preparing the germ, so impress on it his own conditions of body and soul, that these must necessarily be developed in the future child, so as essentially to affect his character and destiny? That he does, is certain. Whatever diseases affect the father, must also affect all the secretions of his system, and none more so than the germs of future human beings. What an obligation, then, rests on every man, to see to it, so far as he can, that the system in which the life-germs of human existence are prepared, should be replete with manly beauty, tenderness and power!

No less important is the *maternal* relation to the child before birth. She consents to receive the germ into her organism. It is placed in its only proper position for growth. It has an inherent power to attract to itself, from the organism in which it is placed, materials for growth to body and soul. These elements, which constitute that growth, are prepared in her system, from the various substances received into it from without. That nourishment must be affected by the conditions of the organisms in which it is prepared and administered. The energies of her nature are taxed to prepare and administer to the growth of the new being, and should be left free as possible to do well the work assigned them. She has taken into herself the germ of a new life, in human form, gladly and thankfully, it may be, (would it were never otherwise!) and by so doing, has pledged herself to the future man or woman to confer on him or her, health, strength and beauty, to body and soul.

Does that woman know the intimacy and power of the relation which she, *voluntarily*, it is to be hoped, assumes to that germ, which, under her forming hand, is soon to appear among us as a living child? Does she know that, from all she takes into her system, in the shape of food, drink, air, &c., the living germ is to extract the substances that must go to form the body and soul of the future living being? When she consented to receive that life-germ of an immortal spirit into herself, did she ask the question, whether she was prepared to forego all practices and indulgencies that could conflict with the health and perfection of her new charge? Did she ask whether her own organism, including body and soul, was in a fit state to receive such a charge, and perform to it the services of a just and loving mother? How few women ever think of these things, when they consent to receive into themselves the elements of a new existence?

Every son and daughter, as early as they can be taught any thing, should be taught to know and respect the part which he or she is to perform in the deep, mysterious process of perpetuating and perfecting the human race. How can parents excuse themselves for allowing their children to grow up in ignorance on this subject? They can comprehend their relations to the future existence of the race, and the duties growing out of those relations. Every male child should be taught to know himself as a *germ-preparing* being, every female, as a *germ-nourishing* being; and the meaning of these terms should be made plain to them, that they may be prepared to discharge naturally and truly the duties of the office assigned to them, respectively, for the highest interest of those who may derive existence from them. No appetites, no pleasures, no occupations, should be allowed to interfere to disqualify them to prepare and develop the most perfect germs of the most perfect men and women.

*Inherited conditions of Parents.* That these enter into the organic structure and constitutional tendencies of children, facts abundantly prove; and that, too, often in most marked and extraordinary ways. Bad conditions are no less likely to be transmitted than good tendencies. Scrofula, consumption, insanity, and idiocy are every where recognised as capable of being transmitted. This fact is acted upon, the world over, by all who are interested in improving the quality and elevating the conditions of all animated existences beneath man, and no pains are spared to get healthy progenitors. Encouragements are given by religions and governments to improve the lower animals. But what encouragement do they offer for the production of the most beautiful, healthy and perfect specimen of the human being? What religion or government offers a bounty for the most healthy and perfect child? Why should they not? Men have certainly more control over the beauty and health of their own offspring, than over the offspring of the lower animals. The subject is of infinitely more importance to mankind than the improvement of the lower animals. Prizes are liberally offered for the best plough, cart, or machine of any kind. Religions offer prizes for the best tracts, pamphlets and books. Why should they not, by similar encouragements, seek to perfect the human being in beauty and strength? What tract, pamphlet or book can be so important as the record stamped upon the body and soul of a perfect child? The child is the true family Bible, in which every parent should read a chapter every hour. Why should not Religion offer a premium for the highest and noblest type of a human being? Would it not do more to regenerate and redeem the race, than it could by spending *all* its energies in efforts to strengthen inherited weakness, to beautify inherited deformity, or to regenerate that which had been badly generated? Had the money that is now spent in war, in government, in *ritual* God-worship, and in sustaining penal establishments, been used to induce husbands and wives to prepare and present to the world more healthy, beautiful, and perfect specimens of human beings, how different had been the result! What object more deserving the attention of government and religion, than that of offering appropriate inducements to men and women living in marriage to give existence to children that shall be healthy in body and soul? The reward should be, not to those who have the greatest number of children, but to those who give existence to children that are, physically and spiritually, most healthy and perfect.

If man were rightly and truly born of woman, he would not need afterwards to be born of God; for to be rightly born of woman is, in the truest and highest sense, to be born of God. Those who receive a healthful and noble creation at first, need no second creation, provided that the first be not deformed by abuse. Society, Religion, Government, and all individuals who would improve and elevate human nature, should aim to procure for every human being, as the richest and most valuable of all boons, a pure and perfect creation of body and soul, at the beginning of life. If Religion would bend her energies to procure for future generations a pure, healthy, natural birth, it would do more to save human kind from torment to body and soul, than it could by spending its energies, as it now does, to heal those who are born diseased. Man should not be "*conceived in sin*," nor "*shapen in iniquity*," and then he would not "*go astray from his birth, speaking lies.*" It is well for Church and State, and all Reformers, to do all that can be done to redeem those thus conceived and thus born from straying into wild and devious paths of transgression; but it would be a much more wisely directed effort which should seek to procure for every child a just and healthy conception, and a true and propitious birth.

Ponder the following facts. A woman, known in the

circle of my friends as healthy, beautiful, and highly accomplished, married a man entirely diseased. She had four children. One died in infancy, a mass of disease; one at seven, and one at eleven, each greatly diseased from birth, and having known no cessation from suffering during their brief existence. The one that died at seven, had more the countenance of one of seventy, caused solely by intense sufferings. One is now living, but her appearance bears the marks of the diseased state that swept away the others. The father died fearfully diseased; the health of the wife and mother was nearly ruined by the diseases of her husband being communicated to her.

I know a man and woman who have five children. The mother has a cancer in her breast, which sorely afflicts her; the father has scrofula, that is developed in running sores. She nursed three of her children, and they drew in the cancer with their food from the mother's breast. His scrofula and her cancer are mingled in them all. They are thoroughly diseased with salt rheum, cancer and scrofula. She now has an infant two months old—full of painful disease, the head and body covered with sores. They both belong to the church, but their religion has never taught them that it is a sin against God thus to inflict disease upon their children.

What greater outrage against Nature could a woman commit, than to consent to become a mother by such a man? None. Let every man and woman, as they would live in the love and respect of their offspring, consider well the physical, mental and moral conditions of those with whom they unite, to become the fathers or mothers of their children. It is computed that more human beings die from diseased tendencies, inherited from parents, who, themselves, had inherited them, than from war, intemperance, slavery, cholera, fevers, and all contagious, adventitious diseases put together.

*Acquired Tastes and Tendencies.* Many diseases of body and soul are acquired, and inherited diseases are made more malignant by abuse. Those whose organizations were originally quite sound, acquire, by unnatural indulgences, diseased conditions. There are few whose natural tastes do not reject tobacco, alcohol, tea, opium, and various other articles of common use, but of great injury, when first they are taken. These acquired conditions, both of body and soul, are transmitted.

*Illustrations.* I know of a man and woman, who, as to riches, move in the wealthiest ranks of fashion. The woman, though naturally healthy and good-tempered, became by indulgence exceedingly passionate, and addicted to strong drinks. Had four children. The eldest, greatly deformed by a fall of her mother, in a fit of intoxication, previous to birth. She died of consumption, at eighteen. The second, a dwarf, a mild and gentle one, died at twenty, of consumption. The third was deaf and dumb, and of a malignant temper. The fourth, a demon in temper, and a drunkard. The mother's conditions were transmitted to her children. She had several miscarriages, caused by her intemperate habits.

I am acquainted with the following fact. A man

and woman, both healthy at marriage, became diseased by abuse of their sexual nature after marriage, he in the lungs, she became deranged in the nervous system and by scrofula. Had five births. The first an abortion, produced by sexual abuse during pregnancy. The living children all diseased with scrofula, or consumption, or both. The parents go on, reproducing, in their own likeness, scrofula and consumption.

*Transmitted Insanity.* The following came under my observation. A woman, who had given birth to several children, became hopelessly insane, through the constant abuse of her nature by her husband. The children were most of them puny and sickly. During her insanity, she became the mother of a living child. It was developed previous to birth, and nursed under the influence of an insanity in the mother so deep, that she seems to have had no consciousness of the period through which she had passed, and had no recognition of the child as hers. The child betrayed the evidence of insanity from its birth. What should be said of such a man? Can man perpetrate a deeper wrong against humanity, and against parentage and marriage? Yet he is counted a Christian, is a member of a church, and in good repute in the community in which he lives!

*Conditions at the time of Sexual Intercourse.* These, too, may, and often do, have a marked influence on the child. The soul should be in its happiest and most perfect state, free from care; the Love element in the entire ascendant; every element in the soul of each concentrated in love upon the other, and penetrated with a pure, intense desire for offspring. The body, in all its powers and functions, should be in full vigor, free from all weariness or lassitude, not excited by artificial stimulants of any kind. Conjugal love, when true, is attracted to purity, to beauty, to all that is sweet, tender, pure, delicate. It can have no affinity to coarseness, vulgarity, uncleanness, or meanness. Marriage love can do nothing but refine, elevate, beautify and adorn all who come under its influence. *Passion*, existing and seeking indulgence without love, as it generally does, is coarse, selfish, polluted, and necessarily tends to degrade and profane both body and soul.

The following cases illustrate the influence of parental conditions, at the time of sexual congress, on the offspring. The wife was a healthy woman, in body and soul, — refined and accomplished in heart and intellect, and of great personal grace and beauty. Her husband was a sober, respectable man when she married. He became a sot. Under the influence and excitement of intoxicating drinks, he sought and obtained passional intercourse with his wife. An idiotic child was the result — hopelessly and helplessly idiotic. The mother attributed the idiocy to the drunkenness of the father; and justly, without doubt.

I know two young sisters, opposite as the poles in their tendencies; one being fretful, impatient, revengeful, and seldom satisfied or in harmony with any thing or person around her; the other is exactly the reverse. Both have the same father and mother. What makes the difference? The difference in the conditions of the parents at the time of reproduction. The union from which the former derived existence was had when the parents were laboring under pecuniary anxieties and trials, that kept them in constant irritation and impatience, and suffering under a sense of wrongs received;—that from which the other sprang, occurred under circumstances directly the reverse. One will suffer, and the other be happy, as the result of the different conditions of their parents at the time of conception.

The following is the testimony of the mother of five children. A stranger asked her one day how it happened that her children manifested such marked differences in their characters. She replied, "I am aware of the difference. It has existed from their birth. They are as different as so many nations. But I know the cause. I can see and feel, in each, my own mental, affectional and physical conditions at the time of their conception and their birth."

*Effects of Artificial Stimulants on the Reproductive Element.* No woman, instigated by pure love, can be attracted to a man of filthy, disgusting habits, such as frequently belong to those who use tobacco, alcoholic drinks, opium eaters, and those who live under the influence of any artificial stimulants. No man, influenced by pure love, can be attracted to a woman, as a husband, who lives on artificial excitements. All such, whether men or women, become impure, ugly, and necessarily repulsive to true love. The sexual element becomes diseased, and, in proportion to their use of such stimulants, unfitted for the sacred function of reproduction.

How can a woman consent to become a mother by a man physically and spiritually polluted by tobacco, alcohol, or any foul, unnatural appetite and practice? How can a man receive as a wife, and become a father by, a woman whose body and soul are filled with enfeebling, polluting disease? Passion, gross sensualism, may bring such together, and enable them to propagate; but pure love, never. Such love cannot be attracted to uncleanness and meanness, of body or soul. The offspring of impure, unclean souls and bodies, must, of necessity, be defiled. Insanity, idiocy, anger, revenge, and diseases of various kinds and degrees, appear in the children born of such unions.

*Drunkenness a cause of Divorce.* No woman, who respects herself or her child, will ever yield to sexual intercourse with a man when he is excited by alcohol, or who habitually or occasionally comes under its influence. She may entail disease and deformity on its body, and idiocy or insanity on its soul, if she does. Drunkenness, in any degree, should exclude a man or woman from marriage, and parental relations. The use of alcoholic drinks should be a sufficient cause of divorce. Drunkenness, of necessity, dissolves the marriage relation; for no man or woman can love a drunkard as a husband or wife. Tea and coffee, alcohol, tobacco, opium, and all artificial stimulants, necessarily derange the sexual secretions; and the day will come, when men and women will so respect the function of reproduction, that they will shun all food, drink, and pursuits, of gain or pleasure, that tend to injure it, and disqualify them to be healthy parents of healthy children, and never connect themselves in marriage with those who thus abuse their nature. Those are unfit to be fathers or mothers, who indulge their appetite at the expense of health. They cannot make a happy home, and those who wish for this priceless boon, will never knowingly enter into conjugal relations with them.

*Solitary Indulgence.* Men are often advised by doctors to marry, as a cure for solitary indulgence. Wo to that woman and to her children who marries a man to cure him of such a vice! If he would not control his sexual passion before marriage, he will not after it. He gets a wife, not to restrain him from pollution, but that he may indulge his sensuality under legalized and social sanctions. In solitary indulgence, he ruined only himself; now, he victimises wife and children to his passion. Death, to a pure-minded woman, were preferable to such a doom. Yet multitudes are sought, in legal marriage, by men whose aim is, to save themselves from what they have come to consider an indulgence which they must and will have alone, if they cannot get legal control over the person of a woman. Such men had better be left to die as solitary sensualists, than to enter into relations by which others must be destroyed with them.

Let the following extract from a letter illustrate the effects of sexual abuse on the entire man:—

" Sir :

"Having noticed that you are in Boston for a few weeks, I have concluded to address you, to get some advice from you. I am suffering as the victim of a solitary abuse of my sexual nature. My anguish is often great. The vice has gained upon me for several years, and has worn out my vital powers of body and mind. The essence of life has left me. I live only in name. My spiritual life has left me. I have spent a great deal on doctors. Their prescriptions have done me no good. Can you restore me to life? Can you rouse up the dormant energies of my mind? I have a soul to save from this lowest hell. My digestive organs are out of order; my memory is very bad; I cannot keep my mind on what I read; I am incapable of studying; I have no relish for society, or for any of the charms of the world. My age is twenty-one. If there is any medicine that will raise my mind from this low condition, and make me myself again, you shall be well rewarded, if you will point it out to me.

"Yours, truly,  ——— ———."

Here is a *living* picture of the natural and necessary results of sexual abuse, whether perpetrated socially or in solitude. The laws of Nature heed not the existence of human enactments, or conventional usages. They are self-executing; ever true in their decisions, and inflexible in their penalties. Those who expend the reproductive element of their nature for sensual gratification, whether in solitude or otherwise, must receive their reward. Human laws and customs may and do authorise men to do so; but outraged Nature, sooner or later, vindicates herself, and metes out to the transgressor a righteous retribution. And men and women who thus prostitute themselves till they are utterly diseased in body and soul, become fathers and mothers! How idiotic, insane, or imbecile, must be their children! The only cure for such persons is, "*Cease to do evil, learn to do well.*" God cannot serve them in any other way.

*Sexual Abuse during Gestation.* The following cases illustrate the abuse often practised by men upon women, during gestation, under legal and conventional sanctions, and the consequence of such abuses: —

"Dear Friend:

"I send you the following fact; use it as you please. I knew a young woman, who was healthy and bright when she married. She had one child, two years old, and another, a few months. While she was developing this child, previous to birth, her husband forced her to yield to his passion very often, regardless of her tears and entreaties to spare her for her own sake and her child's. Her distress would be so great under his abuse of her during gestation, that she could with difficulty suppress her screams. He would threaten to remove her living child from her, if she did not submit. Within a week after her child was born, he insisted on his legal right to sexual intercourse, and threatened to abandon her and take her children from her if she refused him. The child lived a few months, and died. The man soon died of consumption. The woman soon after fell a victim to the same disease, brought on, probably, or hastened, by the abuse of the man, under the sanctions of law and religion.

"These things were told me by the woman, who often sought refuge with neighbors, to free herself, for a brief space, from legalized and consecrated sensuality.

"Your friend and well-wisher, ———."

Mr. L. and his wife, when they were married, had healthy and vigorous constitutions. They had four living children. She destroyed the fifth conception, procuring abortion at four months. Then she had two other conceptions within fifteen months, and destroyed the fetus at about three or four months. Then she conceived again, and could not procure abortion. The child was born fearfully diseased; it lived four months, and then died. The mother died two weeks after the child was born — the victim of sexual abuse, mainly during gestation. He then got another woman, who, in due time, became pregnant. At about eight months, she had a fit, which lasted twenty-four hours. To bring her out of it, two doctors concluded to take the child from her. She died under the operation. The fit was thought to have been induced by sexual abuse during pregnancy. He took another according to law, — a feeble, consumptive woman. Within about eighteen months, she had two abortions; one at three months and one at six, and both, as it was thought, caused by sexual abuse during gestation. This woman is victimized to her husband's sensuality. He has caused the death of two women, and of several children, and is killing his third wife. This man is counted a just, pure, and Christian man; yet, on this subject, his reason is utterly dark, and his conscience fearfully obtuse.

MENTAL CONDITIONS DURING GESTATION. The following extract illustrates the power of the mental and affectional conditions of the mother over the child previous to birth: —

"I know a child, ten years old, who has a great fondness and faculty for telling stories. I have been often surprised at her talent and propensity, they are so marked. The mother informed me that, previous to her birth, she very often gathered around her a group of children, and amused them and herself by telling them stories, which she usually made up as she went along. She became exceedingly interested in her own stories, and excited by her own creations of fancy, and by the absorbed attention of the children. Her daughter has, from the earliest development of her intellectual and affectional nature, shown a decided propensity and talent for reading and telling stories. I have often heard her when she lost all consciousness of her surroundings, in her wrapt interest in her own inventions."

Another case. The eye of a young lady of S. has a protuberance of the size of a pea, just below the pupil, and it rests on the under eyelid. There is no cure for it. It was there at her birth, and does not occasion her any suffering. No surgeon dare attempt to remove it, lest her eye be ruined. In the early period of gestation, her mother met a woman, and was a day in her society, whose eye was similarly affected, which gave to her a very repulsive look. She was deeply impressed with fear lest her child should come into being with an eye thus deformed. Her mind dwelt upon it anxiously, and this fact probably produced the very result she so much dreaded. Her child was born with a similar affection of the same eye.

Yet another. S. W. has no left hand. His arm is developed to the wrist, and there is a little bit of flesh at the end of it, without bones or fingers. The cause: Some months previous to his birth, his mother, whose dread of rats amounted to a fixed terror, came in contact with one, as follows. She went down cellar to get some milk that stood in an arch. As she was opening the door into the arch, she was deeply impressed with terror lest a rat should suddenly spring up before her. With this feeling, she entered, put her hand up to get at the milk, when suddenly a large rat jumped upon the back of her hand. She dropped her milk, ran in terror up stairs, and, in a state of faintness, dropped into a chair. Her husband came in, saw her condition, and concluded she had met with some sudden terror, but said nothing, lest he should increase it. She recovered, and told him the whole story. He treated it lightly, and tried to divert her attention and to dissipate the consciousness of the sensation caused by the touch of the rat; but she often recurred to it. Her child was born. Her first, anxious inquiry was, "Is it a perfect child?" "Yes," was the answer, no one having seen the defect. Her attention was at once directed to the left hand. She discovered that it was not developed, and fainted. That was her ever-present foreboding, lest her child should be born without the left hand. This protracted terror and anxiety probably produced the dreaded result.

LACTATION. Facts show that nursing infants are not unfrequently greatly injured, and exposed to the keenest sufferings, and sometimes to death, through the effects produced on the Mammary secretions by the mental and physical conditions of the mother.

A woman of a reckless, ungovernable temper, had a child six months old. She was excited to anger by some unguarded words from her husband. She rushed to her chamber, where the child was sleeping, others being present. She was so vociferous and boisterous as to awaken the child. It began to scream in terror at the mother's furious and angry look and manner. The mother took it up and nursed it to still its crying, and then laid it on the bed again. In a short time, it was in violent convulsions. A physician was called, who at once concluded that the convulsions resulted from some hurtful substance in the stomach. The mother told him of the child's nursing, and of her own mental condition at the time. The convulsions were attributed, by the doctor, to the effect of the mother's anger on the Mammary secretions. She was directed not to nurse the child at the breast again for twelve hours, and *never* to do it when she was angry, or in any unnatural excitement.

The following was told me by the mother of a child with whom I am intimate. The child is now twelve years old, and from infancy has had a kind of instinctive longing for tea. Her nervous excitability and restlessness have been a source of great suffering to the child from its birth, and of anxiety and weariness to all who have had charge of her, and have made her an object of dislike to her playmates. The mother assigns as the cause of this derangement of her daughter's nervous system, the fact, that she, (the mother,) during the period of Lactation, and a part of Gestation, drank strong tea, by direction of her medical adviser, in order to increase the quantity of the Mammary secretions. The result was, a diseased nervous system, which must entail a life of bodily and mental suffering on the daughter. She will be repelled from the companionship of those whose society will be most essential to her development and happiness.

The above facts, and the following extract from Carpenter, (Sec. 627 and the note,) should be deeply pondered by every mother and father: —

"No secretion so evidently exhibits the influence of the depressing emotions, as that of the Mammæ; but this may be partly due to the fact, that the digestive system of the infant is a more delicate apparatus for testing the qualities of that secretion, than any which the Chemist can devise; affording proof, by disorder of its function, of changes in the character of the Milk, which no examination of its physical properties could detect. The following remarks on this subject are abridged from Sir A. Cooper's valuable work on the Breast. 'The secretion of milk proceeds best in a *tranquil state of mind*, and with a cheerful temper: then the milk is regularly abundant, and agrees well with the child. On the contrary, a *fretful temper* lessens the quantity of milk, makes it thin and serous, and causes it to disturb the child's bowels, producing intestinal fever and much griping. *Fits of anger* produce a very irritating milk, followed by griping in the infant, with green stools. *Grief* has a great influence on lactation, and consequently upon the child. The loss of a near and dear relation, or a change of fortune, will often so much diminish the secretion of milk, as to render adventitious aid necessary for the support of the child. *Anxiety of mind* diminishes the quantity, and alters the quality of the milk. The reception of a letter which leaves the mind in anxious suspense, lessens the draught, and the breast becomes empty. If the child be ill, and the mother is anxious respecting it, she complains to her medical attendant that she has little milk, and that her infant is griped, and has frequent green and frothy motions. *Fear* has a powerful influence on the secretion of milk. I am informed by a medical man, who practices much among the poor, that the apprehension of the brutal conduct of a drunken husband will put a stop, for a time, to the secretion of milk. When this happens, the breast feels knotted and hard, flaccid from the absence of milk, and that which is secreted is highly irritating, and some time elapses before a healthy secretion returns. *Terror*, which is sudden and great fear, instantly stops this secretion.' Of this, two striking instances, in which the secretion, although previously abundant, was completely arrested by this emotion, are detailed by Sir A. C. 'Those passions which are generally sources of pleasure, and which, when moderately indulged, are conducive to health, will, when carried to excess, alter, and even entirely check, the secretion of milk.'

"The following is perhaps the most remarkable instance on record of the effect of strong mental excitement on the Mammary secretion. 'A carpenter fell into a quarrel with a soldier billeted in his house, and was set upon by the latter with his drawn sword. The wife of the carpenter at first trembled from fear and terror, and then suddenly threw herself furiously between the combatants, wrested the sword from the soldier's hand, broke it in pieces, and threw it away. During the tumult, some neighbors came in and separated the men. While in this state of strong excitement, the mother took up the child from the cradle, where it lay playing, and in the most perfect health, never having had a moment's illness; she gave it the breast, and in so doing, sealed its fate. In a few minutes, the infant left off sucking, became restless, panted, and sank dead upon its mother's bosom. The physician, who was instantly called in, found the child lying in the cradle, as if asleep, and with its features undisturbed; but all his resources were fruitless. It was irrecoverably gone.' In this interesting case, the milk must have undergone a change, which gave it a powerful sedative action upon the susceptible nervous system of the infant.

"The following, which occurred within the author's own knowledge, is perhaps equally valuable to the Physiologist, as an example of the similarly-fatal influence of undue emotion of a different character; and both should serve as a salutary warning to mothers, not to indulge either in the exciting or depressing passions. A lady having several children, of whom none had manifested any particular tendency to cerebral disease, and of which the youngest was a healthy infant of a few months old, heard of the death (from acute hydrocephalus) of the infant child of a friend residing at a distance, with whom she had been on terms of close intimacy, and whose family had increased almost contemporaneously with her own. The circumstance naturally made a strong impression on her mind ; and she dwelt upon it the more, perhaps, as she happened, at that period, to be separated from the rest of her family, and to be much alone with her babe. One morning, shortly after having nursed it, she laid the infant in its cradle, asleep, and apparently in perfect health ; her attention was shortly attracted to it by a noise ; and, on going to the cradle, she found her infant in a convulsion, which lasted for a few minutes, and then left it dead.

"Another instance, in which the maternal influence was less certain, but in which it was not improbably the immediate cause of the fatal termination, occurred in a family nearly related to the author's. The mother had lost several children in early infancy, from a convulsive disorder ; one infant, however, survived the usually fatal period ; but, whilst nursing him, one morning, she had been strongly dwelling on the fear of losing him, also, although he appeared a very healthy child. In a few minutes after the infant had been transferred to the arms of the nurse, and whilst she was urging her mistress to take a more cheerful view, directing her attention to his thriving appearance, he was seized with a convulsion-fit, and died almost instantly. This case offers a valuable suggestion,— which, indeed, would be afforded by other considerations, — that an infant, under such circumstances, should not be nursed by its mother, but by another woman, of placid temperament, who had reared healthy children of her own."

To the above facts, I would add the following extract from a letter, to show that a tendency to *suicide*, as well as to *insanity*, may be transmitted from parents to children : —

" DEAR FRIEND :

" It is now several years since I became acquainted with Mrs. ———. She was young and beautiful, possessing a fine intellect, which was well cultivated. She, with one sister, were the only surviving members of her family. Her father, brother, and, I think, one sister, had been afflicted with partial insanity, and had terminated their lives by committing suicide. A few years after, Mrs. ———'s health began to decline, and her intimate friends saw indications of aberration of mind. She was put under the care of a skillful hydropathic physician. While under his care, I spent a few days with her, and helped to administer the treatment; and had I not been well acquainted with her, I should have seen no jar in her mind. Soon after I left, she attempted to jump from a two-story window, and thus to take her life; and again, by jumping into a deep pond. Her husband's life was hazarded in rescuing her. Having thus twice eluded the strict watch that was kept over her, her husband thought best to carry her to another Water-Cure Establishment. On their way, they stopped at a friend's, to make a short visit, and while there, she made a third attempt to destroy her life, and succeeded. Thus ended the life of the third, and, I think, of the fourth member of that family, by suicide.

"I also know a family in ———, where the father and two sons, in good circumstances, took their own lives, through fear that they should come to want.

"If the above facts will help you in demonstrating the truth, that mental, as well as physical, qualities are transmissible, they are at your service."

Society abounds with facts to show that the psychological, no less than the physiological conditions of the mother during Gestation, may and do affect the child; often producing deformities, in the shape of marks on the skin, the absence of a hand, or arm, or foot, or an incomplete or unnatural development of some part of the body. To avoid this, women should be trained to habits of calmness and self-possession, and presence of mind under all circumstances of sudden emotion, and in the presence of deformed objects and startling scenes. These qualities are no where so necessary as in a woman in the presence of her undeveloped, unborn babe, whose happiness for life may depend on her calmness and self-possession. It is not the sudden, transient emotion, that is likely to prove injurious to her babe, but a longing, a terror, an anxiety, or any emotion that is prolonged for weeks or months. The deep, abiding, all-controlling psychological condition should be one of sweet serenity, a holy love and reverence for the new life that is being developed within her own; a tender love and yearning desire for the presence, love and sympathizing caress and support of the father of her babe, and perfect trust in his manhood, and self-abandonment of herself and babe to his manly tenderness and protection. The true husband will show himself worthy such loving trust and self-abandonment, on the part of his wife, while she is preparing to crown him with the dignity and glory of a father. Let all husbands and wives deeply ponder the fact, that their homes, and the happiness of themselves and their children, may be affected for life by the *mental conditions of the mother* during the period of Gestation and Lactation. Let the mother, for her child's sake, be guarded from all unnatural and unhappy emotions and excitements, as she, with her husband, would stand in innocence and honor in the presence of their child.

H. C. W.

## LETTER VII.

### The Welcome Child:

PARENTAGE THE RESULT OF CONSCIENTIOUS FORETHOUGHT, AND NOT OF RECKLESS PASSION.

LENAWEE, June, 1852.

DEAR FRIEND:

For no office in life do men and women need a more careful and thorough training, than for that of parentage, — for on none hangs such mighty results. Yet, for this alone they have the least thought of preparation. They submit to years of severe discipline to become boxers, wrestlers, warriors, or statesmen; milliners, blacksmiths, or farmers. But how few seek wisely and conscientiously to discipline their bodies and souls, with a view to become healthy parents of healthy children, and to fill the station of fathers or mothers with honor and fidelity to themselves and their offspring! Men and women are more diligent to get a healthy crop of wheat, potatoes, or apples, and to grow beautiful and fragrant flowers, than to give existence to healthy children, with beautiful souls, fragrant with love and spiritual life.

How often men and women, even in legal marriage, are brought into the parental relation, not only without any design or desire on their part, but in opposition to their wishes! How often conception takes place against the most earnest prayer of the woman's heart! The husband demands the gratification of his sensual passion. In her heart, the wife repels him, yet, for the sake of peace, and to retain her husband with her, yields. He cares not for the child that may result. Passional indulgence is all he seeks; and even in the sexual embrace, the wife prays in her heart that there may be no conception. But there is, and the unwished-for child is born, conceived and developed in the organism of one, whose heart throbs only with anguish, struggling against the very existence of the tender life that is being formed within her own. What must be the character of human beings thus generated and developed?

When will men and women show a rational, conscientious, loving forethought, in giving existence to their children? In growing grain, fruit and cattle, in commerce, politics and religion, they are considerate, and show great deliberation, and skill, and forethought; but how utterly thoughtless and reckless are they in entering into the relation of parentage! Their children are the offspring of chance, of mere reckless, selfish passion. A child of fierce, ungoverned passion, and the child of love, controlled by a conscientious forethought, and acting in harmony with Nature, — how different their characters! — how dissimilar their destiny!

Let every father and mother, and all who hope to become such, ponder well the two following letters. The first is from a physician and his wife, and the second from an enlightened farmer and his wife. I give them, in substance, as they were written. Every friend of

Humanity must rejoice to see such cases multiplied. By this loving and wise forethought alone, can the reproductive element in man be rescued from the pollution, shame and disgust, now so often associated with it in the minds of wives and mothers, and made conducive, not only to the perpetuity, but also to the purity and dignity of human nature.

"Dear Friend :

"I sit down with my wife to say a word to you on the importance of attending to our conditions of body and soul, in taking the initiatory step in the process of creating a new being in human form. We have three children ; two of them having been born since our conversation with you, and since you urged upon us the duty to have in view the health and happiness of our child, rather than our own sensual gratification, in performing the act in which that child was to originate. You justly dwelt upon the fact, that the child must be more or less affected for life by the physical, mental and spiritual conditions of the parents at the time of sexual congress. It must be so ; and the most sacred obligations rest on those who would assume the holy and exalted relation of parents, to attend to their conditions, of body and soul, when they take that first step in the process of Nature which is to give existence to a rational being, to call them father or mother, and whose happiness is to be deeply affected by their conditions. As you say, 'LET THERE BE LIGHT,' on this point, as well as on others relating to this purest and most potent, for good or evil, of all human acts. Let the most fitting conditions, in both husband and wife, be clearly understood, and then let them be sacredly regarded. None but the unjust and impure can knowingly disregard the fiat of God in this matter, and, for merely sensual gratification, do the deed which is to place them in the relation of parents, without any thought for the welfare of their child. When the desire for a child, and for its health and happiness, rather than sensual pleasure, shall prompt to the act, then, and never before, may we hope to see the earth peopled by a nobler type of human kind.

"We would say a few words respecting our conditions at the time of the act of reproduction, in the creation of each of our children; and if we say the same things, it is because our thoughts, as well as our affections, run in the same channel. We are able to give some particulars in reference to each child; for we have kept a record,— to us a dear and sacred record, — of our physical, intellectual and spiritual conditions, and of our external material and social surroundings, when each was conceived, developed, and born. No written or printed record can ever speak to our hearts as does that; none can ever awaken memories so sweet and precious, for in it are noted the conditions and circumstances that stand connected, in our minds, with the purest and most intense joys of our wedded and parental hearts.

"The conditions under which we gave existence to our firstborn, a son, were far from what they should have been. It was before we had turned attention to the subject. We had no thought that our conditions at the time would affect our child. Indeed, the act was not performed with reference to offspring. We had no wish for a child, and, of course, cared not for its welfare, should one ensue. Our own gratification was the sole motive by which we were influenced. It was in August. Physically, mentally and spiritually, we were greatly prostrated by the heat of the weather and by toil. Our bodies and souls were without life or energy. Our conjugal affection was inactive. We were in a state of wounded pride and hostility towards some of our neighbors. Our vital forces were dormant, or, if exerted, had been for several days in a state of hateful activity. The act was performed. A child was the result. That boy is sluggish, and has a feeble, inactive body and soul. The life-principle of his nature has no buoyancy. He is listless; he has no energy of will, and little resolution; is sullen on trifling occasions, and it is very difficult to divert him from a sense of injury. Life seems dark and gloomy to him. We think we can trace much of his imbecility and suffering, of body and soul, to our conditions at the time he was originated. We made no preparation for the act that was to ultimate in parentage.

"For some time previous to the creation of our second child, a daughter, we had the subject under consideration. We studied to know what conditions in us would most conduce to the well-being of our child. We were both in better physical health than we had been since our marriage. Animal life was active and buoyant. Conscious life seemed but another name for conscious bliss. We were happy in each other, in our friends, and in our surroundings. Our first-born was three years old. Intelligent, genial, happy friends were around us, and daily with us. We sought to turn our thoughts and feelings as much as possible to the one great end we had in view,— A PERFECT CHILD. On this, our souls were concentrated. We felt deeply impressed with the fact, as we never had done before, that each depended on the other for this happy consummation. That each might prepare the other to bestow this blessing, I was led to give all the tender, loving and devoted attentions to the physical and spiritual comfort of my wife, of which my manhood, penetrated by deep, concentrated love, was capable. She did the same by me; and thus, in seeking each to prepare the other for this function, the best possible preparation was secured to ourselves. In proportion as I sought to prepare my wife to become a mother, I prepared myself to be a father. The act in which the two elements were blended, and in which our daughter originated, was consummated in September. Our child was born in June. The hearts of a proud and happy father and mother need not assure you respecting the physical, intellectual, social and spiritual organization and conditions of our child. In her perfect health, beauty, energy, activity, and love-nature, we find our reward for our wise and considerate course in the process of giving her existence. With her, as with her parents at the time of her conception, *conscious life is conscious heaven*. You know and appreciate her, and we need add no more about her.

"When our second child was in her fifth year, our third was born. For one year previous to the blending of our two elements, in which this object of our love originated, we sought to bring our bodies and souls into that state which, in our view, would be most favorable to give existence to a type of Humanity as superior to ourselves as possible. We abstained from all artificial stimulants, drank only cold water, and used mostly a vegetable diet. We abandoned all late social parties, kept aloof from all occasions and scenes calculated to produce unnatural excitement of the intellect or the heart. We avoided all crowded or excited gatherings. We took special pains to keep ourselves in a pure, fresh air. We were often together, and with a few intimate friends, in the fields and the woods, and amid the beautiful, calm, bright scenes of Nature. We were together nearly every hour for about one year, and by all the offices and endearments which our love prompted each to crave from, and render to, the other, we sought to perfect the oneness of our souls, and to call into activity and to blend all the purest, most refined and ennobling elements of our natures. We made our lives subservient to the welfare of the child whom we intended to bring into existence. Our child, for whose welfare we prayed, even before its conception, came to us, — the child of our Love, our Reason, and our Conscience, and not of mere sensual Passion. She is now about two years old; the child of the day, and not of the night; of light, and not of darkness; of a calm, tender, loving forethought, and not of reckless sensuality.

"By me, at this moment, sits the happy mother of my child, with our daughter, laughing and delighting in her smiles and caresses. We think that no such child could come into being as the offspring of passion, that takes note of nothing but its own gratification. Such a child could not be begotten by accident. No woman could conceive and develop such a child, while her soul was crushed in her struggles against its existence, from the initiatory act to its birth. We wanted a healthy, happy child, to be the joy and glory of our home, to represent us in the race, and to be an ornament to the nature we bear. We practically and deliberately sought such a child. There, before me, with its arms in ecstacy twined lovingly around her mother's neck, is our reward.

"As physicians,— for we are both in that profession, in fact, and have much to do in midwifery,—we are prepared to endorse all you have said to us on Marriage and Parentage, and on the transmission of parental conditions to children. Too much attention cannot be given to the conditions of parents at the time of the reproductive act, and during gestation. In blending the masculine and feminine elements, should sensual gratification, or offspring, be the ruling motive? Should mere sensual passion rule, or should the union be consummated under the guidance of Love, of Reason, and of Conscience? Should the gratification of the sexual instinct rule in that relation, or the perfection and happiness of the child?

" During the period of gestation, let the mother be surrounded by the tenderest care, and guarded from all harm. Let her take heed to what she eats and drinks, and to her temper and disposition. Unnatural stimulants, to body or soul, are always hurtful to the unborn child. The mother should shun them, if she regards her child. Let husbands beware how they treat their wives during gestation, and do all they can to save them from excessive toil and fatigue, and from all depression, anxiety, and gloom of spirits. Let them do all they can to surround their wives with comfort, and with all bright, quiet, cheerful, happy influences. Above all, let them abstain from all sexual commerce with them, or excitement of the sexual instinct. Let the life and energies of both be consecrated to the perfection and happiness of the new immortal for whose existence they are responsible.

" But I forbear. We both bid you God-speed in your efforts to discover and publish the true, natural laws that were designed to govern the masculine and feminine elements, as they are embodied in human form, and to call men and women to obedience to those laws. Evermore be true to your favorite text, ' LIKE PRODUCES LIKE,' till the sexual instinct shall be brought under the control of Conscience, and become, practically, the purest and noblest attribute of our nature, and the means of our highest elevation, and truest and most ennobling joys.

"Yours, ———— ————."

---

" DEAR FRIEND :

" We are in the humble walks of life, — without fame, and without property, except the dear little farm on whose fruits we live, and on which is the home of our love. Your views on Marriage and Parentage are known to us, and we welcome them as truths direct from God to all who are living, or expect to live, in conjugal relations. Your teachings on the expenditure of the Reproductive Element and the government of the Sexual Instinct, we accept, and, in our united life, seek to live out. You say, the existence of children is under the control of parents. We know it is true. You seek to bring the sexual instinct and the reproductive element in men under the control of Reason and Conscience. We know it can be done. The following is the history and result of our experience, since we entered into the relation of husband and wife.

" We have lived together in this relation seven years. We have one child, now two years old. We had one hundred acres of land to begin with, and nothing else. About one half of it was covered with a dense forest, with little fencing on the cleared part, and on it a log cabin and barn. Before we began to live together as husband and wife, we often conversed on the subjects presented to us by you, especially on the laws that should govern passional intercourse and the expenditure of the Reproductive Element. It was settled in our minds, that the conditions and wishes of the wife should ever govern that relation; and thus we determined it should be with us. We also settled, that we would have no child until we had prepared for it a comfortable home, in which to give it a suitable welcome.

" Our union was publicly recognized. We at once moved to our log-cabin home. We cleared and fenced our homestead.

We toiled steadily and happily together three years. We had nothing of this world's goods, except what we raised on our farm. We were happy in our rude home. Love made labor light and pleasant. We both labored for an object, that now rose to our vision, tender, bright and beautiful. Each labored for the other, and for the child that each was to receive from the other. The hope of having a home of love and comfort for my wife, and the child she was to bestow on me, nerved my heart and my arm. We toiled together; we grew together. Daily and hourly was the oneness between us made more perfect.

"But we had no child. Our neighbors began to ask us, jokingly, why. We assured them the child would come when we were ready for it, and wished for it. Meantime, we put up a pleasant cottage house, furnished it comfortably, and surrounded it with flowers and fruits, such as we could command. Our cottage home seemed to us an Eden of God, for in it, in anticipation, we blended our souls, our very existence, to form a new being; and in it, we hoped to welcome the angel embodiment of our love. As robins prepare their nest, exerting all their skill to make it comfortable and beautiful to welcome their tender young, so we planned and built ours, with a view to give our hoped-for nestling a tender, joyous welcome.

"On the fourth year, we raised wheat and corn to supply us for two years. We sold off our stock, and so arranged our affairs that we could devote the fifth year to one of the great ends of our united existence,— the creation of a child, to bless us, and be blessed by us. To the best of our knowledge, we did what we could to secure to our child a healthy organization of body and soul. Before the sexual union was consummated in which our child originated, we endeavored, for some months, to get our bodies and souls into as healthful, happy conditions as possible. We both longed for a child. Our home seemed lonely and desolate without one. We needed the sweet smiles and prattle of a child to perfect our natures. We wanted to hear the pattering of the little feet of *our* child on our floor. I wished to see my child nestling in the bosom of my wife; she, to see hers resting on the bosom of her husband. Each looked to the other for this great consummation. This feeling of mutual dependence, consecrated by love, found expression in all loving and anxious efforts in each to surround the other with material comforts, and an atmosphere of sweet repose and heavenly beauty.

"On the first day of May, in the fifth year of our united life, our daughter came to us, bearing, in the health and beauty of her person, in the soundness and vigor of her intellect, and in the purity, gentleness, sweetness and power of her affections, Heaven's holiest, noblest boon to her parents' hearts. Our forethought, our self-control, our tender solicitude and anxious preparation, are rewarded a thousand-fold.

"This child is our family Bible, whose pages we have studied hourly and devoutly. This angel babe comes to purify and ennoble our natures, to beautify and perfect our oneness, to make earth a paradise, to take us by the hand and lead us to a bright and glorious future, by a pathway adorned with all fragrant and beautiful flowers. Where can man find Eden, where can he commune with God, if not by the side of his loved and loving wife, contemplating his babe, as it nestles in her bosom? In the face of that babe and of its mother, God and Nature reflect all their concentrated beauty, sweetness and brightness to his heart.

"But I must stop. Our hearts' prayer is, that every man and woman may be blessed with a home of love, where they may find rest and peace to their souls.

"Yours, truly,

———— ————."

Is the child the result of a voluntary act on the part of its parents? Are its organization, character, and destiny greatly controlled by the physical, intellectual and spiritual conditions of parents at the time of the sexual union in which it originated, and during its development previous to birth? These questions can admit of but one answer. Then did those parents who penned the above letters act rationally, justly and nobly, in thus seeking the welfare of their offspring. Their conduct is worthy of all commendation. Are the wives of those two men happy? Who can doubt it? They fear not the passion of their husbands. That very passion, which is often a source of anxiety, of deep terror, of sickness and death, to wives and their children, is to them an ever-present stimulus to tender and manly sympathy and respect. An ennobling love, and a tender anxiety for the health and happiness of their wives and the mother of their children, control all their passional expressions. Their wives and children are never sacrificed to sexual gratification.

H. C. W.

## LETTER VIII.

### The Unwelcome Child:

QUESTIONS TO BE ASKED AND ANSWERED IN THE FUTURE OF THIS WORLD — RESULTS OF SEXUAL ABUSE TO PARENTS AND CHILDREN.

LENAWEE, June, 1852.

DEAR FRIEND:

UNDESIRED and unwelcome children! Are such ever born? It would seem impossible; so unnatural, so unjust, and so monstrous does it seem, to impart the life-germ, to develop it into a human form, and give birth to a living child, and then frown coldly on the helpless, tender being you have forced into existence, without any choice or will of its own. Of all the victims of human ignorance and crime, none so deserve tender, pitying sympathy, as an unwished babe! Of all the wrongs that can be done to it in after life, none can ever equal that done by its parents before it was born, and at its birth. Those who give existence to a child, when they do not wish one, and when they are not prepared joyfully and proudly to welcome its birth, whether in legal marriage or out of it, deserve to be, and will ere long be, deemed the most criminal of human kind.

Yet, such unwelcome children are not uncommon; and the authors of their being, who dreaded and execrated their appearance in life, as a burden and an encroachment on their pleasures, are held in respect, as just, honorable and Christian men and women. What language can adequately portray the hardened depravity of that mother's heart, who could give the following answer to the question, — "How did you feel towards your first child when it was born?" — "*I felt as if I wanted to slap it in its face!*" What a welcome for a mother's heart to accord to her unconscious, innocent babe! Yet that woman is highly cultivated and highly associated! What must that child, now a woman, think of the mother who could consent to receive into herself the germ of a new life, and develop it under a heart pulsating with repugnance to its existence, so bitter, and so monstrous? What can the daughter think of the man who could be so lost to justice and self-respect, as to become a father by a woman so heartless and so debased?

A father and son, in my hearing, thus addressed each other. The father was angry with his son, and said, — "You have been the plague of my life; I repelled you and cursed you, before you were born, and at your birth!" "Father," said the lad of eighteen, — a sad scapegrace, — "am I your son?" "You are," said he, "to my shame and disgrace be it spoken. You have dishonored me, and will bring my head to the grave in sorrow." "And," said the son, "you hated and cursed me before I was born, and my mother tells me she would have killed me in the womb, if she could have done so without endangering her own life." "Yes," said the father, "from your conception to your birth, we both struggled against your existence, and when you were born, our first feeling was that of deep regret that you had come, and, on my part, a wish that your stay with us might be a short one. You have been violent, headstrong, revengeful and vicious, from your childhood." "Where is the fault?" asked the son. " How could I be otherwise, ushered into life as you say I was? Little love and respect do I owe you for a life you have cursed from the beginning. If my existence was such an offence to you, why did you give it to me?"

Are such parents deserving pity or condemnation? They gave birth to a child when they did not wish one, and they suffer the natural and necessary retribution. The momentary gratification of their sexual passion, when they were averse to having a child, has been fearfully avenged. That unwelcome child, whose existence was so offensive to them, has made even their wealth, their elegantly-furnished home, and their social, political, and religious position, the source of ever-present mortification and anguish.

Not unfrequently have I heard parents, among the rich and the poor, especially mothers, bewail the conception and birth of their children. This lament is not uncommon in the heart, if not expressed in words, and it is felt and heard among all classes. What does it mean? The robber, the slaveholder, the pirate, the drunkard, the warrior, bewail the wounds and diseases, the moral indignation, obloquy and sufferings, that result to themselves, as the natural consequences of their vices and crimes; yet they go on doing the same deeds. So these parents lament the undesired conceptions and births that necessarily result from their sensual indulgence; yet persist in their right to the indulgence, and in the repetition of it. The husband demands sexual intercourse as his right, and as the great end of marriage; the wife yields, both knowing that a child may and probably will be the result, yet the hearts of both pray earnestly against it. The babe is born, — the unwelcome offspring of mere sensuality; but born only to bring shame and sorrow to those who cursed its life with the curse of an undesired existence. The only apology that can be offered for such parents is that which Jesus offered for his murderers, — "*They know not what they do!*" This is true, and no wonder it is true, for what has the family, the school, the church or state, done to give them light? They have, for the most part, been dumb as death.

For many years, I have been accustomed to free conversation with men on this subject. In regard to the intent and the result of passional intercourse with their wives, I have put the following questions to many husbands, solely with a view to get the testimony of their experience as to the manner in which children are begotten, developed, and born; and few have repulsed my inquiries, when they have understood why they were made. Man would be true and noble to his wife and his child, if he knew how to be.

1. What proportion of the acts of passional intercourse was held with an earnest desire to have children?

2. What proportion has issued in conception?

3. What proportion of conceptions has issued in the birth of living children?

4. What proportion of conceptions was joyfully and thankfully welcomed by your wives?

5. What proportion of living births has been longed for and welcomed by both parents?

6. What proportion of those who were born alive died in infancy?

7. Have your wives suffered much during gestation and child-birth?

8. Have you been accustomed to sexual indulgence during gestation and lactation?

9. What has been the effect of such indulgence on the mother and child?

10. Are your wives diseased in the symbols of womanhood?

11. What influence has your passional relations to them had in producing these diseases, and the consequent sufferings both to them and your children?

To hundreds, in different conditions and classes of society, have I put some or all of these questions; and from many received written answers, and from nearly all to whom they have been put, sincere and kindly ones. They bear on all that is beautiful, noble and lovable in manhood and womanhood; to all that is sweet and dear and holy in home; to all that can make home an Eden, where alone the sweet flowers of affection, and the golden fruits of a concentrated, vitalizing love, can blossom and ripen. They involve the character and destiny of individual man, and of states and kingdoms.

Man is not designed to be a brutal sensualist, but a gentle, generous, loving, just and noble being, and such he may and will be, in the future of this world. When he comes to understand his true relation to woman, and the true mission of woman to him, and how to make that relation conduce most effectually to his elevation and happiness, he will not receive her, when she comes to him as a wife, and the mother of his children, as he now does. An unselfish, wise and tender love, not selfish, reckless passion, will watch over and guard from all harm, the wife that trustingly nestles in his bosom, as in the bosom of her God, there to receive and impart eternal life and peace. Woman, then, will not fear the passion of man, but as it is controlled by wisdom, by love, and a tender, manly regard to her life and happiness, for whom it exists, she will find in it the fulfilment of her wants and the completion of her destiny, as a woman.

Let all husbands and wives, and fathers and mothers, and all who hope to become such, ponder well the following cases. They are reported by one who, as a physician, has earned, by observation and experience, the right to speak on the subject of which he treats. If physicians would note down, and report, as this man has done, cases of sexual abuse, and their results, they might give life to many a crushed and despairing heart; and to many a home, light for darkness, beauty for ashes, and transports of joy for the spirit of heaviness, by teaching men the fixed, just laws of God, that were designed to control the expenditure of the Reproductive Element; they might forestal most diseases, by removing their causes, make the earth to be peopled by nobler and more beautiful types of manhood and womanhood; and thus become ministers of grace and angels of mercy to a corrupt and bewildered world. Like Jesus, their mission would then be, "TO SAVE, AND NOT TO DESTROY."

"My Dear Sir:

"Your letter was duly received. You have made an important inquiry of me, which I will here insert, and to which I will attempt a brief answer:

"'In your practice as a physician, have any facts come under your notice, illustrative of the diseases resulting to the bodies and souls of parents and children from sexual abuse?'

"I can assure you, that, from a somewhat lengthy and extensive practice in two of the New England States, especially in the diseases concerning which you ask information, I could furnish numerous cases in answer to your inquiry. Rheumatism, neuralgia, dyspepsia, loss of appetite, universal debility, imbecility, loss of memory, of speech, and of all self-respect, are some of the physical, intellectual, social and moral consequences of an abuse of the sexual element, whether in solitude or in legal marriage. And in regard to children, I have seen idiocy, insanity, physical and spiritual deformity, to my full satisfaction, resulting directly from such abuse. Only two or three specific cases, upon which your question bears, can I give you, for want of time; these must suffice.

"The Case of a Clergyman and his Wife. He, a fine, bright young man, was educated in one of the New England colleges, and graduated with high honors, and after a course of theological studies, entered the ministry, was ordained and settled. She, the daughter of a wealthy merchant of a New England city, had received a polished education, and was the pride of her father's family. They married. He was beloved for his cordiality, and admired for his soul-stirring eloquence in his public addresses to God and man. But not many years had passed before some of his people discovered irregularities in his appearance and conduct. Something seemed to be going wrong with him, which was attributed to his devotion to the duties of his profession. It was finally decided that he was insane. He was sent to an Asylum, remained four months was no better, and was taken out by his friends; remained out a few months, grew worse, was again sent to the same Asylum, stayed another term, was adjudged incurable, and again taken to his friends.

"As for the wife, soon after he was carried to the Asylum the first time, she became insane, and was sent to an Asylum in another State. After a few months of separation from her husband and of kindly care, she became so much improved that she was dismissed, and returned to her father's house.

"It was at this time and place that I first became acquainted with her, while attending a sister, who had long been an invalid from female weakness and disease, supposed to have been caused by injuries received by a fall. From her I learned the history of her sister and husband. It had been decided by the friends of each, that it would be unsafe for them ever to live together again, even should he recover, as it was thought he had so long and so fearfully abused his manhood, that he had for ever lost the power of self-control, and it was not safe for them to see each other. The wife felt the same necessity, and had thus determined.

"But she loved him still, and all the more for her two children's sake; and she knew that he loved her and them, though, through ignorance, he had so fatally abused himself and her, as well as her children. The son was a perfect picture of him, and the daughter of her. Both were in feeble health, and the most perfect specimens of nervous excitability;— the natural and necessary result of the great wrong done by their father to himself and their mother.

"'Do you think, doctor, there is any hope that any means can be used to restore my husband to health, to society, to me and our children, again?' Questions like this the wife often asked me. My reply was, 'I fear not; yet it may not be impossible.' After much importunity, I consented to make a trial, having had experience in cases of insanity, especially those produced by causes similar to such as, I had no doubt, had produced it in him and in her. He was accordingly brought to my house, and remained under my special care and treatment for the period of six or eight weeks; in which time, he had so much improved in health, both of body and mind, that I dismissed him to go and visit his friends in different parts, and to return after a specified time, which he did, much improved every way,— in good spirits, buoyant with hope of a reünion (as he called it) with his wife and children, and of starting again in life, a wiser man.

"I advised him to spend the winter in some employment suited to his capacity, and in the spring, if his health remained firm, it would doubtless be safe and proper for him to live again with his wife and children. He did so; spent the winter in teaching, and when spring came, he again united with his wife, and soon resumed his profession as a minister. He is now settled over a parish in New England, living prosperously and happily with his family, loving and beloved.

"Now for the causes of this insanity and unhappiness. I will give you the substance of his course of conduct, as nearly as I can remember, as he related it to me. When quite young, he entered a college in one of the New England States, and soon, in common with many of the students, acquired the habit, and nightly pursued the practice, of solitary sensual indulgence. This habit he continued through his whole collegiate course. Several times his health became so much impaired, and his nervous system so irritable, (as his family were made to believe, by hard study,) that he had to suspend his studies at various times; but his aptness to learn carried him through, and he received the honors of the college at the end of the term. He continued this habit through his theological studies and his preparation for the ministry, and up to the time of his marriage; after which, he indulged in sexual intercourse excessively, until his insanity became complete, and his wife, pure and healthful when he took her, became the victim of his lust, and shared the same fate,— that of a maniac; and his children, begotten under these circumstances, are irritable, nervous, physically and mentally diseased, — monuments of sexual abuse, and victims of the violated laws of reproduction in their parents.

"When this man first came under my charge, he was pale, feeble, emaciated, dyspeptic; all the symbols of manhood were diseased by nightly and daily abuse. Mornings, he was stupid and imbecile, almost an idiot. I had to pull him out of bed, and shake him about, as I would a man drunk with some narcotic, to arouse any energy or action in him. At times, he would be lively and eloquent, and then gloomy and disconsolate; sometimes entirely avoiding society, unwilling to sit at my table, lest the cause of his condition might be discovered; ashamed of himself, — as well he might be. Such are some of the natural and necessary consequences of sexual abuse.

"At their request, I gave them directions in regard to their future conduct in the marriage relation, which I have no doubt they religiously obeyed.

"Now, my dear sir, if these cases, very hastily, and consequently, very imperfectly, reported, will be of any service to you or the world, you are at liberty to make such use of them as you choose. I have no doubt that similar abuses are the true sources of many of the cases of loss of voice, of dyspepsia, of consumption, and premature prostration of the physical, intellectual and moral powers, so often occurring among ministers and professional men. Their sedentary, studious habits, and want of physical labor in the open air, tend powerfully to strengthen and excite the sexual instinct, and, in their ignorance, they exhaust the very life of their manhood. They are versed in what is called the science of God, the science of Law, and the science of Medicine, but are fatally ignorant of the laws of physical life and health, especially of those designed to govern the expenditure of the reproductive element. They, by indulgence, lose the power of self-control, and their overmastering sensuality hurries them swiftly to destruction.

"Another case was that of a woman who had been married

ten or twelve years. She was small and rather delicate, but was well when she married. She had several children in quick succession, her health gradually failing from the first to the last child; after which, she continued to grow worse and worse, until she became a maniac, at the age of thirty-two. She was carried, by advice of physicians, to an 'Insane Retreat,' and remained three or four months, when she was either dismissed or taken from the Institution, no better than when she entered. On her return, she fell into my hands. I immediately searched into her past history, especially since her marriage, and became satisfied that she came to her then wretched condition through sexual abuse. I endeavored to inspire her with sufficient confidence in me to make her willing to yield to my treatment. I found the vagina much diseased, the womb prolapsed and retroverted, and the whole surface of the *cervix uteri* covered with ulcers and red granulations, and other parts entirely diseased, of which I will not here speak. I immediately commenced doctoring the cause, and the result was, perfect sanity in less than four weeks ; and it is now more than four years since there has been any appearance of the disorder. But her constitution is broken, her health destroyed, and she must drag out the remainder of her days an invalid. A flower was blighted by the cruel demands of unbridled passion. It cannot bloom again, until it shall be unfolded, in immortal beauty, in the spirit land. The kind, but misguided, husband, learned a lesson too late, and all the regrets he expressed, and the bitter tears he shed, can never avail to restore his once healthful and blooming companion to his bosom again. He demanded indulgence continually, without regard to her conditions or wishes, — through ignorance, I believe, — and she yielded, (during gestation and lactation, as well as at all other times,) through the same ignorance of the direful consequences to herself and children, and through the too general belief, that the wife must submit to the demands of the husband, *nolens volens.* How gross, how fatal, yet how general, the error, that woman comes to man as a wife, only as a means of his sensual indulgence ! How few men have any other or higher ideal of

Marriage than that of a licensed, uncontrolled gratification of sensual passion!

"One more case. Quite lately, I was conversing with a young married woman on Marriage and Parentage. I had been the accoucher in her first and only confinement, which was very painful, and I felt quite confident that a double tax had been levied on her constitution during the period of gestation. I said to her—'You ask me, madam, why so many women, being healthy when married, in the course of a few years run down, look pale, and become sickly, and wholly inadequate to the cares of a family; I will tell you. In the first place, their energies are constantly taxed to gratify the sensuality of their husbands, until they become pregnant, and then doubly taxed by the same indulgence and the support of the fetus; and this is continued nearly up to the time of the birth of the child; and then, soon as the child is born, they claim and obtain the same indulgence, while the infant is drawing the life of its mother from her breast, for its support and growth. Even more than this is laid upon the wife and mother, for, in a few months, women sometimes become pregnant again, while nursing their babes; and thus they are taxed with the three-fold burden of administering to the sexual indulgence of their husbands, the support of the infant at the breast, and of the fetus in the womb. Do you now wonder so many fade early, pine and die?' 'O!' said she, with tears and sobs, 'you have exactly described my case. I don't wonder now why I, who was once so healthy and strong, am now so poor and feeble What would I give if it could be otherwise!' 'It can and must be otherwise,' said I. 'O!' said she, 'I should not dare refuse my husband, for the sake of peace. He would be offended with me; for he has often been, and has threatened to go where he could be gratified, if I refused him.' 'Tell him to go, if he will,' said I. 'If he has no more regard for his wife and children than that, he is unworthy of you and them, and fit only to dwell among prostitutes. The time will come when the wife will assert and maintain her rights as a wife, and the husband will feel that he is as much under the control of his wife as she

is of him; and I shall do all in my power to hasten the day.'
'I thank you, sincerely,' was her grateful reply; 'and I can only pray God to hasten that time when men will be more mindful of the health and happiness of their wives and children, and less intent on the gratification of passion. It will bring joy and gladness to the crushed and bleeding heart of many a wife and mother, and the restoration and assurance of life and happiness to many homes, which now are overcast with gloom and desolation.'

"I might add many more cases, going to illustrate the fearful results to the bodies and souls of men, women and children, of sexual abuse, under the impious sanctions of human law and custom; but I forbear. Human legislation may sanction the use of alcoholic drinks, but drunkenness, with its train of poverty, misery and death, must result none the less. So it may license the expenditure of the Reproductive Element, as a means of sensual gratification, and without regard to the wife or child; but, sooner or later, Nature will demand a strict account for such an abuse of her purest and noblest function, and award the terrible retribution of painful disease, insanity and idiocy to the transgressors and their innocent, helpless offspring, who are cruelly victimized to the husband's sensuality.

"Yours, ———— ————."

Mark the contrast between the cases reported in this and in the preceding letters; between the welcome and unwelcome child! The one came in answer to the earnest prayer of two united, loving, longing hearts; the other against the wishes of the parents, who were intent only on sensual indulgence, unmindful of the child that might ensue! The one comes into being as a joy unspeakable and full of glory, around whose birth all pure and loving spirits gather to welcome it into life; the other, as an offence, an object of shame and repulsion, over whose birth hover disappointment and discontent.

A welcome or an unwelcome child! How sweet, how fragrant, how noble, how beautiful, is life, conferred under the auspices of a loving, welcoming smile! How dark and bitter is a life bestowed under the withering influence of a frown! To the one, earth is a garden of sweet flowers and delicious fruits; to the other, a dreary, barren waste!

H. C. W.

## LETTER IX.

### Existence of Children:

TO WHOSE AGENCY IS IT TO BE ATTRIBUTED? — WHO IS RESPONSIBLE FOR IT? — A FATAL POPULAR ERROR.

Lenawee, June, 1852.

Dear Friend:

Three topics present themselves in all inquiries into human life and destiny, i. e., Existence, Organization, Development. Whose agency controls these in regard to children? The preceding pages show that the responsibility for their organization and development, previous to birth, rests on the parents. The question arises, Who is responsible for the child's existence? To ask the question, is to answer it. The agency that gives existence to a child is as obvious as that which ploughs the field, plants the seed, tends the crop, and gathers in the harvest. We know the child is the result of an act of the parents.

Yet, through some strange perversion of their moral nature, parents feel no more responsibility for the existence of their children, than for that of the sun. The first earnest inquiry of the child is, "*Who made me?*" Over nothing do children ponder with more seriousness and wonderment. The answer is generally evasive and untrue. A direct answer is given in children's Catechisms. The first question is, "Child, who made you?" "God," is the answer.

This is usually regarded as the first element of a religious education. Those who have not been taught this are counted Heathen and Atheists. Why? Not because they have not been taught to tell the truth, to be sincere, honest, faithful, loving and kind, but because they are not taught to utter what every man and woman may know to be untrue. Parents who have not taught their children this untruth are considered cruel to their offspring. Many an exclamation of surprise and pity have I heard over children who, when asked who made them, have answered, "I don't know."

I heard a little boy hold the following conversation with his school-teacher: —

*Teacher.* Do you know any thing about God?

*Child.* No. Who is he?

*T.* Did your father and mother never tell you about God?

*C.* No; they don't know him. I never saw him at our house.

*T.* Poor child! Did they never tell you who made you?

*C.* Yes, many times. They say I grew in the garden, and that they found me there.

*T.* I must tell you that God made you.

The child was puzzled at this solution of the mystery of his being, no less than by that of his parents, and asked —

*Child.* Who is God? Where is he? I want to see him, if he made me.

*Teacher.* What do you want to see him for?

*C.* Did God make little sister, too?

*T.* Yes; God made all children. Why do you want to see him?

*C.* I want to ask him why he did n't give her eyes like mine. She never could see any thing. Did God make her blind?

*T.* Yes; God never gave her eyes, as he did you, to see all the pretty things.

*C.* Then I don't like him. Where is he? I want to see him, and tell him I don't like him.

*T.* Poor, lost child! How neglected!

In the same school was a little girl, some three years old, of whom the teacher asked — "Jane, who made you?"

*Child.* I grew on a rose bush.

*Teacher.* No, my child, you did not grow on a rose bush. Rose bushes bear roses, not children.

*C.* Yes, I did; for mother calls me her rose bud, and says she found me on a rose bush.

*T.* Poor child! God made you.

*C.* No, he did n't; mother says I grew on a rose bush.

*T.* Dreadful! Shocking cruelty!

"Why," said a visitor, "what have they done?"

*T.* Nothing; not even taught her who made her.

*Visitor.* They feed and clothe her well, and evidently inculcate kind and loving feelings and principles; and the child looks very happy and contented.

*T.* But they have not even taught her that God made her! She has no idea whence she came.

*V.* But she has; she thinks she came from a rose bush.

*T.* But all know that is not true.

*V.* What would you tell her?

*T.* The truth, at once: that God made her.

*V.* But do you not know that is not the truth, and that God had no more to do in the creation of that child than he would have in its death, if its parents were to give it poison?

*T.* I admit that what you say is according to the facts of Reproduction. Children do derive existence from their parents.

*V.* Why not tell them so? When you say to that child, "GOD MADE YOU," your words convey to her mind an untruth, as really as do the words of her mother, when she says she grew on a rose bush.

Thus, in the first step of what is called a religious education, children, instead of being directed to known *facts*, are led off into the regions of romance; and a fiction is presented to them as a fact. Instead of directing their minds to realities, which would, generally, satisfy their curiosity, and set them at rest on the rock of truth, they are sent off into the world of fancy, in search of one to whom they owe existence. From this false starting-point, they are led on, step by step, into the dark, intricate ways of an infinite romance, until they lose sight of the facts of their being, and are prepared to receive as literal truth, the most absurd and monstrous fictions. It is cruel thus to abuse the minds of children, when they so much more readily apprehend facts than fiction, and appreciate truth than falsehood. An untruth is ever hurtful to the human soul.

The following conversation took place, in my presence, between a Minister and a Layman: —

*Layman.* What do you regard as the essential element of a *pious* education?

*Minister.* To know whence we came, what we are, and whither we go.

*L.* I like that. But a child asks you, "Who made him?" What would you say?

*M.* That God made him, of course.

*L.* A friend of mine had a child three months old. It had some pain in the stomach. The mother gave it some *paregoric.* It went to sleep, and never awoke. Who killed the child?

*M.* The mother.

*L.* True; but what difference in the agency of God in the creation of that child and its death? God established a law, by which life resulted, in one case, by an act on the part of both parents; and death, in the other, by an act of the mother.

*M.* True; but God did not give the poison.

*L.* Nor was it the act of God from which that child originated. Are men and women responsible for the *intended* results of their own acts?

*M.* Certainly. If a man strikes another, intending the result to be death, he is responsible for that result, and ought to be so regarded and treated.

*L.* Is not the existence of this child the result of a *human* act, as truly as the death of him who was struck on the head?

*M.* It is.

*L.* Why, then, deceive the child, by teaching him

to hold God responsible for his existence? Why not refer him to the visible authors of his being, and teach him to hold his father and mother solely responsible? In all common things, you refer natural results to natural causes; but here, you introduce an unseen, fictitious cause, to account for a most common phenomenon, the result of human agency.

*M.* But God connected the existence of the child with an act on the part of the parents.

*L.* In the same sense he has connected death with the use of poison; yet, you say, the mother killed the child, — *ignorantly*, to be sure, — but she killed it. When you teach a child to cast on God the consequence of a human act, your teachings are untrue and most injurious. Better teach nothing, than a falsehood. There is more piety in leaving a child in ignorance of the authors of his being, till his own soul shall render the true answer, than to tell him God is responsible for his existence.

*M.* But would you have parents explain to their children the laws of reproduction?

*L.* If you tell them any thing, tell them the truth.

*M.* But would they understand it?

*L.* As well as they do the laws of reproduction among animals and flowers; as well as adults can.

*M.* But adults can understand the distinction of sex, and its use.

*L.* Children can understand this as soon and as well as they can any facts respecting their physical nature. The process of reproduction is ever going on in their presence. It is much more satisfactory and beneficial to children to be instructed in the facts of this process, than to cast a mist about this most important but most common of human functions, and attempt to satisfy their curiosity by falsehood.

*M.* But, in doing this, we must call their attention to the distinction between male and female, and its object.

*L.* True. What then? This distinction is known to children early in life. All animated nature teaches them on this subject. Unconscious of impropriety, they freely and innocently speak of it, till chided by parents and others, and made to feel and think this most common of all Nature's works, and more intimately connected with the elevation or destruction of the human race than any other, must never be spoken of by parents, or by brothers and sisters, except in secret, and then, only in a whisper; and even then, only by males to males and females to females. They are told it is something to be ashamed of, to be able to think, speak or write about it, as they do about other natural phenomena. So the distinction of sex, with its uses and abuses, must be wrapt in mystery, whose deep secrets it were a shame to disclose. On no subject might children more easily be taught to feel and think with purity and respect than on this, were true and elevating influences brought to bear upon them. But now, the manner in which parents, and others, generally think and speak on this subject, is so false and debasing, that it seems a miracle that any child can escape the wreck of his moral nature in reference to this distinction and its natural and ennobling use.

Of all relations, this is the most absorbing, and designed to be the most happy and ennobling; yet it is looked upon as almost the only forbidden topic between parents and children. How many children are taught by parents to know the nature of the sexual distinction and its object? Not one in a hundred.

*M.* But would it not tend to excite the passions of children, and to ruin the moral purity of their hearts and lives? Even without such instruction, we see how soon they take to practices, both solitary and social, that ruin their bodies as well as their minds. How ruinous, then, to teach them on these matters!

*L.* Precisely in proportion to their ignorance on this matter will be their sensualism. It is certain they will, early in life, have their attention called to this distinction, and they will ask what it means. They will, generally, from some source, early learn how to make it a fruitful source of sensual gratification. The question is not, then, shall they know of it? but, from whom shall they get their knowledge?— from those who would keep their hearts pure, and have them associate the distinction of sex and its great purposes with all that is pure and noble in manhood, or from those who will teach them to associate it with all that is mean, shameful and degrading? There is no other alternative. The knowledge they will have. Shall it be of that kind which shall purify and elevate, or pollute and degrade them? The only way to save human beings from solitary and social abuses of the sexual nature is, to instruct them as early and fully as possible, as soon as they are capable of learning any thing respecting their physical and social nature, what is the nature and true design of this distinction of sex. Let them be taught, openly and promiscuously, in a way that shall beget in them a feeling of respect for an attribute so identified with the perpetuity and perfection of the race, and with all reasonable hopes of the triumph of truth over error, of right over wrong. My only hope of salvation from the physical, mental and moral diseases and pollutions that now afflict human beings, is in the distinction of sex, and the endearing relations, the purifying and elevating influences, that grow out of them. From the outset of life, let children be taught, in the family, in the school, in the church, and through the press, to regard the marriage and parental relations that are based on this element as the most sacred, potential and enduring of all human relations. Let them be taught to reverence the natural laws that govern it, as the most sacred and binding of all the laws of God, inasmuch as on obedience to them depend the organization, character and destiny of man now, and in the great future. Let boys and girls understand their natures, as males and females, and the relations which, by reason of the distinction, they are in after life to assume to each other, as husbands and wives, and to all future generations, as fathers and mothers. Then their curiosity is measurably gratified. They will understand the process by which they are created, so far as it can be known. Their thoughts will not dwell upon it anxiously; they will feel little excitement about it; they will be accustomed to hear it spoken of openly, and as associated with truth, with purity and delicacy, with all manly and womanly feeling, and never with shame and pollution. Then, when prompted by Nature to become husbands and wives, fathers and mothers, they will do so naturally, knowing and appreciating the beauty and sublimity of these relations, and prepared lovingly and nobly to meet the responsibilities and discharge the duties imposed by them. Ignorance in regard to the sexual element in human nature, and its great objects and abuses, has been the source of more crime and misery, and a greater hindrance to the progress and elevation of mankind, than ignorance on any other subject.

No act of human life is replete with consequences so important, as that which gives existence to a human being. No act is vested with so much from which we should suppose the human soul would naturally shrink: the exercise of creative power, not to give existence to a flower or a plant, without the capacity to enjoy or suffer, nor yet to an insect, to live a few days and then go into unconscious dust, but to a human being, capable of happiness and misery, and with a soul destined to conscious, eternal existence. The embryo immortal, once started in its process of development, cannot be arrested in its career, but by a crime against Nature. On it must go, in a journey of unending duration, subjected to all the known and unknown vicissitudes of this state and the next. It is a fearful act, and fearful and eternal must be the consequences, for good or evil, to all who do it, and to all who result from it.

Parents! look on your children. See their nature, and all their boundless relations and liabilities. Look on all they are to do and suffer — on all they are to struggle with as they pass from their birth onward, in eternal progression. Look on them, and contemplate all the certainties and probabilities that are before them, and then fold them to your bosoms, as if to shelter them from all possible harm; and remember, they are your own work, and that existence, with all its relations and duties, and the organization that must, in a degree, control their character and destiny, must be traced to your agency.

How can men and women help regarding reproductive intercourse between them but with profound respect? How can they resort to it for purposes of mere sensual gratification? As a *divine* act, they speak of the creation of human beings with reverence; as a *human* act, it is spoken of as what may be done without a thought of the consequences, but as a momentary gratification of a mere animal instinct. In all the round of human life, I do not believe that any one act is more unnaturally and more thoughtlessly done than this, the most important of all. Of none do men and women generally feel more ashamed; in doing none, do they more often feel the consciousness of degradation and of a loss of self-respect. No wonder; for in nothing do they more abuse and debase their nature. The momentary gratification of a mere sensual appetite is their main object in seeking sexual intercourse, and to talk to them about placing the sexual instinct and the Reproductive Element under the control of reason, conscience, and a wise and tender forethought, seems to them mere foolishness. Carpenter justly says:

"The instinct, when once aroused, (even though very obscurely felt,) acts upon the mental faculties and moral feelings, and thus becomes the source, though almost unconsciously so to the individual, of the tendency to form that kind of attachment towards one of the opposite sex, which is known as *love*. This tendency cannot be regarded as a simple passion or emotion, since it is the result of the combined operations of the reason, the imagination, and the moral feelings; and it is in the engraftment, so to speak, of the psychical attachment upon the mere corporeal instinct, that a difference exists between the sexual relations of man and those of the lower animals. *In proportion as the human being makes the temporary gratification of the mere sensual appetite his great object, and overlooks the happiness arising from spiritual communion, which is not only purer but more permanent, and of which a renewal may be anticipated in another world, does he degrade himself to the level of the brutes that perish.* YET HOW LAMENTABLY FREQUENT IS THIS DEGRADATION!"

The question arises, is it right for parents to bring into existence more than they can rightly care for? The answer is obvious. It is a flagrant violation of the law of parentage, for a man and woman to give existence to children whom they cannot or will not care for, and leave them to the care of strangers and asylums. All such parents deserve, and will ere long receive, the reprobation of their neglected children, and of all who respect humanity. A house full of children is counted as the poor man's blessing; but it oftener proves a curse to the children, for the poor man and woman have given existence to more than they can sustain and educate properly. They have brought them into being, only that they may live and die neglected, ignorant and outcasts, to prey upon society. They are born and reared in a state antagonistic to the wealth, comfort and happiness that surround them. They are made criminal by their parents, to be punished by society.

Nature directs each pair to nurse and provide for their own offspring; and it is clearly a violation of Nature for them to create more than they can properly nurse and care for. But most people think they may rightfully have all they have the power to create, and then leave them to be cared for by others or by no one. To a mother of eight children it was said, "You have enough—all you can rightly care for; it is time to stop." "O!" said she, with resignation, "I must have all God sends." "But your husband, not God, is the father of your children, and it rests solely with you and him, and not with God, to say whether you have any more." No more children were born in that family. The husband and wife were sensible people. But suppose a man or woman, through imbecility of body or mind, or of both, to be incapable of rightly rearing any,—is it right for them to become parents? The desire for children exists, where there is no ability to rear them after they are born. What ought such to do? My answer is, each pair should be held responsible for the nursing and rearing of their own children. What greater crime can a man commit, than to give existence to a child that he cannot or *will not* care for? If any act should consign a man to infamy, this should. Yet men who become parents, abandon their offspring to starvation and wretchedness, and to the doom of slavery, are received into religious and political society, and made welcome to domestic circles, and their company and alliance courted, as though they were true and honorable men. They are often counted the highest ornaments of the church and of society, and elevated to the highest offices; while their children, and the mothers who bore them, are suffering in poverty and neglect. Of all earthly criminals, such are the most deserving condemnation.

Who can help but approve the conduct of the woman in the following instance? The account came from the woman, who, for a time, was an object of general censure:—

"A leading man in a church married, and had one child. He was greatly diseased with erysipelas and salt rheum, all inclining to concentrate in a cancer. The mother was healthy, and knew not of his diseases when she married him. The diseases of the father appeared in the child in about one year after birth. The man wished for more children; the woman objected. He insisted; she refused. He threatened a divorce, and to get another woman; she was firm. Finally, he called a Council of his fellow church-members. He told his story; she hers, pleading as her reason for refusing to comply, the fact that he was so diseased, and that he would entail his diseases on her children; that she owed it to herself and to her children, not to inflict on them such suffering. She presented her living child as a specimen of what, in all probability, future children from such a parentage must be. His plea to the Council was, that ' she violated a command of the Bible, which requires wives to " submit to their husbands in *all* things." '
' But,' said she, ' does this require me to aid you to inflict on my children your diseases? My maternal nature teaches me a

different lesson, and my living child is an ever-present remonstrance against my having any more.' 'But,' said one of the Councillors, 'we are commanded to multiply and fill the earth.' 'Does that require me to aid in multiplying diseases, and to fill the earth with suffering? I have aided to multiply cancers, and my innocent child must ever suffer for my act. As the mother of children of healthy bodies and minds, I should feel proud and happy, for thus I should help to fill the earth with beauty, health and happiness; but I cannot aid further to fill it with disease and suffering.' The man left her and her child, went to a distant settlement, took a new name, and found a woman who was willing to submit to him in all things, and aid him to 'multiply cancers, and fill the earth with suffering.'"

That woman had been saved from much sorrow, had she known the physical conditions of the man who sought her as a wife, before she consented to live with him as such. No man or woman should ever enter into the conjugal relation, till they are acquainted with the mental as well as the physical conditions of the person with whom he or she is to be united. Let the man ask respecting the woman he seeks as a wife, Is hers a soul such as I would wish to be blended with mine in my child? — for the souls of both parents, as a general thing, in their leading constitutional tendencies, will pass into the souls of their children. Why, then, shut our eyes to the constitutional bias of those chosen to mingle their spirits with ours in our children? Men often seek those in marriage whose souls cannot mingle with theirs in their children, because they cannot mingle with them in their own persons. They might have known that spirits which are at war with theirs, in their own persons, cannot harmonise with them in their children.

What do men and women know of the mental, social, moral or physical conditions of those whom they are selecting as husbands or wives, and to be the fathers or mothers of those who are, in all coming time, to represent them in the race? Nothing, absolutely nothing, often. Nor dare they seek to know. It would be counted an insult to inquire into this matter. Man! does your nature prompt you to enter into the relations of marriage and parentage? Shun the society of women whose souls are deformed with selfish, envious, revengeful passion; shun the company of the vain, the gossipping, the envious souls, though dwelling in forms of apparent grace and beauty; shun women of *poor souls*, though they have *purses* of untold wealth, and faces and forms of surpassing beauty; shun such spirits as you would some fatal malady, lest your posterity have cause to curse your memory. If your own soul be pure in its tastes and instincts, it will shrink away from intimacy with such. You could not be drawn even into a *law* alliance with them, for purposes of reproduction. The silent, but all-powerful monitions of your own hearts, combined with the voice that would come up to you out of the future, would save you from such a connection.

To woman, I would say, if your nature seeks the love and companionship of a man, as a husband, beware how you ally yourself to one whose soul is sordid, mean, cowardly, ambitious, avaricious, and whose appetites are unnatural, and whose aspirations extend only to the gratification of an animal nature. Such a man, as a husband, will crush your heart, will crucify your moral nature, and will entail on your children souls which it will take an eternity to cleanse and save. But, alas! for the generations to come, in marrying and giving in marriage, little or no account is taken of the constitutional tendencies, the tastes, appetites, or instincts of the soul, or of bodily diseases. There is one continued effort, on the part of men and women, to conceal from each other all mental and social, as well as physical defects, till, by law, the alliance is made, and the bargain sealed; then, when the law has put it out of their power to repent, all cause for concealment is removed, and the soul to which they are tied comes out in all its deformity. Now, wo to your memory, in the estimation of posterity! The world is full of facts to warn all against such alliances. The human family, itself, is but one great remonstrance against them.

Of all the periods of our existence, probably none is so important in giving tone and direction to our character and destiny, as that which precedes our birth into this state. It is brief; but its every moment leaves its indellible impress for good or evil. Then and there, the elements of the human being are developed, and prepared to enter upon an independent existence in this state. There the question of organic laws, of constitutional and natural tendencies, as to body and soul, is settled, and these must be the supreme laws of life to all. The great future of our being is wrapt up in that brief period. Yet this is the very period of which no account is taken in estimating the causes of human character. The child is little thought of, or cared for, till after its birth. It is thought that human agency begins to act on it after birth, and not before. Governments and Religions do little or nothing for the child in the first brief stage of its being; whereas, that is the very time when it needs all possible care and attention. True, the child can be influenced only through the mother; but through her, its character and destiny may be materially affected by the action of society and its institutions. Let all be taught the facts relating to the child's development during that period, and the direct influence of the mother on it. Let all know how much whatever the mother drinks or eats affects the child; how much every thing which affects the mother's feelings, or mental and bodily conditions, influences the child; and let all mothers be placed in situations where their unborn children may have as good a chance as possible for natural and healthful development, and an auspicious start in life.

Numerous are the cases in which children struggle into life against the wishes of their parents. The moment the mother is assured that she is about to give birth to a child, for various reasons, her soul rebels against it, and she hesitates not to use any means by which she may destroy it, without injury to herself. To prevent, not to promote, the development of her child, to mutilate, not to perfect it, to kill, not to warm and cherish it into life, is her intent and effort. At every step of its progress, the unconscious babe encounters the spirit of murder; and that, too, in the person of its mother. Innumerable would be the cases of abortion, or, in other words, of child-murder before birth, were it not attended with danger to the mother. Doctors, instead of urging men to control their passions, direct their attention to discover means to prevent conception and procure abortion. To kill her babe, the mother endangers herself, and she resorts to medical advisers to help her destroy her children, with safety to herself. Disguise it as we may, to kill a child before it is born, to prevent its birth, even though it can be done without injury to the mother, is no less a violation of the laws of life, than to kill it after it is born. Those doctors who aid women to destroy their unborn children, instead of urging men to control their sensuality, ought to be treated as among the vilest of men. Can a state of mind be conceived more utterly devoid of self-respect, than that which leads a woman to seek the destruction of her unborn child, and which prompts others to assist her?

What must necessarily be the character and disposition of that child, whose pathway into life is beset by a lurking enemy, ever watching to extinguish the first glimmering of the spark of life. He is likely to be, in spirit, what his mother was, and inclined to inflict on her, and on all around, the doom she sought to inflict on him.

It was designed that Love, and *only* Love, should watch over the growth of the child in every stage; but especially in that preceding birth. Nature provides that every step of its progress, from the first act, should be hailed with joy, hope and faith; that it should be welcomed to, and cherished in, the very heart of Humanity, the moment it enters this state; and fondly and reverently cherished, as the sweetest and most beautiful flower of earth,—as God manifest in the flesh. To every child thus born it may be said, by parents, and by all, "He comes to us as a Savior, and we will call his name Jesus." But, Wasting and Destruction are stamped on the brows of many, before they enter into this life. How different the spirit, the character and destiny of that child, whose every step of development, previous to birth, was welcomed with tender love in the mother, compared with that whose steps were watched by deadly hate and murderous resistance! What a staté of society is that which prompts woman to hate her unborn babe, and to seek its destruction! Most unnatural and brutal, though called Christian and civilized.

A perfectly healthy, beautiful LOVE-CHILD, is a joy unspeakable and full of glory to the parents. It is a consummation of our being earnestly to be desired and eagerly and resolutely sought. Who would not be in earnest to perfect his or her nature, if thereby such a priceless boon might be theirs? What a Savior is such a child to the parents! What a God manifest in the flesh to their hearts! In the face of their child, as in a bright mirror, they see a reflection of all that is lovely and great in themselves. If the hope of becoming parents of such children cannot restrain men and women from mean and wicked feelings and acts, and incite them to all that is pure and ennobling, then can no theological motives move them. It is vain to lay before them heaven and hell in the next state; they will not be true to their nature to gain a heaven here. What is heaven, here or there, if it be not one for a man and woman, united by love, to press a child to their hearts, seeing in it all that is good and noble in themselves, and hearing it say, "My father — my mother"? How must such a child regard its parents! By suppressing all evil, and cherishing all good, in themselves, they were prepared to transmit to their child an inheritance of health, of love, of truth, of justice, of true nobility; an inheritance above all riches, and which not all the treasures of the earth could purchase for him. What a relation is this! How exalting! how divine! And such are the parents and children whom God designed to inhabit this earth.

But how many men and women not only pay no heed to themselves, for the sake of their posterity, but, to gain a little wealth for them, sacrifice all that is healthy and beautiful in their bodies, all that is pure and noble in their souls; and thus, while preparing riches for their children, prepare for them all that is deformed, mean, low and execrable, in body and spirit. No amount of gold and silver can compensate for the inheritance of such a *poor* soul. If future generations could speak, one deep, earnest voice would come up from the future to the present, saying, "Give us health and beauty of body; give us rich *souls;* endow us with all noble and generous intellectual, social and moral qualities, and we will take care of the rest!"

How infinitely is a Love-origin to be desired! How above all price is a Love-ancestry! Talk not of an ancestry of princely titles, of knightly deeds in war and slaughter! Talk not of a parentage of wealth, of station and dignity, in Church or State! More to be valued is a lineage of Love, than an ancestry of untold wealth, or of the most honorable titles and standing. This Love-lineage is a foundation on which the soul may build for Eternity!

H. C. W.

END OF PART I.

# PART II.

## Correspondence between a Husband and Wife.

### LETTER I.

#### FIDELITY TO OUR NATURE.

NINA:

THOU art my wife; I am thy husband. That the relation may work out for us and our children perfection and happiness, we must know ourselves, and, knowing, be true to ourselves. In accordance with the demands of our nature, and strengthened and exalted by the relation in which we stand to each other, we meet and hold communion daily and hourly; not in words only, but in a language much more expressive. Yet I wish to record, in the form of letters addressed to thee, my views of Marriage; and I ask thy views on the same subject, in a series of letters addressed to me.

Love for thee, and the desire to secure the highest welfare and happiness of my wife and children, prompt my request. I would record my *present* views and feelings in reference to thee. I ask thee to do the same in reference to me and to our relation, that, in the future of our being, we may be able to call to mind what we were to each other, in the commencement of our united existence. We know what each is to the other now; of the future, we are ignorant. I am thy husband, thou art my wife, now. That is all we know at present. It is enough. Sweetest hopes and holiest aspirations spring up in my heart, from the ever-present consciousness that we hold this relation to each other.

I am not about to record my feelings, wants and intentions, as a human being, a citizen, or a religionist; but as a husband. I would record what, in my opinion, I, as thy husband, owe to thee. Wilt thou not respond to my call? It is the call of Love; and love must respond to love.

As preliminary to what we have to say on the subject of our relation as husband and wife, I have this request to make of thee; that, in thy answers, thou wilt not be influenced by any reluctance to differ from me. Be simply true to thyself, and thus give the most conclusive evidence of thy love and respect for me. No wife can be true to her husband who is false to herself.

Obedience to the laws of thy being, as a woman and a wife, can alone insure the happiness of thy husband and our home. Give to him whatever thy nature prompts thee to give, as a wife; but yield nothing to him, however earnest may be his demand, merely to gratify him, and when, at the time the call is made, thy nature cannot happily respond. So will I be true to my nature as a man. Let the deep love with which each has inspired the other be not only the power that blends our souls, but also the law by which all our outward relations and intimacies in the sanctuary of home shall be regulated. Joyfully yield to me all the love I have the power to awaken, as I will, without restraint, give to thee all thou hast power to call out. If at any time thy wifely love shall grow inactive, and thy nature call not for my caresses as a husband, be openly and frankly true to thyself. Wound not thine own soul! Fidelity to thy reason, thy conscience, and thy womanly instincts, is, in the noblest sense, fidelity to thy husband. Even the fear of wounding thee shall not tempt me to be untrue to myself. On this foundation of perfect fidelity to our own souls, in our intercourse as husband and wife, let all our hopes of the future rest, and then they never will be doomed to disappointment.

Thy husband,<br>ERNEST.

## ANSWER.

Ernest:

Thou hast called me thy wife; thyself, my husband. There are no other words by which we can express the fact, that two separate existences are henceforth merged in one; that a tie stronger than that of kindred blood has bound two souls together; and that this bond is inseparable, not from the force of human laws and enactments, but from its very nature and essence.

It is not the work of human hands or tongues which has made us husband and wife, but a law of attraction superior to our wills, and which we have no power to create or destroy. When we first met, I did not at once recognise in thee the consummation of my happiness. I met thee with indifference, and gave out sparingly the thoughts which lie deepest in my heart. A chance word, which struck upon an answering chord in thee, (which I perceived with surprise and curiosity,) led me on to test still further the points in common between us. The result of this investigation is all told in that I am now writing to thee, as my husband, on questions which can only be truly presented by those who sustain a relation to each other for which there is no other comprehensive word but MARRIAGE, — a relation which those who sustain truly, nobly, fearlessly, will grant is the only one in which the whole nature of man and woman can find a full development.

Some women find their life in intellectual culture; but in such, it is almost a universal fact, that they have powerful natures, which demand an all-engrossing object, and they turn to books for the development which is denied them in the actual relations of life; but books do not meet the fulfilment of their demands. Their standard of manly excellence is high. They are too noble to stoop for marriage, too courageous to fear the stigma of leading a single life; and they give to the silent heroes of the past, the heart-worship which might bring sunshine to the domestic circle of any who could truly estimate its worth. And I say nothing against marriage when I say, they do well. Nothing, in heaven or on earth, can equal a true marriage, as a means of growth and happiness; nothing in the regions of despair can compare with the effects of the legal bond, wherein the heart has no part, for cramping and crushing the noblest powers of the human soul.

From this dark picture, how joyfully does my heart recur to the sense of life, freedom and peace, that flows from my relations with thee, my chosen one! I cannot but be true to thee; for if I differ from thee, I know that thou dost accord to my whole nature the right to its independent thought and action; and therefore, I fear not the loss of thy love, even in a difference of opinion.

How much more am I bound to fidelity to myself, when I know that by this alone can I retain thy respect and love! Thou hast placed before me the highest of womanly excellence. Thou hast said, Strive for that; not for my approbation, though this follows as a necessary result. Thus it is between us, as it is between all who place the truth higher than the individual, that in striving for my own highest development, I secure thy noblest affection, and in my attainments are the reflections of thy nobility of soul.

I am, thy loving wife,

NINA.

## LETTER II.

### THE MISSION OF WOMAN.

Nina:

In this letter, I will take a general view of the mission of woman to man, hoping that thou wilt, in answer, define the mission of man to woman.

In all ages and nations, the fact has been recognised, that woman was made for man. Religion, Science, History, Poetry, Music, and the Drama, in their allusions to woman, base their reasonings and conclusions on this assumption. So with Governments; in their legislative, judicial, and executive proceedings, they assume this as one of the self-evident truths, or fixed facts, of human existence. In Christendom, as well as in Heathendom, woman is supposed to have no rights apart from man; and it is asserted that the sole end of her being, *as woman*, is to develop and perfect man. It is supposed that her own instincts assure her that to this end was she created, and that, so far as she comes short of this, she fails to answer the one great purpose of her existence.

Is this a fact, or has the entire race ever been in error on this subject, both in theory and in practice? The masculine element or portion of the race, in all its manifestations, has asserted and steadily maintained this position. But is it not possible that man may have erred? May not ambition, pride and passion have blinded him to the truth, in this as in other matters, and thus biassed him in favor of this doctrine? In the social, civil, educational and religious institutions with which he has encircled her, man has clearly expressed his opinion of the great end of woman's existence.

But what has woman to say for herself in this matter? The feminine element or portion of the race has generally acquiesced in this decision of the masculine. There have been individual cases of strong and persevering protest among women, wherein they have asserted rights, duties, and a destiny, disconnected with, and independent of, man. They claim that woman has a direct relation to the Creative Mind, without reference to man as a medium through which she is to come at the Divine; that she can be perfectly developed without his aid, and that the utmost limit of progress and happiness which she has power to reach and enjoy, can be attained as well without as with him.

Man has decided that he is the door through which woman must enter the kingdom of heaven; and the jealousy with which he regards these claims of hers, would indicate that he considers all who strive to enter by any other door as thieves and robbers.

On which side is truth in this diversity of opinion? Many questions of grave import are suggested to my mind in connection with this subject. Why is the feminine element embodied in human form? How can its great object be most perfectly accomplished? In what relations, and in what modes of expression, can woman's nature be most happily developed? Do existing social and domestic arrangements, and religious, educational and governmental institutions, truly define the object of her being, and aid in its accomplishment?

There are those who believe that woman alone is competent to answer these questions; that she alone has the right to answer them; and that her decision should be received and implicitly obeyed by men. I believe that *each sex can alone interpret the other;* therefore, leaving to thee the work of defining the mission of the masculine element of Humanity, and of showing how that may be best accomplished, I will proceed to state the nature and design of woman's mission, and how it can be most successfully fulfilled.

The question may arise,—"Has man a right to speak for woman? Can he define her mission, and point to the means of its successful completion?" I answer, that man alone has the ability and the right to explain the great object of woman's existence, and to show how she can most perfectly answer that end. The embodiment of the masculine and feminine elements has no significance, except as each answers to the wants of the other; the organization of each having no object but in reference to the wants of the other. The being who is conscious of a want can alone understand and truly estimate the nature and value of that which is essential to its supply. Man needs refinement, purity, elevation. In vain he looks to man for this consummation. Whatever power man may have to beautify and ennoble woman,—and over her it is almost omnipotent, as is hers over him,—he has little power over his own sex. Woman alone possesses the power to impart to man an influence, without which his nature must deteriorate, and his life be an unexplained mystery. Man has a record which woman alone can read. Manhood is a sealed book, which woman alone can open. The holy mysteries, the deep, eternal truths therein contained, can be interpreted and appreciated only by woman. Woman does not feel the want of the refining, elevating influence of woman, as man does; and therefore she cannot understand and appreciate her own nature and power, as man can, in whom that want is ever present. Man without woman is like a plant without light; he must wither and die. But as the plant inclines to the smallest ray of light, and begins to revive under its influence, so man, whatever be his surroundings, turns to woman, when she is revealed to him, yields to her power, and thereby grows purer, brighter and stronger. His longing for her purifying influence and companionship is the one overpowering want of his existence. She alone can fully meet and satisfy that deep, concentrated want. Who, then, but man, can have the right and the power to speak with authority as to the mission of woman?

The starving man can alone estimate the value of bread. He only who is perishing with thirst can fully realize the worth of water. In like manner, man alone can define and appreciate the power of woman. To him, she holds the relation of supply to an essential natural want; to her own sex, she holds no such relation. From her point of view, she could never take in the full scope of her influence, or realize her responsibility.

Such is the original design of woman, when viewed in reference to man. What influence she is to have on his character and destiny is not for her to determine. Man must decide that, and she will be to him exactly what he makes her.

Instead of cautioning men against the arts and fascinations of woman, it were better to instruct them in the capabilities of their own nature, and teach them how she can be made most conducive to their true development. I repeat it, woman will be to man just what he makes her. If he chooses to make her sex a besom of destruction to his manhood, her power will lay waste all that is noble and manly in his nature. If he seeks in woman a savior, he will find one.

How can woman be made a redeeming power to man?

To a diseased system, even wholesome food may be destructive; but then, the fault is not in the food. A bracing atmosphere will infuse life and strength into healthy lungs, while to those debilitated by disease, it would bring speedy destruction. Woman is an essential element of perfect health and happiness to the soul of man. The feminine element, in itself, is pure, and can no more be corrupted than any other attribute of the Divine nature. Other and corrupting incidents, such as a bad organization or false education, may be connected with it, and pervert it; but the element itself, as embodied in human form, is never impure. Nor can its manifestations to man ever be hurtful, unless they are rendered so by adventitious circumstances. The feminine element, in itself, is natural and perfect, and a true, natural manifestation of it to its corresponding element in any department of life, can never be hurtful to itself or to man, its natural, vitalizing counterpart. The causes of its destructive power must be sought in its attendant circumstances, as in the case of pure air or wholesome food.

As the feminine element is embodied only as a counterpart to the masculine, and has otherwise no significance, and only by the union of these elements can a perfect manifestation of the human soul be obtained, if ever this feminine attribute becomes hurtful to man, the cause must be sought in the conditions of him whose want it comes to supply. Woman has power to meet the holiest, deepest wants of man's soul. An instinct directs him to her to supply those wants, as another instinct directs him to food to appease hunger. He attracts her to himself in the relation of a wife. But shortly he begins to rail against her, finding in her the bane of his life, instead of the completion of his manhood, laying all the blame upon her, and warning all men against her, as their deadliest foe. Whereas, had he looked more narrowly into his own soul, he would have found something wrong in his own conditions, which prevented the healthful and natural action of the woman's nature upon his own. He whose physical and spiritual nature is prepared to receive woman, and to blend harmoniously with her, will find her the "bread of life"; but he whose nature is perverted, and whose wants are therefore unnatural, may find her a deadly poison. Man being diseased, woman cannot be to him what she was designed, and what she yearns to be; and instead of being a refining, ennobling influence, she becomes, without fault of her own, an agent of his ruin.

Man will find among women whatever he seeks. Whether he desires her as a means of mere sensual gratification, or as a household drudge, or as a mother and nurse for his children, or to add grace and dignity to his social position, or a sentimental dependant, to pamper his love of power, he will find among women those who will assume either of these attitudes to him. But if he seeks her as the life-principle of his soul, to add dignity and elevation to his manhood, he will find also, in woman, the satisfaction of his purest aspirations, the noblest fulfilment of his destiny. If he wants a *wife*, in all the deep and consecrated import of that word, she will come to him as the home and heaven of his manhood. Therefore, if man would know what effect woman is to have on his character and destiny, let him look well to the conditions of his own manhood, for she will bear to him, as a general rule, exactly that relation into which he has power to attract her. Let him possess all pure and noble qualities, and he will attract such a woman as can meet and strengthen these conditions. But if he has a gross and impure nature, the woman he will attract will be of a quality corresponding to his own. Woman will embody to him that, and only that, which his soul is capable of comprehending and appreciating. To an impure man, the symbols of womanhood will necessarily have an impure significance. He will find in them only the certainty of sensual gratification. To him, the presence of woman, however pure and perfect she may be, will excite only impure thoughts and feelings; while to the pure, true heart of manhood, her presence, however low and degraded she may be, will excite only tender commiseration and generous sympathy.

Thus, man alone can truly estimate the mission of woman, inasmuch as he alone can be the object at whose elevation and happiness that mission aims. The woman who has done nothing to purify and elevate the opposite sex, in any relation, has embodied the female element in vain. So far as man himself is the cause of this failure, woman may truly, but sadly say, "I came to my own, but my own received me not"; or, if man has welcomed her, it was to make her the agent of his ruin.

The mission of woman! — how beautiful, how delicate, how potent, how sublime! To reveal to man the wealth of his own spirit; to separate the pure gold of his nature from the coarse earth which surrounds it; to give repose to his restless soul; to lead him to his home and everlasting rest in Love — in God! It is a mission of which she may well be proud. In the conscious dignity and divinity of her calling should she go forth to save; for only in her love, her purity and power, can man find his true salvation.

But wo to man when he abuses this holy mission! In proportion as woman has power to save, she has power to destroy. She must bring life or death to his soul. How rich the nature of that man who can fully comprehend and appreciate her mission of love! — to accord to her the welcome she deserves and wishes, and to open his heart to her only as a redeeming influence! Many have eyes, but they see not her true beauty; ears have they, but they hear not the true melody of her voice; they have hearts, but they feel not the true healing power of her presence and her love.

Woman, like God, is practically, to each man, just what he conceives her to be. Let not woman be startled at the assertion, that every element of her physical, intellectual, social and spiritual nature, demonstrates that she received her present organization for the development and perfecting of man. Nor let man be startled by the assertion that he is a helpless dependant on woman. His soul can no more be perfected without her vitalizing and sustaining power, than his body can without food and air. Woman was constituted with the power to beautify and perfect manhood, solely with reference to the want in him which she thus supplies, and he is a dependant on her love and power. He cannot develop and perfect himself without her. He who fails in attracting a woman as a wife, who shall claim his entire manhood, and appropriate it to beautify and ennoble her womanhood, is, among men, like a Sahara on the earth's green surface; and he is but a shallow, pitiful embodiment of manhood, destitute of the first elements of true nobility, who can feel insulted or degraded by this assertion. Every man who has a soul of sufficient power, purity and tenderness to render his nature attractive to the true woman, will recognise this as a fixed fact of his interior and exterior existence. As well might the earth feel degraded by its dependence on the sun, as man by his dependence on woman. Deep and ever-present in the heart of manhood will be the proud and happy consciousness, that without woman he can do nothing.

*How can woman most perfectly develop and interpret man?* She can never truly develop man except in a true relation. Religion, government, and social custom, may sanction the surrender of a particular woman to a particular man, and though they do it in order to make him a nobler and purer being, yet she cannot vitalize and elevate his manhood, unless each is attracted to the other by a concentrated, *exclusive* love. Though the man may love the woman deeply and tenderly, yet the manifestations of her womanhood cannot refine or exalt or satisfy his nature, unless he is fully assured that they are prompted by love. As a friend, a sister, a daughter, and a mother, woman may contribute to man's development and happiness; but she is powerless in these relations, compared to her influence as a wife, for man's wants as a friend, brother, son or father, are feeble, compared to his wants as a husband.

If this be a true delineation of the natural relation of the feminine to the masculine element of Nature, embodied in human form, — if woman exists to contribute to his growth in all high and noble qualities, — why is it that man should ever be cautioned against her influence? Special efforts are made to fortify men against the blandishments and fascinations of woman. She is held up to him by Priest and Parent, Church and Government, as the most insidious and dangerous enemy to his peace. This is all unnatural, and no true, noble man can ever feel or assert it. Was woman made for man? Is she a necessity of his being? Can he be what he was designed to be without her presence and influence? Is man drawn to her by an ever-present and irresistible fascination, as the needle to the pole? Why, then, should he be taught that she is, or can be, his destroyer? Why should he be instructed to guard his heart against her approach and her power? As well tell the needle to guard against the polar attraction, or warn the green meadow against the falling dew. It is monstrous!

Is woman "Heaven's last, best gift to man"? Does she come as "the power of God and the wisdom of God," to develop and ennoble his manhood? Why not, then, hail her advent with a "*Gloria in Excelsis*"? Rather let man go forth to meet her with thanksgiving and the voice of melody; let him open wide his heart to her influence, as one "that bringeth glad tidings of great joy,"—tidings of "peace and good-will to men."

But woman sometimes approaches man as a blighting mildew to his best affections and the richest fruits of his manhood. Whose is the fault? Woman embodies a saving power essential to man. She may err in her modes of manifestation, through ignorance or a bad organization. She may coarsely and clumsily fulfil her holy and delicate mission. But that she so often comes as the harbinger of death, is in a great degree owing to the unnatural conditions of him to whom she comes, and to his erroneous views of the purposes of her mission. So the advocates of Peace, Anti-Slavery, and Non-Resistance, may imperfectly present the truth; but the source of the vexation, unrest, and self-condemnation they arouse, is mainly in the conditions of those whom they seek to bless. The prophets and apostles of old, though they came as harbingers of peace and good-will, were denounced and stoned to death. The outcry against Jesus was, — "Blasphemer against Moses and the prophets," "Infidel," "a despiser of God," "Friend of publicans and sinners," — "Crucify him! crucify him!" Yet he came "to seek and to save the lost." Why was the world which he came to save thrown into such confusion and misery by his presence and his power? He brought them a "savor of life unto life," but they turned it into a "savor of death unto death." So woman, though she comes as "Heaven's last, best gift to man," having power conferred by God to regenerate and redeem; yet man, by his manner of receiving her, and his perverted views of her mission, growing out of his abnormal conditions, makes her a source of degradation and misery. Man may say, "Woman, as a law of life to me, is holy, just and good, but I am carnal, — sold under sin; therefore, that which was ordained to life, I find to be unto death."

Instead, then, of railing against woman, and guarding his heart against her influence, let man accuse himself, and guard his heart and life against himself. Let him resolutely set to work to correct his own tendencies to unnatural, sensual indulgences; let him perfect his manhood in all pure and attractive qualities, and woman will come to him only as a purifying and ennobling influence. She could not present herself in any other light to man, thus appealing to her for help; or, if she did, his refined intuitions would instantly unmask her, and she would stand before him powerless for evil.

NINA, — I have thus endeavored to define the mission of woman, and to show how it can be most perfectly accomplished. I have spoken from an experience which has been enriched and crowned with joy by the presence and power of woman. My heart turns fondly and proudly to thee for the fulfilment of its deepest wants and aspirations. I look to thee to explain the mysteries of my being, for the development of my manhood, to place me in my true position in the universe, and to help me to work out happily the problem of my destiny. Thy mission to me has thus far been successfully accomplished. Guided by thy love, protected by thy tender care, I can confidently traverse the entire course of my endless being.

In the language of one of America's most noble and gifted daughters and wives, who thus addressed her husband in his hour of stern conflict with his material and social surroundings, I would say, — "The first great end of our being is answered. *We have met and interpreted each other.* This most intense and potent desire of each having found full satisfaction in the other, we will wait for the fulfilment of our destiny in all other directions with firm and patient hearts. We may well rest and be happy in each other, since we are conscious of being loved as our hearts crave to be."

In answer to the above, the husband replied, — "My

entire manhood responds to thy remark. We have met and interpreted each other, and thus the great end of our being is answered; for a true and perfect development of our whole nature is the great end of our existence. I had remained a sealed book, even to myself, had not woman, as a wife, appeared to open that seal and interpret that book. To do this for me was thy mission. Perfectly hast thou performed thy work. The mysterious, holy record, stamped upon my being by the hand of my Creator, thou hast read to me. The ever-present inquiry of my heart was, 'Who will read for me this record, and explain to me the deep mysteries of my manhood? Who will tell me why I am a man?' Thou didst come to me and say, 'Give me that record! I can and will read it to thee, and in so doing find my own life.' As thy work of reading and explaining has progressed, the call of my heart has ever been for another chapter, and yet another, for thy words have been words of hope, of faith and consolation."

This answer of the husband, I accept as a true expression of my feelings as to what thou hast done for me. *Why am I a man?* Thou hast answered this inquiry of my manhood truly and nobly, and the desire of my heart is satisfied.

Man is Heaven's best gift to woman, in the same sense that woman is to man, and he has a mission to her. Wilt thou define it, and show how it can be successfully accomplished? Has not woman alone the right and power to answer this question? As a woman and a wife, freely express thy convictions to

Thy husband,<br>
ERNEST.

## ANSWER.

### MISSION OF MAN TO WOMAN.

Ernest:

Thou hast made two statements in thy last letter which will rouse the prejudices of most who read them. First, "that man can best define the mission of woman." I believe the distinction of sex is not limited to the physical organization, but extends to the spiritual nature; and that each sex can best define its own wants, and point to the means of its most perfect development. I believe that woman can best define what she requires from man, because she best knows what he can be to her. Therefore, I endeavor to comply with thy request. In answering the questions proposed by thee, I shall not claim superiority for either sex; the two natures are equally beautiful and noble, but they are unlike.

In thy second statement, "that woman is made for the perfect development of man," a phrase is used which has so long covered a low and degrading idea, that even thy definition will perhaps fail to banish the associations already connected with it. But I think candor will confess that thou hast but stated a general law, running through all orders of animal and vegetable life. An inextricable confusion has resulted from a misapprehension and disobedience of this law. Human legislation has done its best to restore order, but in vain. We shall sin and suffer, until we turn a reverent attention to the voice of Nature, and implicitly obey her teachings. I believe it, in the sense in which thou hast used these words, but in no other or different sense than that in which man is made for the perfection of woman. They are made for each other, without an implied moral, intellectual or physical inferiority in either. In a true relation between the sexes, there can be no question of superiority. Mutual help and dependence will be freely offered and recognised, and harmony and true growth will result to both.

What is the instinct in woman's nature which seeks manhood? To what relation does her instinct point? These are questions that lie at the threshold.

Companionship is the first demand of the child's nature. Its claims are strong, but not discriminating. It must love, and be loved, or its young life is crushed. In young boys and girls, there is no recognition of the distinction of sex; there is the same free, unconscious enjoyment with each other, as when each is restricted to its own sex. As they grow older, the attraction of each to its counterpart becomes more decided; yet Nature, true to herself, leaves them both pure and happy, yet giving and receiving an influence peculiar to each. Still further on, when the girl becomes the maiden, with her character more mature, her nature more positively defined, her need of sympathy and true companionship keeps pace with her development, and among her associates, her intuitions select those most in harmony with her own cast of character. It is the relation of brother and sister into which this want of her nature leads, and it is fruitful of most beautiful results to both.

But she is not yet fully satisfied. In all these friends, she finds something to love and respect, nor would she mar the existing relations by the slightest word or deed. Yet there is still a void unfilled, a want unsatisfied, a clamoring voice that will not be still. It comes from the very centre of her life. She longs to be claimed, *possessed;* to feel the very fibres of her heart grasped in a mighty hand; to hear the solemn assurance which shall fill her soul with rapture, "Thou art *mine,* for time and eternity." From that hour of transfiguration, she walks in "robes of golden light." "I have *loved,* I have *lived,*" is the unceasing music of her soul; and, borne on the mighty wings of this new life, she mounts to heights of heroism that her eye could never reach before. For the first time, she learns the true object of her creation. All previous life, all attainments, all efforts, which have hindered or failed to aid her to this true life, are viewed as time and labor lost. Time itself is obliterated, and existence seems to date from the entrance into this new life. This is the consummation to which all her instincts have hitherto pointed, and in it does she find, for the first time, *true rest.*

To *man* she looks for the power to still these troubled waters. To him her heart utters its earnest, undying call. Her ideal is noble, pure, and lovely. She seeks such, as the worthy recipient of all she has to give. To him she rushes, without question or misgiving, in her eager self-abandonment. She knows that men are bad and false; but *her* chosen one is a world above them all. Her love invests him with all goodness, strength and beauty. He stands in glittering robes, bearing in his right hand the destiny of the heart of Love. In her self-abandonment, she calmly bears reproach, poverty, pain and death, if she may but preserve in her heart the faith that her chosen one is worthy of the sacrifice. She asks only that he may be worthy, and her brave heart will face the darkest fate.

It is true, innocence is sometimes betrayed, confidence misplaced. But even when Love sees its idol turned to clay, the heart is slow to believe that it is dead. I believe that a true woman would rather *love*, even if it were rejected, than live without knowing the depths of her own heart. Bitter tears may mingle in the draught, but she knows, at last, what it is to *live;* and before the solemn beauty of that experience, all former life dwindles into nothingness.

Man! couldst thou but believe in the mighty power that rests in thy noble nature to save her who waits and longs to come to thee, thou wouldst rather die than do aught to mar the glory with which a woman's love invests thee!

Such is the attitude in which Nature places the heart of the true woman towards man. Can her life be perfected without him? She may attain to great intellectual cultivation; she may, in isolation from man, extend a general benevolence which will do much good, and bring much happiness; she may, by constant activity and exertion, save herself from *ennui* and discontent; but she will never fully comprehend the extent or beauty of her relations to God or man, till she is regenerated. She must experience the new birth into the heaven of Love, before she can see with unclouded eyes. Life will then receive a new significance, and, under the influence of this new spiritual sense, the most ordinary life becomes heroic.

Woman can never take the attitude of independence towards man, unless in utter ignorance of her own nature, or under the sting of personal wrong. She would never do such violence to the mighty instincts of her nature. Manhood has abused his trust, else woman never would seek defences against him, or vindicate her "rights." She freely puts herself into his power, in a way that cannot be paralleled by any amount of self-devotion on his part. In marriage, she gives him wealth, without reserve, blushing at the thought of *legal protection* against him whom she honors with her *love*. With a trusting heart, she confides her destiny to the strong arm that she believes will never fail. It is for man to answer whether he has deserved and nobly used such trust. It is for those who jeer at the claims of what they call "strong-minded women," to ask themselves whether the wrongs these women seek to remedy are self-inflicted, or whether man himself does not scoff at those he has betrayed. Nature must be bitterly outraged, when woman suspects and fears the power of man.

The most superficial observer must perceive, that here, as in all cases where powers conflict that were designed to be harmonious, the wrong is generally to be traced to both. It were hardly possible for one to be entirely passive and aggrieved, while the other is uniformly oppressive and unjust.

Are we the beings thou hast described, whose advent should be hailed with open heart and arms? Does the true soul of womanhood shine in the women of our day? The relations between man and woman cannot be regulated by law or plan. He will feel towards her just those emotions which her character is calculated to awaken; and in proportion to the depth and earnestness of her own nature will be the sincerity and permanence of her attractions to him.

It is our painted ball-room dolls, the shallow beauties that parade our streets, — whose estimate of manhood is measured by his dress, moustache, gloves and boots, — who complain most loudly of the fickleness of men. What need has *manhood* of such toys as these? Are these the beings that deserve the name of *women?* Shall man look to such as these for true companionship, for intelligent sympathy, and can he lavish on a toy the wealth of love that waits to meet a living soul? Rather let our young men die in exile, or on the plains of polar ice, than meet a living death in a life-long companionship with these bodies without souls.

My sisters! we must be noble women, if we ever hope to find true men. We must live for higher aims than the superficial shows of life, if we hope to share the highest life of manhood. Until a wiser appreciation of our own capabilities and true destiny can be put into the head and heart of woman, man will toy and trifle and betray. A close observer of the defects of woman has lately said of them, — " We have no better reason for denying intellect to our women of society, than the entire want of evidence to prove its existence. In their empty career of show and frivolous occupation, a prospect never opens to the better life of thought and of earnest purpose. Hour succeeds hour in languid succession, while the wearied pursuer of exhausting pleasure sinks in a mortal lethargy, cheered by no spark of heavenly flame, and enlivened by no vital current of intelligence. Our young ladies have been to school, bu their intellectual culture is as scant as their knowledge of the wicked world is abounding."

Until man finds in woman a character strengthened by obedience to the demands of the inner life, unbiassed by worldly aims, expressing itself in a life which regards the interest of an endless existence, we need hope for nothing great or noble in the relations of the sexes. If woman descends, man will follow. If she remains where she was born to dwell,

> "Breaking to him the heavenly bread
> Of hopes which, all too high for earth,
> Have yet in her their mortal birth,"

he will ascend to meet her, and she will then deserve the welcome of a *" Gloria in Excelsis."* At present, woman has lost the ideal of what she should be to man. She decks her person, and displays her graces, to win — a husband; not love, nor the abiding realities of a sincere and noble heart, but wealth, position, fame. So long as woman holds herself so cheap, she will be cheaply bought.

Shall we blame men for offering the coin that woman seeks? While woman sells herself for gold, she need not expect a more precious medium of exchange. Can men be blamed for offering sugar-sweets to the puny, fawning dependants on their favors? When she waits for *manhood*, we may look for better specimens than society now affords.

It were perhaps to be expected, from a sex so nobly endowed as manhood is, that the strong should raise the weak; that there should be found wisdom of head and heart to point out and pity the follies of their bewildered sisters. But the misfortune is, that woman cannot sink alone. She has drawn after her the head and heart of man, so that, among the conflicting claims of ambition, passion, and a lust for gain, he has lost the ideal of what woman should be. We must look to ourselves for salvation. Virtue will never find protection in human laws. It must put on the armor of self-respect, it must be unfaltering in allegiance to truth and purity, in order to paralyze the arm or tongue that would assail it. Woman must guard well her heart, for out of it are the issues of life. Let her keep her intuitions clear, and be implicitly obedient to their warnings. In the bestowal of her love, let her be deaf to the claims of ambition, or any worldly interest. "For if the young heart be dried up in its fountains of love; if the ways of pleasantness and peace which should lead to the shrine of her affections, where all would worship, be thronged with money-changers, and the temple itself desecrated with unholy barter, then truly is life but a frightful reality of wo. * * * Fathers and mothers lead their daughters to the sacrifice. The young victims, decked in flowers of fashion, gayly dance to the altar, where they willingly offer up heart and affections to avarice, while the parent sanctions, and the priest, in the name of religion, blesses the unholy ceremony. The young heart is entombed in gold with all the honors, and the youthful affections hang in withered drapery over the tomb, upon which we may inscribe, ' Sacred to the memory of the lost Heart, dead ere its prime.' "

If in early life, the blessing of a noble love, the satisfaction of her heart, the fulfilment of her destiny, be vouchsafed to woman, let her thank God on bended knees. But if not, rather than yield to the fear of reproach, or the force of opinion, which sets so fiercely for worldly advantages, the true heart of woman will wait and wait, even though with weary heart and far-searching eyes, she turn from one after another who may seek her love. She will say to them, — "Pass on, pass on, I wait for my Messiah." Even if she wait until her eyes grow dim, and her unblessed brow be crowned with silver hair, — nay, even when she lies down to rest in her last sleep, her unbowed soul will still say, " I wait for my Messiah."

When such is the general type of womanhood, when her fair form is but the fitting temple for her noble soul, when her earnest eyes glow with the holy light of purity, and her lips are eloquent with truth, when dignity is not a studied grace, but the unconscious expression of nobleness of soul, man will learn to honor what he cannot corrupt, he will be compelled to love what he cannot flatter. Man should be to woman an aid to just this level of attainment. In his highly-endowed nature abides all that a woman's heart demands. She must love and honor him, and merge her life in his. He must be great, and pure, and true, or this impulse of her nature will lead her to her ruin.

Man has a right to look to woman for the completion of his destiny, by her power to refine and elevate his nature, to share his intellectual life, to develop his affections in the most endearing domestic relations; woman has a right to look to man for a type of greatness which shall fill her ideal of manhood. She expects from him a generous appreciation of her whole nature, moral, intellectual and physical, and his help in its development. She should awaken in him a wise, tender love, which seeketh not its own. She should come to him as a companion, protector, friend, and lover.

When will man accept this holy mission, and be blessed?

NINA.

## LETTER III.

### WHAT IS MARRIAGE?

NINA:

*What is Marriage?* In what consists the relation of husband and wife, in which we now stand to each other? It is not in the fact that we have a license from the Church or State to live in this relation, for no such license has ever been asked or desired, and by our mutual understanding of the matter, never will be; nor in the fact that a priest or magistrate, as the mouth-piece of society, has assured us, before others, that God hath joined us together, and that we must remain so, till Death or Divorce makes us otherwise, for no such ceremony has been performed on us, and never will be. Nor does our marriage consist in the fact that we live together as husband and wife; for all these things are done by men and women between whom no true marriage exists. It is not in the power of Church or State, priest or magistrate, to make thee my wife; that can be done only by a power infinitely above them all. And yet, how many, with and without a license, are living together as husband and wife, between whom there is no marriage! No human law, or license, or authority, or social custom, can make that right which would otherwise be wrong, nor that wrong which would otherwise be right.

What, then, is marriage? No logical definition, of universal application, can be given, for the heart alone can truly apprehend it. Words are nothing; marriage may express all that is good — it often stands for all that is evil. It may be the most vitalizing, improving, happy relation into which human beings can be attracted; and it is often the most debasing and blighting. What, then, are the facts with regard to this relation? I must speak for myself; yet I am assured that, in speaking for myself, I speak for thee; and that thou, in like manner, wilt speak for me.

These, then, are the facts touching my relation to thee. My nature has a certain want, and the power to attract and assimilate to itself a natural and healthful supply. That want pertains to my physical, social, intellectual and spiritual nature, and it is fulfilled in thee. A restless and ever-present longing pervaded my entire being. That restlessness has given place to absolute repose; that intense longing has found a satisfaction still more intense. My ideal of beauty, purity, truth, justice and love, I longed to see embodied; I found them so in thee, as I found them in no other being. I longed to find my highest object of love and adoration incarnate in a living, visible, tangible, actualized relation. That incarnation I found most beautifully presented in my relation to thee.

Love invests its object with light and beauty, with a holy consecration, seen and felt only by the husband. To him, the wife is the embodiment of the feminine element, and this will seem to his loving heart to be the most exalted, most sacred and attractive attribute of the Divine nature. She comes to him to meet his highest aspirations for true development,—as the vitalizing, consecrating power of his soul. Impelled by my experience, in my relation to thee, my heart renders this definition of a wife—THE MOST PERFECT AND ATTRACTIVE INCARNATION OF GOD TO THE HUSBAND. The great Invisible and Intangible is made more beautifully and attractively visible and tangible in this, than in any other relation.

In thee, Love and Wisdom are manifested in the flesh to me, as they are in no other being of the past or of the present. I go no more, in spirit, into the regions of abstraction, to wander, in thought, through the boundless void, to find an object on which to expend the energies of my soul in love and devotion. I find that object in thee, my wife, as I do in nothing else.

Worship is a necessity of my being. I must worship something; so must every man and every woman. My soul cannot stoop to worship times and places, stations and titles. I see no God in them. They are all the work of men's hands. But I worship the true and the beautiful in thee, without one shrinking doubt as to my right to do so, or as to whether God will accept this devotion to the most attractive embodiment of my conception of his attributes as being paid to him.

Our souls, I believe, are substance, as truly as are air, light, electricity and magnetism. The same law of attraction governs souls that governs all material bodies. Human souls are attracted to one another in four distinct relations; there may be others, but those are marked. The broadest relation is that which exists between *human* beings, in contradistinction from the brute creation. This I would call the *Human* Attraction. This attraction individualizes itself in *particular friendships*, in a dearer and stronger sense than in the human. Then man is attracted to woman by a force stronger and dearer than that which draws him to his own sex. This I would call the *Sexual* Attraction. This attractive force individualizes itself in marriage; and this is the *Connubial* Attraction. A masculine soul and a feminine soul, in marriage, are absorbed each into the other. The essence of each enters into the other; permeates, fills and thrills it, leaving to neither an isolated, separate existence. Thought responds to thought, will to will, heart to heart. The advent of man and woman to each other, as husband and wife, is the advent of the true and natural Savior to the soul of each. The entrance of two souls, each into the other, thus making of two one perfect being, — *the blending of the masculine and feminine elements, according to natural law,* — this is MARRIAGE, as my heart defines it.

This is true of our relation. I cannot feel that, as a man, I have an existence apart from thee. It seems to me that, as an embodiment of the masculine element, without thee I am nothing; and that in thee, as the life-principle of my manhood, I live, move, and have my being. To dwell in thee is to dwell in Love. As my soul rests in thy love, it rests in God. My hopes, my longings, my aspirations, as a man, look to thee for fulfilment. In the bright mirror of our mutual love, I see heaven and earth; and the fair stars and the sweet flowers, as therein reflected, appear brighter and more beautiful. Thy love illumines what is dark, and beautifies what is deformed. Thou hast revealed to me the depth and power of my manhood, interpreting it truly, being to it daily the way, the truth, and the life. My God, my heaven, my eternity, are associated with thee; and as seen and felt in my relation to thee, they have their deepest and most ennobling significance.

Such are my present feelings towards thee; so near and dear, so priceless, so beautiful and gracious, art thou now to me. Wilt thou ever thus continue? My soul turns to thee, now, as necessarily as the needle to the pole. Other forces may draw it away for a moment, but they have no permanent influence. Their power is soon exhausted, and then my soul turns to its great central attraction, and, sternly true to itself, looks to thee, and finds absolute repose.

Of the future, I cannot speak; of the present, I have spoken; and these are the expressions of one who is proudly conscious of perfect fidelity to truth and justice in all he has written.

With true love and devotion, with conscious dignity and elevation of soul, I subscribe myself,

Thy husband,
ERNEST.

## ANSWER.

ERNEST:

In thy last letter, thou hast given many suggestive topics of thought and feeling. Thou hast well said, that in entering upon the relation of marriage, we asked not of Church or State the sanction which they have no power to bestow. The only sanction, in the sight of God, is the fact that love, pure and undefiled, has drawn us to each other, has made us willing to renounce every worldly treasure, to live in accordance with its high demands. Fortune, friends, kindred, country, fail to compare with the mighty influence which has made us one.

Society could not effect this union; yet we have not slighted its demands. We have accorded to it all it has the right to claim. We have announced the fact that we are living in the marriage relation. We would not be mistaken for the poor and grovelling natures that seek, by evading social regulations, a stealthy gratification of the senses. We have nothing to be ashamed of, nothing to conceal.

Marriage is holy in the sight of God; and if the heart's deepest, purest worship and affection are elements in the true marriage, then are we married. We have recorded that fact in the public register; we have publicly recognised each other as husband and wife; and more, the world has no right to claim. Thou hast given the deepest depths of thy nature in giving thy ideal of marriage. Nothing less is due from me; and when I speak for myself, I know that I utter the voice of my sex; for, allowing for the difference produced by circumstances, the wants of the human heart are undoubtedly the same in all. Passing over the ideal of the dreaming girl, who, without knowledge of herself, knows not in what character her own will find its counterpart, I give thee what the *woman* asks for.

It is a necessity of her nature to rest in strength and wisdom superior to her own. She may not be weak, but she demands strength and reliable energy of will and action, as the basis of her confidence. With this, she needs a large and loving nature, requiring and granting unlimited freedom of expression and action.

With these general elements, — leaving out the minor particulars, wherein individuals may differ, — with these wants fully met, and with that powerful mutual attraction which endears each to the other personally, which we call love, the growth and perfection of each may be insured in marriage. When these wants are met, the real treasures of the heart burst out in uncontrolled affluence. The rock is smitten by the hand of God, and the waters of life must flow out.

But there is no *demand*, and no *surrender;* each acts out his or her own nature, in its fullest perfection. Love identifies each with that which is most beneficial to the other, in an unexpressed and inexpressible harmony of will and purpose. They live in and for each other, neither fearing to accept a freedom which each is willing to grant.

The great mistakes, so often made in what are called marriages, result from a thousand causes; but chiefly, that persons do not understand their own wants; and, secondly, that they are not true to their own natures, when they do understand them. A young woman must know her own temper and disposition, she must understand what qualities of mind and character command her highest respect, and seek in marriage such, and only such, as she can fully and entirely respect; for, without that basis, where and what is love? It is no longer a noble tribute of homage to her heart's highest ideal of goodness, but a superficial attraction, which must end in *ennui*, if nothing worse.

I have thought that young people, both men and women, often mistake their own wants in marrying their *friends*. As they grow up, they naturally seek each other's society, and find a sympathy and understanding which they cannot find in those of their own sex. This goes on, till some circumstance occurs to separate them; and to avoid that apparent calamity, they marry. If they would have the courage to go apart, and remain wholly separated from the personal presence and influence of each other, time would reveal what and how deep was the real attraction between them. So true it is, that those who might spend their lives in harmony as friends, hate each other when they assume a more intimate relation.

I would, then, ask every young man and woman to consider well whether, in choosing a companion for life, they find in the object of their present choice, the deepest wants of their hearts satisfied. If they do not, let them beware of the fatal step, which, according to the regulations of society, is irrevocable; for, as truly as the heart lives, those deepest wants will assert themselves. They will demand satisfaction, under circumstances of pain and suffering which will rend the very fibres of the soul. It is the will of God, written upon the soul, that its laws shall be observed, and a bitter and fearful penalty is the price of their violation.

The lower considerations of worldly wisdom, — such as fortune, family, social position, &c., — I cannot mention in this connection, for these considerations have no place among those who seek only for a true development of themselves in marriage. Of those who can profane the sanctuary, I have nothing to say.

Here, then, I have given some idea of what marriage should be. The husband is to the wife the ideal actualized. No other man is like him, or ever can be. He is nobler, more tender, more perfectly adapted to the wife's delicate intuitions, than any or all other men.

She does not question whether she loves him; she loves him before she knows it, and her answer to his yearning heart is, not, "I *will* be thine," but, "I *am* thine, already." To his voice, his step, his touch, his glance, her pulse bounds, and, in heart, soul and sense, she is her own no more. With the power of attraction between them, with the noble strength and tenderness of manhood, and the no less noble trust in her husband, which her own strength and tenderness enable her to appreciate, does not marriage show itself to be ordained of God? Does not every heart yearn for it, as its only true satisfaction? Does not every single life seem poor and lonely compared with it?

And if it can bring joy to one manly heart to know that to his own chosen one, he embodies all these wants of her heart, that to her nature he is the complete fulfilment, then that satisfaction is due to thee, my noble husband.

From thy loving wife,

NINA.

## LETTER IV.

### PERPETUITY OF MARRIAGE.

Nina:

We are one. My hope, my heaven, my God, are associated with thee. The very essence of our souls has entered, each into that of the other, as a life-principle, to fill us with the consciousness of perfect repose. Into this dwelling-place, distrust and unrest can never enter. We are one in love, as God is one.

How long is this oneness to be continued? For ever is the emphatic response of our hearts; and to raise the question of its perpetuity, seems but an insult to our love, — a cruel outrage upon the deep and sacred tenderness that each feels for the other. But we have undertaken to discuss the question of marriage between us, that, if possible, we may ascertain the fixed, natural laws by which this relation should be governed, and by these regulate our connubial life.

It is said there are no fixed laws by which the manifestations of love are to be regulated. This may be true as to the particular modes and forms of expression; yet there is a general law, fixed and eternal, by which all demonstrations of true conjugal love will be governed, and that is, THE GOOD OF THE BELOVED. In its very nature, Love can never, except in ignorance, seek expression at the expense of the health, purity and happiness of the loved one. It is a feeling that "seeketh not its own"; but, as to time, place, and mode of manifestation, looks solely to the welfare of the body and soul of the object. It is a condition or law of the soul, existing between the husband and wife, which merges each in the other, and makes the happiness of each dependent on that of the other. This law was designed to govern all expressions of love, in all relations. In its very nature, the feeling is self-forgetting, seeking, not its own good, but that of the loved ones. But I would confine myself to a consideration of the laws that were designed to govern all expressions of love in the marriage relation.

I believe that marriage was intended to be an enduring relation between two individuals, from the facts daily presented to our notice, even if there were no internal evidence on the subject.

It is true, there are many instances wherein Church and State sanction the solemn vow, before God and man, which the heart does not ratify, — that two, who claim the name of husband and wife, shall remain true, in heart and life, till death shall part them; or, perhaps, unconscious of this want of true union, they choose each other for a specific external advantage, and learn their mistake too late; or, perhaps, a love, which was deep and true at first, is crushed by neglect and abuse. Domestic life is full of the victims of ignorance, worldliness, or an insane curiosity and sensuality.

But is it the law of our nature, that the union of one man with one woman should last while both remain in this state of existence? I believe it is. My faith rests on *the nature of the union itself*. As defined by us, marriage is the actual blending of two souls, a masculine and feminine, according to natural law, each being attracted to the other by a power over which neither has control, so long as they remain within the sphere of each other's attractive force. They know not how nor why they are thus blended, since it came by no will or effort of their own. As they did not will themselves into this union, they cannot will themselves out of it. Therefore, the relative conditions of their souls, under which the union was formed, remaining the same, the union itself must remain.

But may not these relative conditions change, and thus the union be destroyed? Through ignorance or carelessness, this may be. These two souls were attracted by love to each other, under certain harmonious relative conditions. The conditions of one are changed, for better or worse, without a corresponding change on the part of the other, and thus the harmony is lost; the oneness ceases; the marriage is null and void, as a heart-relation. But this only goes to establish the fact, that perpetuity is the law of Nature. These are the exceptional cases which we mark, when some counteracting influence has interfered to disturb the harmony which first made the twain one, and should keep them one and inseparable. The law of love, of harmony, would preserve each from deterioration, from all unkind suspicions, feelings, thoughts, words and acts, and carry both together onward and upward; for, in true marriage, both souls are involved in one destiny.

*Each desires the union to be perpetual.* Of all the harmonies the universe can furnish or the mind conceive, none is so perfect, so purifying and ennobling, as that made by the blending of two souls in marriage. Its sweetness never cloys; its oft-repeated strains never weary, but, the more often repeated, the more the soul of each longs for and enjoys them. The human heart can never weary of loving and being loved; nor can it weary of the presence of the beloved object, for it is to each the visible presence of that for which each most earnestly longs, — the presence of Love, of God. If either wishes separation, there is no longer true marriage in the heart. Where there is true marriage, universal experience testifies that it longs for an endless perpetuity; and the very existence of this desire demonstrates to me the fact, that Nature designed the union to be perpetual. The want is natural, and Nature creates no want for which she does not create a supply.

I cannot entertain the thought, that the oneness now existing between us can ever be destroyed. Such a thought would disturb my soul's deep repose, and hang around my future the canopy of death. The present joy of my relation to thee is in the security that it will not be disturbed. So long as we wish our marriage union to remain, it will remain. But its perpetuity depends upon ourselves. If we wish for its continuance, we shall use the means to secure that end. What some of these are will be stated in due time.

It will suffice to say here, that a relation so tender, so delicate, so intense, so absorbing, may be disturbed. The power that attracted each to the other must be perpetuated and constantly renewed, or the oneness will cease. To thee, I embody the ideal of the man whom thy nature craves as a husband. Thou hast described what constitutes that ideal. If I am truly thy husband, and wish our union to be perpetuated, I shall never relax in my efforts to be all thou hast judged me to be.

By the power with which thou hast invested me, I have drawn thee to myself, to be the life-principle of manhood. If I would hold thee in this relation, and call out thy deep and tender love towards me, I must continually exert this attractive force, as the sun pours its light on the earth, to develop its hidden powers in sweetest flowers and richest fruits.

Thou canst not continue to love me, if I become unlovable. No matter what promises thou hast made, if the man to whom thy love was given ceases to be worthy of it, — if thou canst no longer find in me the husband thou hast once loved, — if I fail to concentrate the deep heart's love which once enriched and ennobled my life, — that moment our marriage is cancelled, and thou hast ceased to be my wife.

Be it mine, then, to incarnate thy ideal of a husband, and thus to retain thee within the influence of that love which first attracted thee. In thus fulfilling my relation to thee, thou wilt likewise fulfil thine to me; and thus we shall accomplish the one great desire of our hearts, THE PERPETUITY OF OUR PRESENT ONENESS.

From thy husband,

ERNEST.

## ANSWER.

Ernest:

In thy last letter, upon the perpetuity of the marriage bond, thou hast so truly interpreted the sentiments of my wedded heart, that I find hardly any thing to say in answer, but Amen! Yet, I will try to forget what thou hast written, and state my own views upon this subject, if for no other purpose than to show how fully they coincide with thine own.

In former letters, we have defined the wants of the soul that crave fulfilment in marriage. In the fact that these wants do find, in true marriage, their entire satisfaction, lies the answer to the question proposed in your last. We strive to attain, through marriage, a more perfect development of the elements of our being, than we can attain without it. A relation which fails to meet this want is either defective or altogether spurious.

But when we realize our ideal in marriage, we find, to the whole being, a larger activity, higher objects of aspiration, and the infinitely exalting consciousness of losing our separate, independent existence in that of another; not by the sacrifice of independent thought and action, but by a unity of will which turns all conflicting forces into one harmonious effort.

To speak from my own experience, marriage has revealed to me the perfect embodiment of those qualities constituting my ideal of manhood. What those are is known to thee full well. And does not every strong and tender-hearted woman ask for strength and tenderness combined, wherein to find her rest? A world of meaning is conveyed in that one phrase, "*to find her rest.*" She needs an intellect, strong by natural endowment, and enriched by knowledge of men and books; a moral nature inflexible and incorruptible; a heart of large philanthropy, yet capable of a single, intense affection. In such a nature, she will have freedom of thought and life; her heart will find its wildest dream of happiness fulfilled.

Such has marriage proved to me. How strange, then, sound the questions, Dost thou wish this happiness prolonged?—Art thou willing to cast all this aside, and set forth again, an adventurer, to find new treasures? We would laugh at the gold-hunter who should leave an unwrought mine of wealth beneath his hand, in search of other gain; and shall one expect the possessor of more than a thousand Californias to neglect the unwrought wealth which God has showered on her life? When the flower asks no more for rain and sun, then will I tear from my heart the life thou hast infused therein. It were an unutterable sorrow, if our paths in life were separated; but only insupportable under the thought that our union of heart is at an end.

We pray that the ties which make us one may never be broken, and in this very prayer is the pledge of its fulfilment. We pray, and we act in accordance with it. Our love for each other is a love for the attributes of God, embodied. By this love, we are pledged to every effort of self-development. Our aim is not for the approbation of each other, but for the abstract right, and true, and just, and lovely. While we embody these attributes, we do our highest duty to God, to ourselves, and to each other, and for the happy, glorious result, we find our own hearts drawn into even closer bonds of love.

This, to my mind, is all that marriage can effect for the individual; and such an influence is one that time and place and death can never mar. There is but one response from heart and mind, one cry for the endless continuance of our marriage bond, as we hope for infinite progress in all the attributes of the Divine; and as we hope for a happiness for which there is no other name but—HEAVEN.

Thy wife,<br>NINA.

## LETTER V.

### VARIETY IN LOVE, OR POLYGAMY.

NINA:

It is settled between us that our oneness will be eternal, if our present desires and wants are truly answered; also, that the perpetuity of our oneness depends on our knowledge of and fidelity to the natural laws by which marriage is designed to be governed. The question arises — *Is exclusiveness a fixed law of mar-*

*riage?* I ask not, Should either marry after the death of the other? but, Can a woman be the wife of more than one man, and can the relation of husband be truly sustained to more than one woman, at the same time? To this, my heart and my head give a negative answer. Reason and affection assure me that polygamy is unnatural, and therefore wrong.

What says the heart? Is there a husband whose love is concentrated on one woman as a wife, who can willingly allow another man to be to his wife what he is? He loves her — her alone — above all others, and he earnestly desires that she should return his affection. The very fact that another can claim her interest or win her affection, enough to make marriage attractive, strikes a death-blow to a true lover's peace. It is equally true of a woman's heart. Hence the origin of that expression of feeling commonly designated jealousy. As a husband, my nature is complete in thee. My capacity for happiness is full; and as that capacity enlarges, thou, nurtured by the love I bear thee, wilt grow with its growth. If we are true to ourselves and to each other, neither can outgrow the other. I can never seek an enlargement of soul that cannot be shared by thee. The first object of our lives must be to perfect the harmony between us. In every step of my course, the wife of my soul must stand by my side. I can desire no honor, no station, no heaven, apart from thee. If thou art delayed, I must be delayed with thee. We are one in love, in will, in purpose, in destiny. Be it ours to eternize this oneness. We will stand, go back, or go forward, together.

With this fullness of satisfaction in thee, how can I desire another, as a wife? There is no room for another in my nature; it finds in thee all it can receive from any woman in marriage, and it repels the thought of any other in this relation. The existence of the desire for a second person in the marriage union, while the first one lives, proves that the first relation has ceased, if it ever existed. It seems to me that marriage-love is, in its very essence, exclusive. Men and women have a nature that can be shared by every other man and woman in the ties of friendship, in perfect accordance with the law that binds men and woman together, as such. But in marriage, this general tendency of each to the opposite sex concentrates itself on one, and therefore excludes all others from the privileges and endearments of that relation. The glory of marriage is its exclusiveness. The soul conscious of refinement, purity and dignity, will shrink from sharing the relation with more than one.

Much is said about *variety in love.* It is said that the passional nature of man needs a fuller satisfaction than a single object can afford; that some men must suffer, unless they live with more than one woman as a wife. But the history of polygamy, under whatever name, and by whatever or by whomsoever sanctioned, demonstrates that it is unnatural, since its consequences are evil, and only evil. It renders men imbecile, in body and soul, and tends to a disproportion of the sexes. Woman can never attain nor keep her true position in a state of polygamy.

The only marriage that commends itself to the

instinct, the reason and the heart, is exclusive; and therefore, this alone will elevate and purify man or woman. Tell me if thy reason and heart respond to these sentiments of

Thy husband,<br>ERNEST.

---

Ernest:

The question of "variety in love," as presented in thy last letter, can be settled by referring to the point from which the discussion first started, i. e.: the definition of marriage, and its natural and legitimate modes of manifestation. We have described the attractions which find their fulfilment in marriage. But there is another element, the natural result of the former attraction, pertaining to the physical nature, which claims attention, inasmuch as its demands have a powerful, controlling influence over the whole marriage relation.

The IDEAL of Love and Marriage, in every young heart, is with *one* — never with more than one. Social discord and wrong may introduce other notions, but I understand a deep significance in the old story, that for Adam there was but *one* Eve created. The idea of a truly married pair seeking for a third party in their happiness is absurd. In this view of marriage, I take for granted that the spiritual element predominates. In every true marriage, this must be the case; and it is false to speak otherwise on the subject.

True love finds in one beloved object the embodiment of its ideal. The whole nature, intellectual, affectional, and physical, willingly accepts, in this embodiment of the ideal, a true marriage. And from this willing, mutual self-surrender, flows the confidence which gives and takes without reserve.

Is the marriage tie capable of extension? If a man finds in half a dozen women equally powerful attractions to marriage; if each exercises an equally deep, vitalizing, elevating influence on his life; if the union with either one would be enough to bless his life, were all the others exterminated, then, it is said, he has a right, if all equally desire it, to be the husband of them all! But what does experience prove in this matter? The case is not even supposable. It is absurd in the statement.

The *sentiment* of love finds satisfaction in *one* object. The *passional* element, which borrows the holy name of love, may crave a wider range. When men say they "need variety," they say, in other words, that in them, the passion has the ascendency over the sentiment. The man in whom the need of variety exists, should not take the high social rank implied by the desire for a true marriage, but descend to that level in creation wherein animal passion makes no discrimination in its objects, and finds equal satisfaction in them all. Men who advocate "variety," know that true, pure marriage-love cannot be felt to more than one; but they wish to find, in their various attractions to woman, a sanction for what were otherwise unqualified brutality.

Woman never entertains the idea of the personal relations of marriage, except as a *secondary* experience, if I may so speak. Her love must be won through the bestowal of her confidence in the character of the man she honors. Her spiritual wants must first be met; then follows the growing personal attachment, which, at last, places her a willing gift, soul and body, in the keeping of the husband. Marriage is, to her, eminently a spiritual experience, so profound, so peculiar, so exclusive, that it rarely finds but one realization in life. Now, imagine the experience repeated with, perhaps, a dozen individuals, and we turn with disgust from the picture. How much worse, then, when a man seeks the gratification of his passion among various objects, for whom he never experiences the love which distinguishes man from the animal, in the relation of the sexes! Nothing can save him or them from an overwhelming degradation.

I am told there are women who seek such relations themselves. If this be true, and I do not doubt it, I can only class them with those other unfortunates, whom society has so deeply wronged, and who have so cruelly wronged their own souls, that the idea of purity and dignity is lost.

Those who advocate variety in love are not the ones most anxious to elevate and develop woman to the highest limits of her nature; and when they argue against her strongest instinct, that of *personal sacredness*, they rob her of that which is as essential an element in a pure nature as is the perfume in the flower.

In this protest against variety in love, every voice of my nature joins. It is a deep injustice to the nature of woman, and a profanation of the holy name of WIFE.

Ever, thy loving wife,

NINA.

## LETTER VI.

### DIVORCE.

Nina:

Intimately connected with the perpetuity and exclusiveness of marriage between one man and one woman is the subject of Divorce. This has ever been a perplexing question to statesmen and churchmen. So far as it is a subject for the action and management of human government, it must, like all other matters connected with relations based solely on the demands of the inner life, be attended with difficulty; but so far as it relates to the affections, to conjugal love and its actual manifestations, it is a question of easy solution by every pure and honest heart.

Divorce is the result of violated law, as are other evils. Men and women come together in marriage without a knowledge of each other, or of their needs in that direction. Instead of appreciating marriage as a necessity of their being, an essential condition of growth and happiness, they often regard it as only a civil institution, a contrivance of human ingenuity for human convenience, — a source of gratification to an excited, ungovernable passion. When that passion is satiated, the great end of the relation, as they view it, is answered. Man, too often, takes no heed of the capabilities and qualities, in any other direction, of the woman whom he is about to receive as a wife.

Man pays more heed to the qualities of the ship, the

house, the shoes, the hat, the coat, the horse, sheep or ox, he is about to buy, than to the physical, intellectual and spiritual conditions of the woman he is about to take as a wife, and to make the guardian and protector of his manhood. Woman, often, is far more solicitous about the qualities of the gloves, shawl, bonnet and fan she is about to purchase, than she is concerning the qualities and conditions of the body and soul of the man whom she expects to receive as a husband, and the father of her children. Consequently, society is full of inharmonious and most fatal alliances between men and women, under the name of marriage, — alliances as unnatural and monstrous, and as fruitful of evil, as a union between liberty and slavery, truth and falsehood, purity and impurity, — alliances in which no compromises can ever produce harmony or happiness.

*How to prevent these misalliances?* This is *the* question. Divorce is the result of, and a supposed remedy for, unnatural and inharmonious relations between men and women, under the name of marriage. Divorce, as an experience of the heart, is to the soul much what dyspepsia is to the stomach. Man mistakes the excitement of passion for conjugal love; woman mistakes vanity, ambition, a desire for a home or a social position, for the same. They enter into intimate personal relations as husband and wife. The counterfeits of love, which precipitated them into their unnatural and inharmonious outward union, soon reveal themselves, and both find that they stand in an outward relation to each other which their souls have never sanctioned. In her ignorance and blindness, woman takes to herself what she hopes may prove the bread of life to her soul, but she finds it a deadly poison.

There is but one way in which these unnatural and discordant alliances can be prevented, and divorce be forestalled. The *intuitions* of men and women must be more perfectly organized and developed; the *sexual instinct* must be refined and more delicately attuned; then would they be able to select a natural and healthful supply for that want of the soul which points man to woman as a wife, or woman to man as a husband, with as much certainty as the instinct for material food directs us to select that which is wholesome.

The instinct which points men to women and women to men, for a true development, is all dark, bewildered, gross; and, in its grossness and want of delicacy of perception, it points them to a relation based mainly on sensual indulgence. Disappointment, sickness and disgust of heart, ensue; the twain that fondly dreamed of oneness become antagonisms; neglect, abuse, outrage, follow, and civil government is asked to come in and cut the outward bond, and save them from the effects of their ignorance and passion.

Had that deepest, noblest and most potential instinct of the soul been truly, delicately and nobly formed and directed, had it been so enlightened and refined that it would have guided the soul to select for itself the true element of conjugal life, it would have elevated to heaven instead of casting down to perdition. In such a relation, divorce has no place, no significance. It belongs only to unnatural conditions and false relations between the sexes. Under the guidance of an enlightened, refined sexual instinct, the only power that can bring the two elements into true and vitalizing relations, where marriage is but another name for love, for harmony and perfect trust between two souls, it were as unmeaning to talk of divorce, as to talk of it in reference to the relations between the needle and the pole.

But such is not the condition of society in reference to the relation between the sexes. What is to be done to meet the existing necessity? What *can* be done? Men and women will come together — they *must* — it is a necessity of their being. They are ignorant, they are bewildered. They will come into false relations. Children will be born of such unfortunate alliances. Who or what is to manage these matters, correct these abuses, and secure individuals and society against all possible results from the perversions of a relation on which all rational hopes of human progress must be based? Of all agencies, governments have proved themselves most incompetent to correct these abuses, and save individuals and society from their direful consequences.

There is but one remedy — LET THERE BE LIGHT! The nature, extent, power and object of the distinction of sex must be understood and appreciated; the sexual instinct must be refined, ennobled, and brought under an enlightened reason and a tender conscience; the true object of the presence of the reproductive element in man must be better understood; the fixed laws by which God designed its expenditure should be regulated must be known and obeyed; man's true mission to woman and woman's to man, be known and more truly estimated; and the gospel of a true marriage and parentage be preached to all; — then, and not till then, will the twain that leads to oneness reveal its power to bless and to save; and till then, divorce, as an experience of the heart, will continue to desolate the inner life, and, as an outward ordinance, to bewilder the head of the statesman, and grieve the heart of the philanthropist.

NINA, this is a most painful subject to one who is conversant with the domestic relations of men and women. *Experimenting in marriage* is the order of society. The results are fearful to those who experiment, and to their offspring. While men and women go on to experiment in a relation which is the basis of the perpetuity, and must be of the perfection, of the race, they will have, and must have, governmental interference to save them and society from the consequences that would result to men, women and children, by leaving the parties to repeat their experiments as often as insatiate passion and stupid ignorance might dictate. The evils of divorce, as an experience of the inner and outer life, will continue to increase, until every true and pure-hearted man and woman is satisfied that relief can come, not from human legislation, but only from a knowledge of, and obedience to, the fixed, unchanging laws of God, designed to govern conjugal relations.

Meanwhile, the truth will stand, that marriage, like the pulsations of the heart and the contractions of the lungs, is the work of Nature. There is a power that brings a man and woman into this relation. When this power ceases to act, to make the twain one, marriage ceases, as an experience of the soul; and where there is no union of soul, there is no marriage, and all outward conjugal relations should cease. The mental, moral and physical conditions of a man and woman may be harmonious, when they are drawn into the relation of husband and wife. They may be pure and healthful, and the union be a happy one. Love may bind them together. But perhaps, by some great change of his nature, the conditions of the man are changed. His moral nature may be wrecked in the conflict of life, or his social elements may enslave him to low and brutalizing appetites, so that his intellect becomes imbecile, and the whole type of the man is changed. Can the wife, who loved in him the embodiment of all high and holy qualities, which he once was, still love the man, who, in all respects, fails to meet the ideal that first won her maiden heart? The man she loved is changed; he is no more. Her *ideal* is not changed, but the man to whom she gave herself as a wife has ceased to embody that ideal. Reason and Nature answer, at once, and say, "She cannot love him as she did!" But, without this love, is she, before God, his wife? By all that is sacred, she is not! The man in whom her soul found embodied its ideal of purity, nobleness, and manhood, has become a loathsome sensualist. The man has made himself repulsive to her wifely heart; by his sensualism, he has separated himself from her soul of conjugal love, as the sinner, by his sins, has separated himself from his God. She may pity him, and weep over him, but she cannot love him and come to him as a wife. Love cannot attract her heart to that which is not lovely, and he is so no longer. Now, what shall she do? Is her body to belong to the man who has no power to retain her affection? *Not for one moment!* She is not his wife by love, only by law and outward form; and the surrender of her person is but legalized prostitution, frowned upon by a just and holy God. Come what may, when love ceases between those who have been pronounced husband and wife, let the outward expression cease. Where a deep, holy, conjugal love does not unite the souls of a man and woman, however strong the demands of passion, let there be no surrender of the person, for the unhallowed purpose of mere sensual gratification. Let every woman be fixed, as God is, never to live with a man, as a wife, whom she does not love; let every man be equally true to the voices of his nature, and an untold amount of misery would be saved to both.

Human laws come in and dictate the grounds of divorce. What have they to do with the question of divorce, as a heart experience? Just as much as they have to do with marriage, and no more,—only to sanction what Nature and Nature's God have already accomplished. But they ought never to *coerce* those to keep together, as husband and wife, who require such bonds to unite them, for these are, by the laws of God, no longer one. Love is departed, and with it, marriage; and no human laws can make them one. *There is a twain that leads to oneness*, by a fixed law of human existence,—the law of Harmony, of Marriage. If human enactments attempt too much, and license the union of two as husband and wife whom God hath put asunder, men and women must set them at nought, and obey the higher law written on their souls, which forbids all personal surrender to sexual indulgence, without love.

Human legislation may forbid them again to assume the external relations and to enjoy the outward rights and privileges of marriage, each with another; but it cannot control the wants and action of the soul, which remain the same as before. The fact that they have been once bewildered and mistaken, does not destroy this want of their being. The soul of each must ever demand, in order to its growth in purity and all goodness, that which the soul of one of the corresponding sex can alone supply. They will necessarily attract and be attracted, until the soul of each comes into a natural, harmonious relation.

The rock on which so many fond hopes are dashed, the one fatal error which is so fruitful in direful results to many bewildered, but trusting hearts, is, that men and women commence living in the outward relations of husband and wife, and become parents, in utter ignorance of each other, of their own wants, as male and female, and of the only basis of a true conjugal relation, and regardless of that corresponding attraction and union of heart, without which, the outward personal surrender is an outrage to body and soul, that must, as a general rule, end in disease and wretchedness to all who thus live, and to their offspring. Would that parents might study to guard their sons and daughters against the possibility of mistaking passion, or friendship, or a desire for a home, for wealth, social position, or any other feeling, for conjugal love! Let them attend to the organization and true development of the sexual instinct, and seek to bring it, as they do other instincts, under the control of reason and conscience; let them ever impress upon their children the certain degradation and ruin that must ensue from an external connubial relation, however sanctioned by Church and State, which is repudiated by the inner life of the soul; — then might we hope that the State would not be so often invoked to annul the outward bond, where there is no union of heart.

If human laws enter to regulate the intimate relations of the sexes, and presume to say to a woman, "You shall love this man, and you shall not love that man," or, "if you do not love that man, you shall surrender your person to him in the passional relation, and continue to become the mother of his children," then they go beyond their appropriate function, and usurp a power against which every pulse of true manhood and womanhood revolts.

But, if there are children, what must the parents do? Live together, as friends, who have in those children, on whom they have entailed existence without love, a mutual care and responsibility. Be to them *parents*, in the deepest and widest sense possible. Give them every attention and advantage which they have a right to claim from the authors of their being; and in order to do this, keep your own souls free from degradation, by a firm, unwavering fidelity to the highest impulses of your nature. Cease to be a wife, in external relations, to the man thou dost not love, but be a mother to the child for whose existence thou art responsible; cease to be a husband to the woman thou dost not love, but ever be a father to the child who has derived its being from thee.

It is asked, "Has not Jesus laid down the only true ground of external divorce? Has he not pronounced adultery the only sufficient cause of separation from 'bed and board?'" But, I ask, what is adultery, but the proof that marriage-love, that true, divine, exclusive element of the soul, is gone? What loving husband ever seeks the gratification found in adultery? Jesus *has* laid the true foundation of divorce to be *the absence of love*, and adultery was the form in which it manifested itself in the case before him. In this, Jesus taught according to Nature. Adultery is a sufficient ground of divorce, because it proves the absence of love. Whatever demonstrates the cessation or absence of love between a man and woman, proves that the relation of husband and wife never existed, or that, if it ever did, it exists no longer. There are many other proofs, less censured by human laws and customs, on which a true man or woman must rely, and by which they must govern their relations. Where conjugal love exists between a man and woman, there is marriage. Though external surroundings may prevent the public recognition of it, yet, before God, those two souls are one, — are husband and wife, — as truly as if they openly lived in that relation. There is but one true cause of divorce from the inner or outward marriage relation, and that is, THE ABSENCE OF LOVE.

But, to a true marriage, whose conditions are faithfully sustained, there will come no divorce. To maintain, strengthen and eternize our mutual love, we will live and die, and so cherish the divine oneness between us, that no coldness, no darkness, shall chill the warmth or dim the beauty and the brightness of our united hearts.

Thy husband,

ERNEST.

## ANSWER.

Ernest:

In my last letter, I said that marriage between two was the law of Nature, and that this marriage must be consummated first in the spiritual union, and afterwards actualized in the personal relation; and that the latter relation is only the natural consequence of the former.

Thou hast said that human law should sanction what Nature has accomplished. It consummates marriage between any two who stand up before a minister or magistrate, with a request to be made man and wife. It asks no questions whether love, or policy, or sensual passion, or ambition, or avarice, be the ground of the union. Clumsily and blindly, it puts the chain around the two, rivets the link, and solemnly pronounces them ONE.

How is it about divorce? The law suddenly grows critical and particular. When these two come back, and ask the same power that bound them to set them free, the law says, "If you are guilty of any particular sin, so gross, so palpable, that human eye can see it, and human testimony can prove it, I will set you free; but not otherwise. No matter how your hearts are changed towards each other, no matter what personal wrongs and outrages you have committed under the sanction of my name, if you have not committed the particular sin I specify, I have no redress, no relief for you."

There are those whose morals are fashioned by a higher model than human laws; and the omnipotence of the law of marriage, and the insufficiency of knowledge as to the true grounds of divorce, have produced in men's minds a most distorted idea of their true position. It is usually understood that, by marriage, — that is, by the performance of a marriage ceremony, — a wife passes over to the care, keeping and protection of her husband; that the bestowal of her heart upon any other, is a wrong to him to whom human law has assigned her.

Suppose two are married, under this impression, who think they love each other. As time rolls on, and each matures and develops, they diverge in sympathy; and perhaps the husband or the wife may be so constituted by nature, that the deepest wants of the heart cannot be met by the other. Without abuse or outrage, love yields its place to friendship, respect, and kind feeling. If this takes place in the wife, her nature will not demand the personal endearments of marriage. She will promptly say to her husband, that such expressions belong to *love*, not to friendship; that they are disagreeable to her, and that only by restraining them can either be saved from degradation. He tells her that she is wrong; that when she married, she gave herself to be his lawful, wedded wife, and that his nature demands the gratification of all its wants; that he has a right to such gratification, and her scruples are only foolish nonsense, which should not weigh against his wishes; that they are useless obstacles in the way of his enjoyment; and that the world would agree with him, that his demand was no more than just.

To such arguments, the wife generally yields; not willingly, but by compulsion, for where is her refuge? She applies to her protector for protection against himself, — but in vain. It were well if every husband realized that in thus removing "obstacles," he has planted an element ruinous to himself. He has taken the first step towards turning respect into contempt, friendship into hatred, and liking into loathing.

If women dared to give their experience on this matter, as they one day will, they would agree with this statement. From the hour that a wife realizes that her husband claims her person, when he knows he has not her heart, she is a slave, not less degraded than any ever bought or sold upon the auction-block; and she entertains to her master the feelings which such a relation must produce. Marriage, to her, becomes the name for all that is debasing and disgusting.

What, then, is she to do? Human law lent its sanctions to ratify her marriage. *Now*, an equally clear and unmistakable voice within tells her that that marriage is null and void. She appeals to human law to annul it; but it is silent as the tomb. She has prayed in vain for mercy of him who has taken it upon himself to cherish and protect her, and what remains to her? Either to bow her soul to a pollution too deep for any name, or to disregard the power of human law and a still more cruel public opinion, and leave the home where the shelter for her head must be purchased at the cost of her self-respect.

This is her last resort. But, before this, let her try every argument, every reason, which manhood can comprehend or generosity feel, in behalf of her own rights. Let her show, by appeals to nature and reason, that it is a mistake to suppose that marriage takes from the wife the control of her own person. It is a natural, inalienable right, that was ordained of God before human law was made, and can be annulled by no enactments of men.

If there are children, let her plead to be their true and faithful mother. To this end, let her keep herself pure and undefiled; let their children be a mutual care, and let them have every attention and advantage which they have a right to claim from the authors of their being. A man must be less than human, not to listen to this deep, agonizing petition from the mother of his children.

But if he be less than a man, that wife is bound to fidelity to her own soul, at every cost. She will stand guilty before God for the neglect of her instincts; and if there is no alternative but separation or legalized prostitution, then, I say, in the name of God and virtue, let her depart!

I have stated an extreme case, because there are men, or rather, beings who have the name of men, so degraded as to demand a gratification of their passion without love, because the law has given them possession of the person of the individual who bears the name of wife. But, thank God, there are *men* who deserve the name, — who ask not what the law allows, but who govern themselves by the one only law of the heart.

There are numberless other cases, where affection on either side is wasted by neglect and indifference on the other; but they are all various manifestations of the one great cause — THE ABSENCE OF LOVE; and they all point to one only remedy — SEPARATION; or, at least, suspension of the marriage relation.

Human laws may forbid those who have been disappointed in one alliance from being attracted to others. It is in vain; the pulsations of the heart can never be controlled by such enactments. Though governments forbid the outward expression of it, they cannot prevent the soul from attracting and being attracted. The heart may suffer under a false relation, but its power to love nobly, purely and truly, is not thereby destroyed; and I should utter my protest against all arbitrary restrictions put upon a true love relation. Yet, I am not so blind as to imagine that all the world is ready to act upon the law of spiritual attraction; for, to nine-tenths of human beings, these words have no significance. But, in these letters, we are not laying down laws for the nation, but defining our ideal of true marriage.

It is a bitter sorrow to find the hope of young love blighted; but that is light, compared to the sting of finding our holiest instincts disregarded in marriage, a deaf ear turned to the agonizing cry of the soul for mercy, and the very core of our hearts wrung by a sense of wrong and outrage.

ERNEST, I have written a long letter; but my soul is deeply moved, and I have not said half I might. I cannot imagine the sense of self-degradation I have here described as ever occurring in our relation, any more than that the blue heaven could descend to stain its purity with the dust beneath my feet. But I speak from my knowledge of woman's nature, — her instincts, her demands; and I have heard deep and heart-rending revelations from those the world considers happy. I know full well what depths of misery may lie behind a smile.

Thy true wife,

NINA.

## LETTER VII.

### THE TRANSIENT AND PERMANENT IN MARRIAGE.

Nina:

That there is a transient and a permanent in the relation of husband and wife, as in all other relations, must be evident to the most superficial observer. We believe our relation is a true one. All true relations are as permanent as the wants and necessities on which they are based. Natural wants originate natural relations, and all natural relations are true. A natural want cannot lead us into a false relation. Ignorance in regard to such wants may, and does, lead human beings into relations that are false and ruinous. But all false and unnatural relations are transient, and must pass away; only the true and natural will endure. Of course, all hopes of happiness, based on false relations, are doomed to disappointment. Only those which are based on true ones can be actualized.

What, then, are the *transient* elements of our relation, and what the *permanent*? Among the transient, ONE IS WEALTH. As a means to happiness, and a connecting link in that chain which binds us together, wealth is a nonentity. Our souls, as they were merged by love each into the other, ignored the idea. Gold and silver we saw not. A power, independent of wealth, and all that wealth can procure, drew us together. Just so far as wealth is a basis of marriage, so far is that relation transient and uncertain; for that, at any hour, may take to itself wings, and leave only disappointed ambition and a bitter dissatisfaction in its place. I am far from indifferent to the advantages of wealth, both to ourselves and to the children in whose lives we hope to live, and in whose bliss we hope to be blessed. I rejoice to see thee, my wife, amid the artistic beauty and elegance with which wealth can surround thee. But such beauty and elegance are only artistic and external, and, of course, transient. They cannot satisfy the wants of thy deep and earnest soul. They would soon lose all power over thee, and thou wouldst yield them up as worthless, to be clasped to the bosom of thy beloved. Thou wouldst see more beauty and elegance in the eyes of him who thus holds thee in his keeping,—more to refine, exalt, and satisfy thy nature,—than in them all. Thou wouldst rather behold thine image engraven deep in the manly heart of thy husband, than to see it reflected from the most dazzling mirror that wealth could purchase. There is a depth in our souls, which neither wealth, nor any thing that wealth can procure, can ever reach or fill. In that depth, not in bank vaults, nor in mines of gold and silver, are garnered our priceless stores.

How utterly powerless, then, is wealth, to increase or diminish the strength and happiness of the marriage relation! How surely and how soon the loving heart grows weary of its glitter, and proudly and fondly turns to the answering love and sympathy of the loved one! Knowing this, let the desire for wealth never send me away from thee! May the wish to grow in oneness, till each shall have no life apart from the other, and thus to perfect our marriage relation, be the ruling motive of our hearts! The pursuit of wealth, when it separates or alienates a husband and wife, is a complete sacrifice of the permanent to the transient, the inner to the external life. Love is all that can insure happiness, and satisfy the soul in marriage. That will give us heaven, despite our outward surroundings. We will be rich in each other's love; we will glory in this vast possession. This is a wealth for which it is worthy to struggle, for it is a possession above the power of time and fate.

Is *social position* more permanent, as an element of happiness, than wealth? It is no more permanent, and equally incapable of giving repose. The struggle for social standing is often intense. Health of body, and peace of mind, are often sacrificed to attain it; and when attained, what is it? Nothing. We seek to be admitted to a particular circle in society. We are admitted, on condition of compliance with the established rules of the order. What have they to do with the deepest wants and experiences of the heart? Absolutely nothing. The impulses of the heart must often be crushed and crucified, in order to our acceptance among those with whom we seek association. Should men or women, whose great aim is social position, dare to be true to the deepest and holiest instincts of their nature, they would forfeit their standing, for the simple reason, that social position does not award its favors to fidelity to truth and justice, but to fidelity to its behests.

Men and women may be bewildered and dazzled by a

brilliant position in society, and by the homage of admiring associates. Our superficial aspirations may be met by this, but there is a depth in every heart which this can never reach. If there be no answering voice to the deep, enduring, ever-present wants that are there, life becomes a living death. Wealth and position, with all that glitters in their train, can never answer to those living wants. A husband or a wife must seek, above all other possessions, the entire heart of the wife or husband. When this pursuit is abandoned or endangered, for even the most brilliant social position, the one who tries it is the destined victim of an enduring heart-desolation. To stand in conscious dignity and purity before his wife, will be the highest position to which the husband will aspire. So with the wife in regard to the husband.

Be thou my soul's eternal possession, and may I be thine, and this will be all my nature craves. May we each embody to the other all of the Divine which the nature of each demands, and thus will our souls find perfect repose.

Thy husband,<br>ERNEST.

## ANSWER.

Ernest:

In thy last letter, thou hast fathomed the depths of life, and with a firm and fearless hand brought to light the true riches. Thou hast shown the difference between the real and the superficial with so just a discrimination, that hardly any thing is left for me to say, which can add force to thy thought.

As a true Reformer, thou hast discriminated between abstract right and wrong, and then applied thy conclusions to the questions of daily life. Thou hast taken the standard of perfect manhood and womanhood, and by it measured every passer-by. This thou not only hast a right to do, but art bound to do, as a rational, independent being. Each one is bound to live up to his highest ideal. In society, manifold claims compel us to take the attitude of discrimination, in order to ascertain to what extent they are binding, and how far they should be resisted. The only rule by which to judge them is one's own ideal of truth and justice. I have entire respect and confidence in the result of such applications as thou hast made of thy standard to the practical questions of life. Social wrongs are every where about us, but I am not content with examining them and passing sentence upon them as wrong; I would know what is the first cause from which these wrongs have sprung. For instance, in the illustrations thou hast adduced of the transient influences of wealth and social position on the happiness of marriage, — whence comes the undue weight which these considerations have at present in society? Was it a good or evil tendency in the human heart? Is the present bewilderment on these subjects an evidence of total depravity, or a perversion of a natural and worthy impulse?

To take thy last example first: What has made

equality in social position so essential to marriage? It seems to me to arise from a very natural want. In marriage, we wish for a companion whose cultivation, tastes and associations are so nearly equal to our own, that we shall not feel at a loss for society *at home*, or be shocked by associations disagreeable to our tastes. This is the broad, general reason for looking among our own accustomed associates for companionship. But perhaps we may be connected by ties of blood with those every way inferior to ourselves. Our own natures, tastes, aspirations, fit us for a nobler, more refined circle of friends. To this we turn, as to a native element. Here, by this very fact, we have a right to be; and here, if we are true to our strongest attractions, will our permanent ties be formed. Thus far, there is nothing to be blamed; but the moment we imagine that mere personal intimacy with this or that set of people, reputed to be genteel, is a test of individual merit, or can supply the want of it; the moment we seek society better than our own, from motives of personal advancement, or from any motive but an *inward* necessity, that moment we lose dignity and self-respect. People expect to attain an eminence by the aid of a neighbor's skirts, to which they could never reach by their own two feet.

Then, if in marriage this is a secret motive, the desired end may be gained, but what beside? If not fitted for it by nature and personal merit, it becomes a cold, cheerless, mighty mansion for a dwarf to dwell in. Long since have we ceased to look for the great men and women of the world among those who call themselves the "aristocracy." Let every true man and woman, in selecting companions for life, be governed by the simple and natural wants I first stated in this letter, and forego all the éclat which contains neither the promise nor the fulfilment of happiness.

How is it about *wealth?* To sober, high-minded people, wealth has this substantial value: it enlarges the field of benevolent action in a two-fold way — first, by direct gifts; and second, by leaving the possessor free from the necessity of *engrossing* occupation. A benevolent man, whose time is at his own command, has an unbounded sphere of usefulness; but if the claims of wife and children, who are dependent on him for their daily bread, compel him to a single occupation, his action, in other directions, must of course be limited, however large the benevolence of his heart may be.

As a secondary consideration, wealth favors self-culture, by securing those advantages, and such external surroundings, as a cultivated taste selects. All this may be right, and may be used as a means of imparting happiness and knowledge to others less fortunate. These are the objects for which wealth is truly desirable.

The perversions which shallow natures make of these means of self-culture and usefulness are too often illustrated to need enumeration here. Self-aggrandizement becomes the aim of life, and display, and the hollow admiration which that wins, supplants the nobler desire which buries self in the welfare of others.

A nature which can be satisfied with the latter possessions, to whom they become essential, so that true worth, without them, is unattractive, will often marry for wealth; and if an inscrutable Providence sees fit to let a life flow on in undisturbed possession of this phantom of happiness, the heart will grow poorer and smaller upon this insufficient food, till the realities of another life shall tear the scales from off those blinded eyes, and unfold the wrappings which have converted a being, once fresh and full of life, into an embalmed relic of antiquity. Thank God, that to us, nothing external or superficial has lent a moment's fascination! Wert thou poor, friendless, and an outcast, thou wert all the same to me; for that which I love in thee is nothing that man has given or can take away.

Thy wife,

NINA.

## LETTER VIII.

### HARMONY OF DEVELOPMENT.

Nina:

The beauty and entireness of our relation, as husband and wife, depend upon ourselves. There are privileges belonging to this relation, that can be accorded to none other, without a profanation of the highest and holiest elements of our nature. The attraction of men and women to each other, *as such*, has its privileges, and its fixed, just laws to govern it. The marriage attraction is also designed to be regulated by just, immutable laws. In marriage, each earnestly seeks to be owned by the other. The husband and wife long to be claimed, each by the other, body and soul, and to have that claim asserted and maintained. The more absolute the claim and the possession of each over the other, the more entire is the satisfaction. Each ever longs to hear, in every possible form of expression, — "I am thine, thou art mine." The entire abandonment of each to the other, in body and soul, is the source of the most intense enjoyment of connubial life, and of the most perfect happiness of which the soul is capable, in the present state.

But how often, through ignorance or other causes, is this confidence abused, especially on the part of the husband! This very abandonment, on the part of the wife, of body and soul to the tender love and care of her husband, which should make her more sacred in his eyes, and secure to her his most tender and loving reverence, and thus make her heaven complete, is often made the source of her deepest degradation. Every fibre, organ and element of her being should be sacred to him. She has consecrated her entire womanhood to his care and protection. This priceless wealth is eagerly and joyfully given and received. Shall he take and use it to the intellectual, moral and physical ruin of the loving, trusting giver? It is a lamentable truth, that a husband often proves the most fatal influence to the wife's health and happiness, — an influence from which there is no escape, except in death. Marriage, to both, should be the beginning of life and health. How often is it, to the wife, the first step to a lingering and painful death! Often, a short time, perhaps a single year, produces visible changes in her mental and physical conditions. Freshness, strength and vigor have departed, and a careworn brow, and languor, and ill-health, betray a great violation of some of Nature's laws. Perhaps the husband, perceiving the change, inquires the cause. She knows it full well, but she shrinks from wounding his pride, impeaching his knowledge, or chilling and alienating his affections, by telling him the truth. She suffers, in silence, the utter prostitution and ruin of her soul and body. He who should have been the Elixir of Life to her, has become her Death-Potion, which is fast precipitating her into a premature, but longed-for grave.

Such is a picture which may be seen in any neighborhood, among all classes. Why is it that woman so often dates the beginning of her downward course with marriage? Her intellect becomes enfeebled and bewildered; science and literature become less attractive; her social and moral nature becomes inactive, and she disappears from the social circle of which she was the life, not to give life to the still dearer home-circle, for there, too, clouds and darkness hang round about her. Proudly and fondly she gave to her husband all the treasures of her womanhood, and he has used them to her destruction.

But the wife cannot sink alone. The husband, who

has cast her down, must fall with her: God hath so decreed. Every abuse of her nature is as great or a greater abuse of his own.

The essential element of the marriage relation is *oneness, harmony*, — harmony in the intellectual, affectional and passional elements of their natures. If, in aptitude and opportunity for intellectual development, the husband excels the wife, and he takes no pains to extend his advantages to her, and make her his equal and companion, and thus maintain their oneness, he will soon find himself associated with one, in the most intimate, and important, and ever-present relations of life, who is incompetent to meet his constantly-growing wants in that direction. Her intellect he leaves to barrenness, while he sedulously and successfully cultivates his own. In this, he neglects and abuses his wife, whose right to intellectual development is equal to his own.

So in regard to her social and affectional nature. He cannot enlarge, refine and elevate his social nature, while he leaves her to a limited and inferior circle, without wrong to her and to himself. The husband, if he is wise, will mingle in no society in which the wife cannot stand by his side. He will enter no circle where she may not enter; he will seek no social enjoyment in which she may not participate. Just so far as he cultivates his social nature, and leaves hers to barrenness and desolation, he brings ruin on the home of his love and happiness. If necessary causes confine her at home, his love will keep him by her side. It is certain ruin to his soul's peace to leave her to isolation, anxiety, and an ever-present longing for his sympathy and society, while he is away, mingling in the exciting scenes of general society, however intellectual and refined they may be. He who sacrifices the society of wife and children to general society, sacrifices the substance to the shadow, the pure diamond to the common pebble.

So of the passional element. If the husband enjoys this at the expense of the wife, all harmony of desire is outraged. His passional nature becomes monstrous and unnatural, and seeks its gratification at the expense of the wife's health and happiness. But in another letter, I shall show how our harmony in this relation is to be preserved.

ERNEST.

## ANSWER.

Ernest:

Since thou hast proposed, in thy last letter, to treat more fully, in succeeding letters, that part of the subject which pertains to the physical conditions of marriage, I will limit myself, in this reply, to the ideas suggested in the latter part of your last communication, in which you describe the unhappy results of a neglect of the social and intellectual wants of woman.

In a former letter, I have said that Love strikes its first roots in the spiritual nature. The maiden finds in her hero a wisdom to which her intellect does homage, while her heart is won by his attractive goodness. She looks forward to marriage as the blessed bond which shall insure to her his presence evermore. She will then have an ever-present counsellor and friend. His knowledge will supply her ignorance, his intellectual wealth will supply all her wants; and her growth and progress will be stimulated by his sympathy and encouragement. She foresees the time when domestic cares, or physical weakness, will limit her to the walls of her own house, and when the busy whirl of life would leave her entirely in the background, were it not for the influx of fresh life which Love daily lays before her. Visions of domestic happiness flit before her mind, of busy occupation for herself in preparing comforts for the beloved, while he will cheer her labors with social conversation or a book. To young or old, there is a charm in such a picture of home life. Full in the expectation of such happiness, the bride leaves the home of her youth, her early friends, the position in life where leisure, books and every means of culture were at her command, and joyfully lays them all upon the altar of her love; rejoicing that she has, within herself, resources wherewith to render home attractive to him, whose happiness is now her greatest object in life. As time wears on, her cares increase, and less time is left for self-culture. She tries to inform herself by conversation with her husband; but he finds her ill-informed, her reasoning unsound, in consequence of defective information and limited observation, and he therefore prefers other society, from whom he can gain something for himself. He talks with her about minor matters, of private and personal interest, but leaves for persons of greater knowledge the discussion of the deep questions of life. Club-rooms become the scenes of his greatest intellectual activity and enjoyment, and he looks upon his home as a place of refreshment for his body, of relaxation from mental activity; a place in which he has much to receive, and little to impart.

Thus, by slow degrees, the bonds of true companionship are severed, and life presents to them no longer *one* aim, *one* destiny, and *one* hope, but separate paths, objects and satisfactions. According to the tendencies of her nature, the wife becomes a devotee of fashion, frivolous, worldly, and neglectful of the serious duties of life, seeking abroad what she fails to find at home; or perhaps the native energies of her soul assert themselves superior to such common-place attractions, and she leads her independent life of thought and action under that name which has formerly been a by-word of reproach, a "blue-stocking," and in later days implied in the epithet of a "strong-minded woman." Perhaps the Church, and active works of benevolence, bear evidence of the disappointed hopes which seek an unselfish satisfaction; or, perhaps, from want of inward force, she loses all hope, all aspiration, and all effort, and sinks into the mere household drudge and nursery-maid.

Who is to be held accountable for this wasted life? Not she who has brought heart, mind, youth, strength, high hopes and noble aspirations to the home of her beloved; but he by whose neglect she has failed to become what her natural endowments and previous culture fitted her to be. In associating her life with that of her husband, she has yielded to such claims as *must* engross her time, occupy her thoughts, and enfeeble her physical powers. But shall such a free gift of herself be the wreck of all her deepest aspirations, dependent as she is, for their fulfilment in her new relation, on the ties of social companionship?

Her duties in domestic life are well defined, and neglect of them meets unmerciful censure from the world's people. Has the husband, then, no domestic duties, involving the happiness and development of his wife? Did he marry for a housekeeper and a mother to his children, or did he seek *companionship* for life? In some, a thoughtless neglect, in others, a low estimate of the capabilities of a woman's nature, leads to an entire separation of life and interest between man and wife.

He who loves wisely, as well as deeply, will as generously share with his wife the food of intellectual life, as the daily bread. When he gives her his right hand in marriage, it should be a symbol of the fact that, to her whole nature, he will be a guide, a comfort and a strength, which shall never fail.

But again, I must recur to my home in thee, to renew the assurance that I am speaking from experience, in giving this ideal of what the true husband should be. I am a wife, in all the dignity, power and purity which that name implies. Yet, withal, I have such a sense of rest in thy strength, such respect for thy judgment, and such faith in the love which makes my advancement thy first care, that I almost fancy myself a little child, whose education thou hast undertaken, and for whom thou dost feel a father's solicitude. I am, indeed,

Thy " CHILD-WIFE,"

NINA.

## LETTER IX.

### LOVE AND PASSION.

Nina:

In my last letter, I spoke of the abuses practised by the husband, by disregarding the social and intellectual development of the wife, while he pays every attention to his own. I come now to speak of the *passional*, or purely *sexual* element of our nature, and of the necessity of perfect harmony in its action, in order to the perfection of marriage. If either demands that which the other has not the power joyfully to bestow, discord must ensue. For, if the husband demands the gratification of an unreciprocated want, it must tend to draw around a relation, intended to be bright and living, the shadow of death.

No human relation is under more fixed and certain laws and conditions of life and health, than that of marriage. Unswerving fidelity to these laws is the only condition of happiness in this relation. The passional nature, as an element of marriage, comes under equally just and fixed laws, whose violation converts this source of buoyant life and health into a source of the keenest suffering.

But, before proceeding to define these laws, I wish to say one word more touching the distinction between *Love* and *Passion*.

That there is, in fact, such a distinction, is obvious. Marriage-love is the deepest, tenderest, most absorbing element of the human soul. The highest and holiest effort of the love-nature is seen in the blending of two souls in marriage. To this deep, tender, abiding element of the soul, the *passional* nature will be ever in abeyance.

Where marriage-love exists between two healthfully organized and developed beings, the desire for the expression of love through the passional nature, and the desire for offspring, are natural results. It seems to me there must be a defective organization, where this is not the case. But, while connubial love may not exist without this desire, mere sexual passion may exist, in the most ungovernable degree, without love. In man, this desire or passion is designed to be under the control of wisdom or reason. In a perfectly organized man or woman, the desire for sexual gratification would exist only as the effect of pure love; and parentage would result only from marriage. But men are fearfully diseased in this respect. They seek this enjoyment without love; they stimulate, in every possible way, this element of their nature, and thus enlarge the power and desire of gratification. Reason, Conscience,

Love, Justice, God, are all sacrificed to this sensual element.

The only limit to their indulgence is the capacity for enjoyment. Wife, children, health and life are all sacrificed to sensual desire. How large a portion of the children, born among the most religious and civilized races, are the offspring of mere animal passion! They are neither conceived nor developed in love.

The passional nature should always be in entire subjection to true love, which is always in harmony with wisdom. Instead of this, the love is generally in subjection to the animal passion. In this case, the natural and inevitable consequence will be intellectual, physical and spiritual degradation to both; and an outrage to all who are born of it. Great and most hurtful mistakes are made, in the discussion of this question, by calling animal passion by the name of *love*. The animal desire is often accepted as marriage-love; and if the union of two, for this purpose, is sanctioned by the Church, the demands are considered to be those of love.

This is the sort of love that demands "variety" for its satisfaction. Uncontrolled by wisdom, justice, purity, love, and therefore essentially gross, impure and brutalizing, this passion seeks its gratification with any and every one, to the fullest extent of its capacity.

But, that I may preserve sound and pure the health of mind and body so freely and generously confided to my care, I shall give thee more clearly my idea of the true and imperative dominion which my love for thee asserts over the inferior elements of my nature.

Thy husband,

ERNEST.

## ANSWER.

Ernest:

Thou hast shown the action of selfishness in the pursuit of the opportunities of improvement, and hast made it seem, as it really is, the most direct foe of connubial union. The same spirit, wherever it is displayed, is equally fatal to the peace of her who becomes the victim. But sometimes the sacrifice is active, sometimes passive. The wife may be called upon to renounce a cherished hope with less conflict than to obey a positive command. This is true in the personal relations of marriage. There are many ways in which "marriage is a lottery," according to the old saying. An affectionate husband may make so great demands upon his wife as to undermine her health and destroy her capabilities of enjoyment or usefulness; or he who promises to love, cherish and protect her, may have so low an idea of the nature and offices of love, as to understand no finer mode of expression than through the passional nature; or, after a little while, it may appear that there was no *love* at all, but only a fierce, imperative sense of personal possession, which acknowledges no law or limit superior to itself. Under all these forms of marriage, woman is a hopeless victim, and helpless, also, except from her own resources. She may truly love her husband, yet the capacities of her nature for passional enjoyment may not allow her to respond to all his wants. It is the testimony of many wives, that their husbands, under these circumstances, will not accept such reasons; and if the wives persist in obedience to the instincts of their nature, they show coldness and neglect, and sometimes threaten to leave their homes, and seek among strangers the sensual pleasure denied them by their wives. When once such words cross a husband's lips, his claim to the respect, love and confidence of his wife is forfeited.

We have before classified, in its proper level, the animal passion which seeks indiscriminate gratification. In reply to such a threat, no woman who respects herself would hesitate a moment to assent to his proposition. But it should not end there. If he cannot govern himself according to the laws of reason, justice, self-respect, and the tender considerations which belong to the office of a husband, let him cease to *be* a husband. Never again should a *wife* receive him who can endeavor to frighten and manage her into subjection to his passions. Men say they cannot control these wants; that they are implanted by Nature, and it is intended that they should be gratified. In healthy organizations, when the natural laws are obeyed, they *can* control them, and all sound men know it. Women are taught that a part of their duty consists in sacrificing health and happiness to this sensual enjoyment in the husband. It is no more a duty, than it is to supply intoxicating drinks to the sot. In either case, her whole power and influence should be used to aid him in gaining ascendency over these lower elements of his nature. She should be gentle and affectionate, but firm and persevering in her course. If there is a spark of true manhood left, or even the memory of true love, it will thus be rekindled, *not* quenched.

If there were less reserve between those who intend marriage, there would be less difficulty afterwards. Young men and women should read and think, and have a standard of right and wrong upon this matter as fixed as upon any other moral question; for, surely, there is no one whose influence on themselves, and on future generations, is more direct or abiding. Those who are anxious to develop themselves rightly, will find no difficulty in presenting subjects pertaining to the most intimate relations with true delicacy and propriety. Now, men and women marry in utter ignorance of each other's views and expectations as to the very relation which will most speedily wreck their happiness, if it is abused. So long as they do this, the history of martyrs will continue to be written.

It is vitally essential that a young man should understand the action and reäction of his passional nature. If he be a true, high-minded, loving husband, he will wish to preserve, to the end of life, that perfect trust and confidence which will lead the wife to feel that she has no need of protection against her husband; that respect which often dies in the most intimate hours, while it remains undiminished in all external relations; that tender self-abandonment of first love, which bears in itself the germ of immortality, and can only be destroyed by neglect and outrage. The wife should never dread the coming of her husband, or be wearied with his presence. She should feel that the gentle assiduity with which the lover studied to anticipate and meet her wishes, is only exchanged for a nearer and dearer relationship, by which that tenderness can be expressed with tenfold significance. In marriage, under such influences, there is dignity, self-respect, and an elevating power to the husband; and freedom, joy and heavenly rest to the wife. Are not its attractions enough to render those laws by which it can be secured sacred to every pure and noble heart?

Thy wife,

NINA.

## LETTER X.

### THE REPRODUCTIVE ELEMENT.

#### ITS EXPENDITURE CONTROLLED BY FIXED LAWS.

NINA:

Our happiness, as husband and wife, must depend upon ourselves. Whether our marriage shall be a source of intellectual and spiritual growth, and a means of assimilating us more and more to the Divine, or of degradation to ourselves and our children, is for us to determine. That it may be only for good, we must know and obey the natural laws by which our relation is intended to be governed; especially as to the expenditure of that element which prompted us to enter into this relation. What is that element? To ask this is to ask, in another form, what constitutes me a *man*, and thee a *woman*.

The distinctive difference of sex lies in the power of man to prepare the germ of a new existence; and in woman to receive, mature and give life to that germ. Either sex, in which the power is wanting to fulfil the offices appropriately belonging to each, is defective in the essential elements of manhood or womanhood. It is certain, that Nature designed the race to be perpetuated and perfected here. In the economy of our physical and social nature, arrangements that aim at this end constitute a marked feature of humanity. The distinction of sex, and all the endearing relations that grow out of it, look to this end. Indeed, it seems the *sole* object of this distinction. The power of reproduction is indeed shared by man with all other animals, and even vegetable existences; yet, it is none the less an essential and important element of our nature.

It is too evident to need proof, that the parental relation was provided for in our social and physical organization. Those who do not enter into the relations of marriage and parentage, cannot be said fully to answer the great end of their being. We may know that the power to reproduce constitutes an essential ingredient in Human Nature, and that those who lack this power are wanting in an essential element of manhood or womanhood, from the condition and character of those in whom, by violence or abuse, the power to elaborate and secrete, or to receive and nourish into life, the germs of Humanity, is destroyed or paralyzed. This power in man to prepare and impart, and in woman to receive, cherish and develop, the germ of a new being, and thus to add new members to the great human brotherhood, makes each an object of sacred and abiding interest to the other. Each has a want, ever-present and ever-controlling, which can be met only by that which the other can impart. The husband would be represented in the race: he would hold to his heart one to call him father. In every truly organized and well-developed man, this is a deep and holy want; an earnest call, which can be answered only by a living child, the result of a union, in the person of the wife, between that element which makes him a man and that which makes her a woman. It is from this want, and the effort to fulfil it, that the attraction between the sexes has its origin. It gives magnetic power to each over the other.

No truly developed and well-organized man will seek a woman as a wife, whatever be her personal charms, or her intellectual endowments, if he knows her to be absolutely incapable of crowning him with the dignity of a father. He will seek such as a *friend;* but as she cannot fulfil this deep and holy want of his nature, she will not attract him into the relation of *marriage;* for the reproductive power is the only one that can bring us into the parental relation, which — marriage excepted — is the most important and exalted of which we are capable. On this rests our only hope of deliverance from the multiplied forms of disease and deformity, of body and soul, to which the race is now a victim. The power of reproduction is the basis of the purest, most intense, and most permanent happiness of life.

This power to reproduce is a primary, essential attribute of the soul. The body, so far as it is adapted to this end, is but the physical symbol through which the soul manifests its creative power. This power is the basis of true manhood. Without its presence in the physical system, the soul is necessarily imbecile and deformed, in all its manifestations. The expressions of intellect are feeble, dull, obscure, timid, and without energy; the outward demonstrations of affection are indelicate, repulsive, cold, and without life; the whole soul, in man and woman, is crushed and powerless, in all its intellectual, social and moral expressions. Take from a man the power to elaborate, secrete and impart the germs of new beings in human form, with all the attributes of perfect souls and bodies, and take from a woman the power to receive, nourish and develop those germs, and who would look to them for physical, intellectual, social or spiritual beauty, strength, nobleness and efficiency? Their wills, their intellects, their judgments, their reasons, their consciences, their affections, their entire being, is stunted. The vitalizing element of their manhood or womanhood is taken from them. Their souls, as well as their bodies, are mutilated by violence, or by an abuse of the sexual nature in mere sensual indulgence.

No man or woman can be truly great, intellectually, socially or morally, in whose physical organism this reproductive power has been wanting during childhood and youth. That soul must, in all respects, necessarily be deficient in all the noble, generous and highest qualities of manhood or womanhood, in whose development this power, in the bodily system, had no part. The man who respects not the health and comfort of the symbols of womanhood in his wife, but sacrifices them on the altar of his sensuality, is sure, sooner or later, to receive his reward, in a cheerless, sickly, lifeless home, and in the diseases and deformities of his children. Men and women will not always trifle, as they now do, with an element so essential to the healthful and noble development of the entire man or woman.

How sacredly, then, should such an element be regarded by all, especially by husbands and wives, fathers and mothers! With what solicitude should we seek to know the fixed laws of our being, by which it should be regulated! What scrupulous and unswerving fidelity should mark our obedience to them!

NINA! we must come to a true knowledge of ourselves, and maintain perfect loyalty to our natures, in this respect, and then we need have no apprehension as to the harmony and perpetuity of our life-giving relation. Thy husband,

ERNEST.

## ANSWER.

ERNEST:

THE thoughts expressed in thy last letter suggest to me the propriety of adding what is rarely acknowledged, even between those who are truly married. If I had heard expressions like thine on the difference of sex, years ago, I should have been shocked and pained. I think women generally would now be equally so, should these letters of ours ever fall under the public eye;

because we are taught to banish every thought or word which may remind us of this distinction. The idea is general among women, that they are attractive to men only for social qualities, which fit them to shine in general society or to adorn domestic life. Woman feels degraded by the thought, that her physical organization, as a woman, can add to or diminish the power of her attractions. I always felt this, and I know most women do. I believed that only the sensual eye considered those things, and only the meanest form of love took them into account. But, ERNEST! thanks to thy true and manly heart, thou hast taught me a higher truth than that. By the power of a pure and manly love, thou hast shown me that, to the lover's heart, every function, every organ, every capability of my nature, intellectual, moral, social and physical, combine to make me what I am, — the fulfilment of thy deepest wants, the satisfaction of thy wildest dreams of happiness. With the love I bear to thee, with the respect which no other man has inspired in me, with a trust which knows no limits, with the earnest striving to be to thee, in all respects, the wife of thy soul, can I for one moment resent the thought, that one great cause of this deep and holy relation between us, is the fact that I am physically, as well as intellectually and spiritually, organized so as to meet the yearnings of thy heart for a full and perfect manifestation?

The ultimate design for which woman is constituted, mentally and physically, as she is, can be no other than to fulfil the relations of a wife and mother. If she were meant for an isolated, self-dependent existence, she would have been differently organized, in all respects. Therefore, as the consummation of every created being is to fulfil the ends of its creation, every woman falls just so far short of the fulfilment of her destiny, as she fails in fitness for the relations of wife and mother.

The affections of a woman, her attractive forces, her susceptibility to the attractions of others, are all indicative of the same fact; and when, at last, the true husband is revealed to her, she has no choice but to own her sovereign. He, too, influenced by her love, walks with manly strength and dignity, for on his soul has dawned a vision of beauty and power. His heart pays homage to the loved one, as he claims her as the rightful owner of all he has to give and share.

Then comes the blending of their souls and bodies in the existence of a new being, which must, in that case, bear the impress of the authors of its existence. No wedded life can be perfect without this consummation; no life is complete, no future is full of promise, without this object for which to toil and expend the vital forces.

But no child of love will be dear for its own sake, merely. Because it is, to the mother, the child of a beloved husband, and to the father, the image of a beloved wife, — this makes the consecrating holiness of parentage. In fact, this is all that constitutes *human* parentage superior to the instinct of an animal that protects her young. It is the glory of our humanity, that all the relations in which we stand to each other are stamped by the *soul*. The animal, as such, belongs to the brutes. *Human* beings are designed to reproduce human beings, with all the attributes of soul that belong to them as such. In the reproduction of human beings, all the rational, affectional and moral powers that belong to them must take part, or the offspring is not, in the truest sense, human. If only the animal instinct is concerned in it, mere animals, not human beings, must be the result.

I think, as you know, that no woman has a right to marry, knowing her incapacity to be a mother, without a full acknowledgment, at least, of the fact. Then, if her beloved chooses to sacrifice that part of his being to her, he can do so; but she has no right to compel him to such a sacrifice by concealment. It is a falsehood; and few women are courageous enough to tell the truth in this matter. So of a husband; though I think there are many women who would not be in any wise influenced by the knowledge of that defect in a husband.

It seems to me, that the element in a woman's nature which seeks to embody itself in a child is not generally in a state of such strong and active development as it is in man. It lies dormant in every perfect nature, to be sure; but, as I have known woman, the desire to be a mother does not take a distinct form among the clamorous wants of her nature. I think a woman's love is always, at first, a pure element of the soul, and has no care nor thought for the body; and, oftentimes, the *personal* surrender costs an effort, even where the love is true and deep. This has been the testimony of all the women whose interior lives I have known. Well would it be for their happiness, if husbands, when they first receive to their bosoms the loved ones their hearts would sacredly cherish, would remember this fact, and not demand this personal surrender, until, by other endearing expressions, such as love prompts to give, it shall be a cheerful, willing offering to their love, and this most intense, concentrated expression of it shall be desired by their wives.

For myself, I cannot assume the same peculiarities. To me, the love which is deep, pure and strong enough to attract me into the relation of a wife, obliterates all thought of person. Why stop to look at the setting which surrounds the jewel? When I yielded up my *soul* to thee, my husband, — when I said, into thy keeping I commend my *spirit*, — the physical person, which is but the outward symbol of that soul, went with it. When love for thee cast out all fear for the safety of my deep spiritual life and health, when placed in thy hands, it also cast out all fear for the safety of my physical life and health. My entire physical, as well as spiritual nature, was entrusted to thy care. *Nobly hast thou responded to my trust in thee! A faith, on my part, that has known no bounds, has been met, on thy part, by a power of self-control that is perfect.* I have never felt the sacredness of my own nature, as a woman, in all its functions, till since I have realized that herein lay the very nucleus of my power over him whom I would call my own through all the ages of our future being.

I would that every woman might be comforted by this assurance, that Love consecrates the entire being of its object. Passion does not, of itself; but the mother cares not for the personal comfort of her infant with a purer eye and heart, than does the husband regard the wife who inspires in him a sentiment of absorbing, purifying affection. I rejoice that I am capable, by natural organization of soul and body, to meet all the wants of thy being; and that thus the yearning of my heart for thee, as a husband, may be fulfilled by my fitness to become thy wife, and the mother of thy child.

Thy wife,
NINA.

## LETTER XI.

### THE REPRODUCTIVE ELEMENT.

#### ITS EXPENDITURE TO BE GOVERNED BY MUTUAL LOVE.

Nina:

I cannot apologize to thee for particularizing and laying down rules that seem to me just and natural, for the regulation of my passional nature: for what wife would not bless her husband for fixing such limits, that she may be assured that she will not be victimized to his sensual indulgence? It can but add strength and brightness to her hope of the complete fulfilment of her happiness in marriage, to know that she has committed herself to the care of one who has determined to hold his passional nature in abeyance to his love, and his selfish gratification in absolute subjection to her health and happiness.

We have before stated, that the only sanction for the expenditure of the reproductive element in man is MARRIAGE-LOVE — a love which must not be mistaken for friendship, and which demands other modes of manifestation than friendship suggests; a love which can only find its full and perfect development in marriage. Church and State may sanction a union, and render its fruits legitimate, according to human law; but, before God, every child not born of MARRIAGE-LOVE is illegitimate, whether human laws pronounce it so or not.

An expenditure of this element cannot be made, in any inferior relation, without serious and permanent injury; for then, it is purely sensual — a mere waste of physical life and nervous energy, since the higher elements of the soul take no part in it. It is a mere excitement of the physical organs, and a drain upon animal life, which reason, conscience, and the moral nature, repudiate, as a waste of the most costly physical element of manhood, unsanctioned by love, and destructive of harmony between the soul and body. The physical man seeks a gratification which the spiritual man condemns.

There is no form of disease so painful and so loathsome, and ruinous to the vital energies of body and soul, as that resulting from the gratification of the sexual passion, unsanctioned by love; while the passion, instigated and controlled by love, is productive of no evil. Intemperance, war, slavery, unsuitable food, dress and habitations, exposure to heat, cold, and excessive toil, have doubtless caused many diseases, and much suffering; but the world has yet to learn the full extent of the injury done to body and soul by sexual intercourse, uncalled-for and unwarranted by marriage-love.

It is idle to plead the sanction of Church or State, or any custom, book, or creed. Human Nature, penetrated and sustained by the great Life-Principle of the universe, holds steadily on her course, sternly executing her laws, and punishing every infraction of them. And no law seems more obvious and just, than that the passional relation should be under the absolute dominion of marriage-love; that every expenditure of creative energy, not prompted and justified by harmony between man and wife, must, if persisted in, bring disease to the body, idiocy to the intellectual, and destruction to the moral nature.

But conception, and the existence of a new being, may result from passional intercourse, in which the woman is passive, or positively averse to it, and the man excited solely by sensual desire. How large a portion of human beings, even in the most civilized and refined nations, are the offspring of sexual intercourse, without love! Ask that man or woman, "Are you the child of Love or Passion?—Did you inherit a full measure of the love-nature from your parents, or only the sensual?" A true answer is given in the *life* of each individual; and we are forced to the conclusion, from the history of the race, that the act in which the human being originates is seldom sanctified by pure love and harmony.

Is it to be wondered at, that there is so little of the deep, true love-nature among men? Can we wonder that the passional element is so strong and all-pervading in human nature, and the desire for its gratification so ungovernable? Deep, pure love, that seeketh not her own, does not prompt to the intercourse from which the new existence sprung, but passion, — mere sensual, selfish, loveless passion. With such a type of manhood and womanhood — a type so imbecile to love, yet so strong to propagate as mere animals — we need not wonder that the earth is filled with pollution and crime. *Passionally*, men are giants; *affectionally*, they are dwarfs. They may be strong in intellect, but they are idiotic in love. Earth never can be blessed with any higher type of Humanity, till the passional intercourse is brought into subjection to marriage-love — a love that ever acts in harmony with wisdom. What greater crime can a man commit, than to give existence to a child by an act in which love, on either side, has no part, and in which both are governed by mere passion? Such a child is from the beginning a victim to the sensuality of its parents. They withheld the bright inheritance of love, which, by right, was his, and in its stead, entailed on him the fearful legacy of fierce, insane, ungoverned sensuality. The child had a claim to be formed in the image of God; they gave him the likeness of a brute.

"GOD IS LOVE;" and man should be love, and would be, if, from generation to generation, this were the controlling power that called him into being. To be born of love, is to be born of God; and the love-child is the only God-child. Those only who truly love, can give existence to the children of God. There is another and deeper meaning to the phrase I use. The pure affectional and spiritual relation, between man and the Father, can exist in none with such power, depth and beauty, as in him, who, by the holy birthright of a strong love-nature, is fitted to perceive and fulfil all the relations arising from his near alliance with the Infinite. In him, love to God will be no abstract principle, but a warm, life-giving, blessing power of generous action for his fellow-men.

God will be manifested to us in the living relations of life, especially in those of Marriage and Parentage. The husband and the wife will be, each in the other, the most vitalizing, most endearing, and most potential and useful manifestation of the Infinite. Each will be an ever-present, ever-speaking Revelation of God to the other. The child will come as a Divine Revelation to both; — THE TRUE FAMILY BIBLE.

What a life had ours been, if we all had begun it with a deep, rich love-nature! To commence an eternal existence, with souls all penetrated and guided by this element, were a parental inheritance in which any one might rejoice with joy unspeakable. Such a legacy would be the guaranty of a happy destiny — a birthright passport to the kingdom of heaven.

Thy husband,
ERNEST.

## ANSWER.

Ernest:

One needs no better proof of the long distance which the race has wandered from the straight-forward line of truth and purity, than to realize that such a statement as that in thy last letter could or need be made, in vindication of true love. It is lamentable, but true, that it has assumed, or rather, humanity has put upon it, numberless masks and disguises; that this ministering angel has been driven from our door, wounded, grieved and bleeding, and what was sent to be our high-born guest, has been compelled to the degrading, menial service of the brute.

True love is the same, in all ages and all climes. Its works are ever recognized under the greatest inequalities of outward position. Its wants, its hopes, its aims, its satisfactions, are the same. It claims the possession of its chosen object; it asks no higher blessing, it acknowledges no worthier aim, it can have no deeper happiness. To such love, the mutual health, happiness and development of each is the chief end of marriage. Must we not see the discord that enters at once into a relation where such love inspires but one? Is it not insane to enter upon such a relation, when no all-conquering power impels both alike to merge their being into one?

I should say, whatever be the solicitations of family or friends, or whatever the worldly considerations that urge to such an ill-matched union, a woman will be guilty of less sin to commit suicide than to submit; for, wrong as this may be, she deals only with her own life. In marriage, without love, she exposes herself to become a mother to children whose birth will awaken no deeper thrill in her heart than gratitude for safety from her peril, and the maternal instinct which she shares with all the animal creation. Unless she can look her child in the face, and, before God and her own heart, say that it is *most* dear to her because it is the child of him who made her a mother, she has not the marriage-love which should have blessed her in its conception. The relation of a mother is holy and beautiful beyond the power of words to describe; but it is a relation into which a woman has no right to enter, except by the royal highway of love. It will be observed, in marriage, that those who become mothers under the only holy sanction of maternity, love their children as new representatives of their husbands; while those who give birth to children without love, become selfish and narrow in their love for them as their own offspring. The *husband* becomes the *father of the child,* and he is the husband less than ever.

I can hardly imagine the emotions of a woman who finds herself about to become a mother, under the consciousness that no deep love in the heart of her husband has prompted to this holiest of all relations; or if she finds the tax upon her physical powers too great to make her willing to undertake it. Against all the instincts of her soul, depressed, heart-sick and disconsolate, she gives, for the first supplies of the new being, *silent tears*. Nature, ever faithful to her trust, seizes from the passive tide of life the nutriment necessary to develop the young frame; but, through the minute nervous channels, flows an ever-strengthening tide of sadness, perhaps, at best, of resignation to her fate, which will infuse itself and interpenetrate the very nerve-fibre of the young existence, preparing it, by a bad organization, for a fretful, joyless childhood, a nervous and uncomfortable maturity, and a stern and heartless old age. Have you never seen a young infant's eyes that looked as old and sad as if they had been often closed by grief? — faces that haunt you with their prematurely sad and earnest gaze! To me, these eyes tell of hours of solitary anguish on the part of the mother, when Nature must give way, and yet there was no help, but still to bear on in silence.

ERNEST! it is to the thoughtless sensualist and heartless father that those pleading eyes will turn, when, in the future, the long catalogue of sin committed against the mother shall stand unrolled. For all the tendencies, born of these violations of the mother's instinct, neither she nor her child is responsible.

If this be so, there is but one way for those in whom true love gives no sanction for the marriage relation. They may live together as friends, but never pass over the limits assigned to friendship, as they value their own souls, and as they hope to stand acquitted before the highest tribunals, in this life or the next.

Thy wife,

NINA.

## LETTER XII.

#### THE REPRODUCTIVE ELEMENT.

###### ITS EXPENDITURE TO BE GOVERNED BY THE CONDITIONS OF THE WIFE.

NINA:

My advent to thee, as a husband, involved the entire and unconditional surrender of myself to thee, as thy exclusive possession. My manhood is now thine, joyfully bestowed, and as joyfully received. As a necessity of my being, I have put at thy disposal all the elements of my nature as a man; thou hast received them, and assumed the responsibility of disposing of them, to the best interests of our relation, to the perfection of our own natures, and the development and happiness of our children.

The moment that witnessed this surrender of myself to thee, as a husband, beheld also, in my heart, the feeling that I might not dispose of any element of my nature, except to develop and perfect thine, in thy relation to me as a wife, and the mother of my children. This feeling has grown and strengthened in me, till I can truly say, with all the deep earnestness of my nature, that I am no more my own; I belong to my wife, in all the elements necessary to constitute me a man and a husband; and the more constantly she consecrates all I am and have to perfect and perpetuate the oneness of our hearts, our hopes and our destiny, the more shall I be brought into harmony with the just and the good.

I cannot think of my union with thee in reference to my own sensual gratification. An essential ingredient of my happiness is, that it is all shared fully by thee. The first, great aim of our marriage, so far as I am concerned, is, to perfect the development and happiness of my wife; and only as that end is promoted, can it bring happiness to my heart. I love thee, Nina, with a love that can bring no satisfaction to me, except as it brings purity, self-respect, and a higher life to thee, and as it imparts health and happiness to thy whole being. Mere sensual gratification forms no ingredient in a true marriage relation. True love merges self in the perfection and happiness of the loved one. PROGRESS, not pleasure, is our aim.

Is this condition of the soul an essential element of marriage? Is this the feeling thou wouldst cherish and strengthen in the bosom of thy husband? "This, and none other," is thy answer. What, then, is one of the laws by which the passional expression should be governed? If what I have said with regard to the surrender of the husband to the wife be true, then the answer is obvious:—*The wife must decide how often, and under what circumstances, the husband may enjoy this passional expression of his love.* This, it seems to me, is a natural law by which he should sacredly govern *this* demonstration of love. Only as she calls for it may he rightfully respond. If her call is less frequent than he desires, then he should hold his sexual element in subjection to her wants and happiness, and seek the fulfilment of his love in the thousand other expressions, which, as a husband, his nature prompts him to give. I repeat, the call for this deepest expression of love should ever come from the wife. The right of response belongs to the husband. A woman may love her husband deeply and tenderly, and yet be unable, at all times, to respond to his passion. For a husband, under such circumstances, to insist, is to prostitute himself, and sacrifice her health and happiness.

Nor will a man, who truly respects himself, and who pays due homage to the nature and womanly feelings of his wife, ever urge upon her this expression of his love, when he knows that her only enjoyment is the consciousness that she is administering to his happiness. Is it just to herself and to her husband for a wife to wish to administer thus to his wants? Ought she to consent to yield her person to gratify a passion, which, for the time being, can have no claim upon her, because it is unanswered in her own nature, and which, if allowed, will tend to strengthen in him the feeling, that a wife is bound to submit, under all circumstances, to his sensual demands? He should not, and he would not, if he were manly, and truly respected his wife, ever receive such enjoyment, knowing that her affection for him, and her desire to make him happy, in his own way, are the only motives for her self-surrender. He outrages her nature, and, if the outrage be often repeated, she must sink under it. How many wives have ruined their own health, and brought desolation upon homes that otherwise had been full of life and beauty, by yielding to the solicitations of their husbands, without a similar answering call from their own natures!

It is a common and fatal mistake to suppose that, by such compliance with a husband's wishes, his love will be retained and strengthened. His *passion* may be cultivated and enlarged, but his *love* will find no food in the gratification of any such demand. A man of justice and honor, who is worthy to be the husband of a pure, trusting, noble-hearted woman, could never thus abuse the love and confidence of a wife.

What is the difference between this expenditure of the sexual element, and that caused by solitary indulgence? Is this solely for sensual gratification? So is that. Is this in its nature purely sensual? So is that. Is the one a *solitary* indulgence? So is the other; for the wife is passive, and has no more passional enjoyment than if she were a corpse. All who have attempted to establish a distinction between the two have failed. He who expends the life-principle of his manhood in solitude, does no greater violence to his nature, than he who solicits and takes the same indulgence with his wife, when she has no pleasure in it. In both cases, he sinks himself below the brutes, which never practise the former, and never the latter, except in answer to the call of the female. Among animals, the female instinct is the controlling power. Is it granted to man alone, the most exalted type of animated existence, who boasts of reason and immortality, of being an intimate partaker of the Divine, and in whom love is designed to act in harmony with wisdom, to ignore the wants and wishes of the female? I do not believe it. In the human species, the male should be at least as observant of the wishes and conditions of the female, as he is in the lower orders of animals. But, unfortunately, it is not so; and the unhappy consequences are visited upon the sinners and their offspring. If a man is to be considered pure, honest, noble, manly, who thus demands sensual gratification, against the wishes of his wife, then is he to be so considered who commits the crime of rape. If the one deserves the gallows or the dungeon, so does the other, also; for the latter violates every sacred obligation binding on man, as a husband, a father, protector and friend. Unreciprocated, passional excitement is a solitary indulgence, and, as God is just and true, it will be visited and punished as such. Passional indulgence, *demanded as a right,* is a rape upon the person whom the husband has promised, before God and man, to cherish, honor and protect. This is committed under the sanction of legal marriage; but justice, though it waits, is sure to come at last. Ruined health, a cheerless home, and love turned to loathing, will be the reward for such violations of Nature's laws.

WOMAN'S RIGHTS! True and earnest spirits are intent on discussing this subject. When it shall come to be fully understood what is involved in it, many, both men and women, who are now so anxious to bring it fully before the world, will shrink away. They will not have the knowledge, strength, nor courage, to meet the great and final issue of this question. So long as it is confined to woman's political, pecuniary and social rights, it will not conflict, materially, with the selfish passions and interests of the opposite sex.

But the discussion cannot stop here. It must enter the sanctuary of home, where man and woman dwell together as husband and wife. To perpetuate and perfect the race, combined with individual development and happiness, is the great object for which marriage was designed. In reproduction, the function of the husband is to prepare and impart the germs of new beings; that of the wife, to receive, nourish and develop them. But who shall determine for the wife, when, how often, and under what circumstances, she shall take charge of the germ of a new existence, and assume the office of a mother? Human law and custom give to the husband the power to settle this question. Was a case ever known in which a wife appealed successfully to the law for protection against the husband's passion? Society and government accord to the wife no voice in the matter. Both say to her, "In this, we consign your person to him whom we have empowered to control you as a husband. When he desires a child, or wishes for sexual intercourse with you, you must yield. We shall never protect you against the demands of his passion." It is to such a fearful power that woman surrenders her person, in legal marriage! From the hour that she does so, how often is her course downward, with a crushed and bleeding heart, to an early grave!

There is no tyranny on earth so crushing to soul and body, and so fearfully disastrous in its results to the physical, mental and spiritual improvement of the race, as that often exercised by man over woman, in legal marriage. In a true LOVE-MARRIAGE, where love acts in harmony with wisdom, there can be no oppression. In regard to passional intercourse, and to reproduction, the husband will say to the wife — "THY WILL, NOT MINE, BE DONE." Passion will ever be in abeyance to all-controlling love; that will consecrate her person, and make her health, her happiness and life, dearer to him than they can be to her. He can never urge on her maternity, till she calls for it. If he love her with a pure, self-forgetting, noble love, he can never, intentionally or unintentionally, impart to her the germ of a new existence, till she demands it, and is ready cheerfully and joyfully to receive, nourish and develop it, and return it to his grateful, manly bosom, a living, healthy, perfect child. But, in what is now recognised by law, religion and social custom, as marriage, the wife, as to *rights*, is too often considered a nonentity, in the function of reproduction.

Just so far as man is ready to accord to woman the absolute right to control her person, as a wife, in regard to maternity, will he cheerfully acknowledge her rights in all other directions. Till woman has her rights here, it will be of small account, so far as her true growth and happiness are concerned, to secure her rights in minor matters of life; for all other rights are of little consequence, so long as this one central right of womanhood is denied.

NINA! reveal all the depths of thy soul to me, in relation to this question. Thou hast done it often, *even before our union was consummated*. But put thy thoughts on paper, that they may descend as a legacy to our children, and that other men and women may be induced, in entering the marriage relation, to have a perfect understanding, that THE CONDITIONS OF

THE WIFE ARE EVER TO CONTROL THE PASSIONAL RELATION.

But I must close this letter, already too long. Let me, then, renew the assurance, made long before our union, that, as thou must bear in thine organism its results, thou hast a right to control our sexual intercourse. As God is my witness, I will be true to this promise, believing, as I do, that to violate it would be to disregard one of the fixed, unchanging laws of marriage intercourse, and to trifle with the holiest rights of a wife. Thou wilt help me to consecrate the energies of my manhood to all tender and healthful expressions of love — love, such as thy nature, as a wife, ever longs to receive, and mine, as a husband, ever longs to give.

Would it not be well for every woman, before she marries, to learn whether views like these will regulate her husband's relation to her? and, if not, what advice dost thou give?

Thy husband,

ERNEST.

## ANSWER.

ERNEST:

In answer to thy questions, these thoughts suggest themselves: God, in making human beings, has given to each a power of self-government, which needs, which admits of, no other rule — a conscience, to govern the movements of both soul and body. The body which enshrines each soul, is a direct gift from God, for which the possessor is accountable only to God. He says, " I give a fair, unsullied temple, wherein I place a spotless soul. Use and train the one and the other to the utmost of their high capacity. But thou, and thou *alone*, art responsible for the use or the abuse of it. Confide to others, if thou wilt, the keeping of thy treasures; but it is to thee alone I look for an account of thy stewardship." With this understanding of herself, a woman comes to the experience of life we call LOVE. She finds her ideal, at last, embodied. She says, "Here, accept all I have to give; take me to thyself, soul and body, for time and eternity. Thou art wiser, holier than I; do, then, for me, what I cannot do for myself. Be my *husband*, my guide; and in this relation, endow me with a power and glory I can never know but in being thy wife. Make my virgin soul into the wife; make the wife a mother."

He accepts the gift. The higher and the lower elements of his nature receive a new impulse. Intoxicated by the possession of this treasure, he pours out the fulness of his love in its intensest modes of expression. She finds less passion in her love than in his, and positive enjoyment ends in endurance, and fast approaches to repulsion. What must she do? She must gently and firmly confess the truth, and place the choice before him, of self-restraint on his part, or of disgust on hers. LOVE will waste no time in its decision.

Woman alone knows the limits of her nature in this

respect; she alone is responsible for its voluntary functions. No man, though in the relation of husband, may exact that of her system which she is unwilling to accord. Man, in assuming power over his wife's body, not freely and cheerfully granted, assumes what God never gave to him; and in the wreck of health and happiness which will have to be atoned for in future time, his guilt will be heavier, in the sight of God, than that of any usurper of the power of nations. A loveless, cheerless home is his. The love of no woman, however pure, concentrated and intense it may be, can possibly continue to adorn and beautify the life of that man, who can demand of her an unwilling surrender of her person to his sensual gratification. Her respect for such a man must cease; and when that is gone, love goes with it. What then is left to the home of the miserable sensualist?

It is a woman's *right*, not her privilege, to control the surrender of her person. Thou hast truly said, that, of all woman's rights, this is the most sacred and inalienable. No language can truly express the injustice and cruelty of that man, whose selfishness could allow him to inflict on a woman a maternity for which her own soul did not yearn. Such an enforced maternity, no matter by whom or by what sanctioned, is the deepest wrong a man can possibly inflict on woman. Her first and most sacred right is to decide under what conditions, and how often, she will accept the passional expression of her husband's love, and receive into herself the elements of a new existence. Love will lead every husband in whose heart it exists to recognise this right, and, at all times, scrupulously to regard it. And the wife, when once convinced of this fact on the part of her husband, will ever find her heaven in yielding up her person to his keeping; and, with a faith and love that know no fear, will ever breathe into him the perfection of her self-surrender. The deep, earnest expression of each to the other will be, "*Thy will, not mine, be done.*"

A man has no right to compel his wife to lie or murder. He has no more right to compel her to yield to his passion, and thus to lie against the instincts of her nature, and kill the yearnings of her soul for true companionship, by urging upon her a passion which swallows up all other forces of her nature. No matter whether the violence that enables the man, under the name of husband, to enforce upon her the conditions of maternity, be in his own superior muscular energy, or in the shape of civil law or social and ecclesiastical sanction, the outrage upon her person is the same.

With these principles granted, she is accountable to God, in her own soul, for her fidelity to her nature in this respect. The man who respects not this fidelity is worse than a thief or a robber, for he tyrannizes over the loving, trusting being, whose confidence he won but to betray. She shall say who shall be, to her, the guardian of life and honor. She shall be the interpreter of the demands of her own nature. Man can perpetrate no deeper wrong to himself, to his wife and child, and to his domestic peace, than to urge upon his wife maternity, when he knows her nature rebels against it. Nor can woman commit a greater crime against herself and her child, than to consent to become a mother, when her nature not only does not call for it, but actively repels it.

Let the wife say to the husband, "Show me thy love in some gentler way; let my head repose upon thee as upon a rock of trust; let me feel thine arms around me, to defend me from all harm, not to bring it to me." Then again, when her nature prompts, she will say, "I am ready to be the true, healthy mother of thy child. I am now willing to take into myself the elements of a new being." And when again he makes the same request, and she cannot answer to it, let her say, "Wait till I have force enough regained to embody a new soul as it ought to be embodied." Who but a ruffian would disregard such a request? Who but a being less than man would say, "No matter how *you* feel, *I* wish to be gratified." The wife should be the regulator of *this* marriage relation, for only in obedience to the laws of her nature can she hope to continue to be the loving, healthful, happy wife.

What elasticity would come to many a wife's heart, could she be assured that he, who now denies to her all right of choice in this matter, would never again claim what she could not freely grant! CLAIM! What a word! Do we demand of God the perfume of the flower? Can we snatch, by violence, the sunshine over our heads? No more should a man claim of woman what love alone can rightfully bestow.

*Freely to give, freely to receive*, is what love requires; else, with rash and sacrilegious hand, the flowers are plucked from the altar of God's inner temple. The sanctum of a wife's person is one of which she alone stands High Priestess. No hand but hers should ever raise the veil. If it is thrust aside by violence, no matter by whom or by what the deed is sanctioned, the accursed intruder were better dead at the portal!

I advise any woman, who knows before marriage that the man of her choice accepts no law for the government of his passions except his own will and pleasure, to trample her love under her feet, and bury the remembrance of it in deepest oblivion, rather than bear the touch of unhallowed, sensual desire. Those noble words of Consuelo, when she discovers and is convinced of Anzoletto's infidelity, are the words of every true woman. She flies from his embrace, and says, in the paroxysm of wounded feeling and conscious dignity, "Out of my sight, out of my house, out of my heart, for ever!"

ERNEST! thou hast said all that can be said in defence of the noble and pure instincts of woman. I have little to add to what I have already said. I have, in a former letter, appealed to the highest elements in manhood to preserve and cherish the freshness and beauty of young love. Manly passion is not in itself repulsive or unwelcome to the purest heart of woman, when it is the voice, as it ever should be, of a love unspeakable. When it is this, there will be no question as to who shall rule triumphant in the passional relation. In this, as in other expressions, a quiet, delicate, unfailing intuition will be a constant and unerring guide, which, if carefully obeyed, will never lead us into clumsy errors. In a union made of coarser elements, there is no hope of better things. Sorrow and suffering must ensue, and ever and ever must the turbid stream of life flow on, chafing its troubled waters against obstacles which are self-imposed.

There is a higher life for us here, even in the bonds of flesh. God meant us to be happy, beautiful and good, and it must be a faint heart, and a spirit of most earthly mould, that will not seek to know and obey the simplest, as well as the most secret, of Nature's laws.

You have truly said, that woman must regulate those relations in which her whole nature is put under such severe requisition. The pleasure of a moment may take a year out of her life; and shall she have no voice, and never be consulted, as to the functions of her body, the emotions of her soul, and the changes which may, by the birth of children, be made in her eternal destiny? The lover, when his too ardent gaze is met by a look of pain or embarrassment, turns away, and drops the clasped hand, to reässure the maiden whom his impetuosity has repulsed. Let the husband, under all circumstances, be thus observant and thus tenderly considerate, and old age will find a love still young. Love will then be the memory of the present life, as it will be the joyful anticipation of the future.

    Thy wife,

          NINA.

## LETTER XIII.

#### THE REPRODUCTIVE ELEMENT.

##### IS OFFSPRING THE ONLY JUSTIFIABLE END OF ITS EXPENDITURE?

NINA:

I have noticed two laws, which seem to me fixed, for the government of the passional nature: — MUTUAL LOVE, and THE CONDITIONS OF THE WIFE. Of these, I cannot speak doubtingly. They seem as obvious as those which require air, food and light for the life and health of the body. I have shown that all that is noble in manhood points to the subjection of the *passion* to the *sentiment* of love. I would now call thy attention to another law, which, perhaps, would be equally plain, if we were prepared, by a healthy organization and development, to see and appreciate it; but of which, bewildered as we now are in regard to the nature and objects of the sexual instinct, it is not easy to form a true estimate. In the future of this world, it may be that human beings will find as little difficulty in deciding this question, as they will in deciding by what laws any other human relation was designed to be governed. Their more refined and clearer intuitions may guide them, without the process of reasoning.

*Is reproduction the only object for which the sexual element may be rightfully expended?* The question is important; none can be more so. If the affirmative be true, most men must be brought under condemnation, as guilty of a crime against Nature. But this should not deter us from impartial investigation. Let truth be known; let the facts of Nature be brought to light, and let us look them steadily in the face, however they may conflict with educational ideas or hereditary propensities.

Let God be true, though all men be proved to be false. Immutable principles of justice and equity can never be made to conform to us; we must conform to them, or suffer. To know the laws of life and health, with regard to the passional nature, is essential to human welfare; and inasmuch as on no other relation does the existence and improvement of the race so essentially depend, it must be of more importance to know and obey these laws than any other. It is certain that, thus far in the history of the race, more suffering and anguish can be traced to violations of this relation, than to any other source. The question, then, Is it right to expend the most costly element in the system, except for reproduction? is one of paramount importance, and will ere long be so regarded and spoken of, by all who respect the nature they bear, or who desire the progress of human kind.

*The perpetuation and perfection of the race* are the two great objects of sexual intercourse. The purest enjoyment is indeed designed to be experienced in this intercourse, when prompted solely by love and a desire for offspring. But, unless such pleasure is mutual, the offspring of such a union must be imperfect and distorted in its constitutional tendencies. Mere sensual gratification is generally the sole object. No desire for offspring, no thought of such a result, no anxiety for the welfare of the child that may ensue, enters the mind of either party. Of all the connections between even those who live in the legal relations of marriage, and who are regarded as pure-minded, truthful men and women, and examples of fidelity to their passional nature, three fourths are, probably, had for mere sensuous enjoyment. They would be disappointed, should offspring ensue; and, sometimes, would willingly destroy it, if it could be done without injury to the wife and mother. The following considerations I submit to thee, that we may come to a more perfect knowledge as to the true object of the sexual relation. My enjoyment shall be laid on the altar of thy conscience. I can, rightfully, and without injury to myself, control or forego this indulgence; and, in this matter, I prefer to be governed by thy more refined intuitions and truer sense of right. As God is my witness, thou shalt never be victimized to thy husband's pleasure.

Offspring and preparation for offspring are, undoubtedly, the great objects of the reproductive element. Whatever other objects may be connected with it, they are but incidental. Its presence in the system is essential to a perfect development of soul and body. The more perfect and healthful is this element, and its action when retained in the system, the more perfect and healthful will be the development of all the powers of body and mind. This influences men and women to enter into true and intimate relations. It divides the race into male and female. It gives to each a magnetic power over the other, the possession of which is a never-failing source of happiness, and to which each is equally happy to feel in subjection. In the highest relation into which they are impelled by this instinct — that of marriage — its operation is unlike all other elements of our nature; for the more absolute and unlimited this magnetic power of the wife over the husband, the more complete is his happiness. So of the power of the husband over the wife. But, to answer these ends, and to invest each with this enchantment in the eyes of the other, the element on which the sexual instinct is based must be retained in the system, or, if expended, must be replaced. The soul recognises the sexual distinction only through this element. This is the distinctive symbol of the soul's manhood. Take it away, and the soul of a man feels no more interest in the soul of a woman, than in one of his own sex. As the element, then, is *useless when expended*, except for the continuance and elevation of the race, and is of essential use in the economy of life, when retained in the system, does it not seem that its expenditure for any other purpose must be unnatural, and therefore wrong?

*Then, the cost to the vital forces of replacing it, when wasted for mere pleasure, must be taken into account.* This secretion is composed of the most refined ingredients of our physical nature, the brain and the nerves not excepted. To form it is the highest function of the vital energies. At the period of puberty, it is elaborated and secreted in its natural organs, and the human being is prepared for reproduction. There it should be reserved, to impart life, energy and beauty to the entire man, till he is drawn into a relation in which it may be expended for just and natural purposes. But if a man begins to expend it for sensual gratification, before the brain, the muscles, the nerves, and other parts of the system, are matured, a heavy tax is laid upon the vital forces. The energies of the nervous system are called into requisition to supply the waste. The labor imposed on the passional nature is excessive and unnatural. Consequently, those parts of the system which are called into activity to sustain the life and health of body and soul, are left to droop, and soon become too imbecile to perform their office healthfully; and thus the entire man is sacrificed, to repair the injuries caused by sensual gratification. The brain becomes exhausted. It is the organ through which the soul acts in every direction. If the mind is intent on sexual indulgence, the brain is ever active to exhaust its forces in that direction. It becomes dwarfed and imbecile, as an instrument of thought and affection, in any other direction. The results are, loss of memory, indecision, imbecility of reason and judgment, cowardliness, inactivity, idiocy and insanity. When men will candidly observe the consequences of an abuse of the sexual element, they will be astounded to find how much idiocy and insanity result from it.

It is said, "If polygamy be wrong, and the expenditure must occur only in marriage, and then only for parentage, and a healthful preparation for this relation, what is a man to do? He could have this enjoyment but a few times in his whole life." True; he can rarely have the *expenditure*, but the preservation of this element in the system is an ever-present enjoyment, by the glow of life and healthful energy which it inspires. In all ages, men who have sought to perfect themselves in physical beauty, strength and activity, have been abstemious in this respect. Witness the athletæ of Greece, the gladiators of Rome, the wrestlers, boxers, and runners, of all ages. They knew full well, that the life-energies required to supply the means of indulgence should be restrained, for the perfect development of the body in beauty, activity and power.

In the animal kingdom, in all the orders below man, the instinct of reproduction leads to the expenditure of this element; and why should man, endowed with reason and conscience, as well as instinct, reverse the order, and unfit himself for reproduction, and bring disease and death to body and soul, by the frequency of his sensual indulgence? In man, the reason has become perverted, and instinct blinded, or such ruinous results as society now presents would never have occurred.

In domestic life, why is the wife pining for expressions of love she cannot get? As a wife, her nature ever calls for the presence, the caresses, the approving smiles and gentle tones of her husband. She has given herself to him, and she would have him assert and maintain his right of possession by ever folding her in his mantle of love and tenderness. She pines for this fulfilment of her nature, oftentimes in silence and desolation. Her husband *did* love her, tenderly and truly—perhaps he *does*. Why does he not express it, in all the ways natural to love?

Time was, when absence from his wife was a source

of constant uneasiness to him, and nothing but absolute necessity could keep him away. Now, the most trivial reasons can prolong his absence. Time was, when, after a short absence, he met her with eagerness, and folded her to his heart with rapture. Now, he can be away days and weeks, and yet return to her with measured steps and greet her with formality. She would fly to his bosom, to be folded and sheltered there; but in his altered manner, she meets no response to her outgushing heart. Once, when around the domestic circle, the husband's manner, air and conversation, were unconstrained, natural, joyous, and inviting to the utmost freedom. Once, his wife was his home, and in her presence, he had all his nature called for. Now, he is better satisfied when strangers are there. He is cheerful with them, but silent and moody with her alone. Formerly, he delighted to share her domestic cares, and surround her with all the comforts he could command. Now, his interest in domestic matters is diminished or dead. Formerly, he sought no society where she could not join him. Now, he can go forth and leave her to wait and watch for his return, in loneliness and anxiety. Why this cloud on the once bright heart of the wife? Ask that husband how he has treated her, in reference to passional intercourse, and all is explained. The very life of his manhood, that which made him a tender, respectful lover, and, at first, a devoted husband, and which would have continued him so, had he lived truly with his wife, has been expended in mere sensual indulgence, till, as a husband, he is imbecile, — as a lover, well-nigh an idiot.

Once, as a father, he was tender and fond, and never felt himself more truly noble, and more worthy the esteem of his fellow-men, than when folding in his arms the child of his love. Once, in presence of his child and its mother, no frown could darken his brow, no danger blanch his cheek, no personal sacrifice or suffering appal his heart. That mother and that child were to him, *heaven*. All is changed. The smile and prattle of his child thrill his heart no longer. He seldom takes it in his arms, and reluctantly, if he does. He can see it in the bosom of its mother with indifference. The child no longer watches at the window for his return. Ask for the *secret* record of that connubial life, and you will find that the life-element of his fatherhood has been expended in selfish indulgence. His paternal, as well as connubial instinct, has been sacrificed to sensual pleasure.

Once, that man was active, prompt, accurate and successful in business. His promise was sacred; he was trusted and trustworthy. His wife and child were omnipotent in his heart, to prompt to all noble, manly deeds. Now, his blunted faculties do not deserve the confidence which his former activity and accuracy had won. The world wonders and speculates upon the gradual but thorough change which time has wrought; but none, save the stricken wife, has power to reveal the true and secret cause.

Thus, by an abuse of the sexual passion, man is disqualified to meet his responsibilities, to perform his duties, and wisely to share in the enjoyments of life. He must consecrate this element of his being to the one great natural object of reproduction, and true refinement and elevation; and when not needed for that, it should be sacredly preserved, as an ever-present incitement to all true, gentle and heroic thoughts, words and deeds, that he may fulfil and honor the relation of a husband and father.

There are many phenomena in the life of man which excite a momentary astonishment, and for which none can account, but which Religion and Public Opinion are content to refer to what is called a "wise and mysterious Providence." Failures in business, without any apparent cause; imbecility and folly in plans and purposes, and indecision in execution, where strength, wisdom and promptitude were expected; dyspepsia, rheumatism, gout, apoplexy, paralysis, consumption, and disease in various other forms, and a premature and agonizing death, where a healthy, vigorous youth gave promise of a long life, free from suffering; a morose and selfish temper, where, in youth, a loving and manly spirit reigned; domestic circles converted into scenes of discontent, strife, cruelty and blood, where was once the promise of enduring peace and progress in all goodness; women, whose girlhoods were seasons of health, beauty, and joyous life and activity, become prematurely nervous, fretful, sickly, helpless and deformed; half of all the children that are born alive, dead under five years of age, and half of the remainder dead under fifteen; the many premature births; the sufferings and deaths in child-birth; the inconceivable amount and variety of disease and suffering peculiar to the female organism; idiots, born of intellectual parents; insane, born of the sane; diseased and deformed, born of the healthy and beautiful; hating, revengeful and bloody spirits, born of the loving, the forgiving, and the gentle; — these, and many other facts connected with human life, are ever before us, and ever marvellous. No visible, natural cause for them being known, they are attributed, generally, to a special Providence.

But there is a natural, though, as yet, hidden cause for this ever-deepening, ever-widening, ever-rolling river of human disease, suffering and pollution; a cause that will ere long be known to all, and which it will engage the attention of all the true and the just to remove. That cause will very frequently be found in THE UNNATURAL AND MONSTROUS EXPENDITURE OF THE SEXUAL ELEMENT, FOR MERE SENSUAL GRATIFICATION. It will be seen that its retention in the system, except for offspring, and a healthful preparation for parentage, is what adds health, energy, activity and beauty to the body, and gentleness, power, generosity, courage, nobleness, to the soul; that it is this which makes human beings deep, earnest and constant to love, calm, self-possessed and strong to endure, wise and sagacious to plan, bold, prompt and indomitable to execute; while its expenditure, for mere sensual pleasure, renders them imbecile and powerless in feeling, in thought, and in action.

THE SEXUAL ELEMENT — the object of its presence in man — its action on the whole being, in perfecting its development — its retention in the system, and the effect of such retention on the body and soul, in all their functions — its expenditure for offspring, and its effects when thus expended — its expenditure for mere sensual indulgence, and the effects of such an abuse of it, on men, women and children, and on all human relations — a true, scientific investigation of these subjects, will, one day, command the attention of the good and the great of mankind.

NINA! since we first felt attracted to each other as husband and wife, on no subjects have we interchanged our thoughts and feelings so often, so freely, so fully and so pleasantly, as on the nature, the object and the power of this element of our being. We have sought to know the fixed, natural laws by which our sexual intercourse was designed to be governed. The effects, on body and soul — on the beauty, the comfort, the power, the sweet repose and satisfaction of our relation — of its retention in my organism, except for offspring, have been deep, vitalizing, ennobling, and intensely joyous and elevating. Deeply and tenderly as we have loved each other, its expenditure for sensual pleasure would have changed entirely the tone of our connubial life.

Oft hast thou said to me — "*Ernest! there is no lottery in marriage to me. I am sure, as of my own existence, of every manifestation of love, respect and tenderness.*" Oft have I asked thee to describe to me the effect, on thy soul, of thy husband's treatment of thy person. Thy answer, most grateful to my heart, has ever been — "*It is the deep, abiding, inexpressible sense of the majesty, the purity, the nobleness, the dignity and manliness of thy love to me. In the government of the sexual element of thy nature, I constantly recognise that it is not thy will, but mine, that is accomplished; or, what is more true, that Love has made our two wills into one, and nought but a deep, tender, respectful, grateful feeling pervades my heart when I think of it.*" This deep repose, trust and respect, this willing and joyful surrender of soul and body to the love and care of thy husband, could never have made thy home thy heaven, had sensual gratification been his object in the expenditure of the vital force of his manhood. Thou hast said, "*Marriage, to me, is no romance, but an ennobling fact. I have known its purest and most perfect joys; I have experienced its deepest satisfactions.*" Why? Solely because thy husband has made his sensuous, momentary pleasure, entirely subservient to thy health, thy wishes, and to thy true and perfect development of body and soul, and sacredly consecrated the most vital element of his nature to its true and natural use. Thus, and only thus, can the husband make his home an Eden of Love to his wife, and to himself and his children, into which no subtle foe can ever enter.

But, *is* it an abuse of the sexual element to expend it merely for sensual enjoyment? This is a question which human beings should be deeply concerned to settle. A wise observer of human nature has said that it is a well-known fact, that "the highest development of the individual, or the highest degree of bodily vigor, is inconsistent with more than a very moderate indulgence in sexual intercourse; while nothing is more certain to reduce the powers of body and mind, than excess in this respect. These principles, which are of great importance in the regulation of health, are but results of the general law which prevails equally in the animal and vegetable kingdom, viz.: *that the development of the individual, and the reproduction of the species, stand in an inverse ratio to each other."*

Is this the fact? Does this expenditure, even for offspring, tend to hinder the most perfect development of the individual? *If so, then the question is settled;* it *is* an abuse of the sexual nature to expend its vital energies for any purpose but that of reproduction; for sexual intercourse, for mere sensual indulgence, is then an excess, which surely tends to undermine the soundness of both mind and body. If the above be true, such an expenditure, for mere gratification, is an excess, as much as the unnatural appetite which leads a man to overload his stomach, for the prolonged pleasure of his palate. A diseased and inactive stomach will soon betray the wrong committed.

NINA! since I was first conscious of marriage attraction to thee, on no subject have I pondered so deeply as on this. What is true of ourselves is true of many others, at the commencement of their married life. Both have great life and vigor, both are sound in health, both have strong natures, with the elements of long life and enduring happiness. Both have, in the conditions of soul and body, an inheritance worth more than all the wealth of earth beside. A deep responsibility rests upon both, to their children and to each other. The true husband is called upon, for his own sake, and for that of his wife and children, to renounce or resist all preconceived opinions and propensities, if, by acting upon them, he risks their health and happiness. The happiness of home must be in proportion to the development of the individual. Whatever injuriously affects this, must mar the beauty of our home. I can neither affirm nor deny the proposition, that the development of the individual and the reproduction of the species stand in an inverse ratio, though this seems to be the conclusion to which the facts of life, so far as known, must lead. But a child is the want of our nature, and an essential element in the happiness of our home. This, Nature allows. We are authorised, if we choose, to sacrifice (if sacrifice it be, which I cannot affirm nor deny) so much of our own development as is necessary for reproduction; for the loss is more than made up by the presence of the child. We stake, it may be, a trifle of individual growth, but we gain a crown of parental glory.

Can we, then, in justice to our individual development, waste, in mere sensual indulgence, the element on which our connubial and parental relations depend, when our only compensation is the momentary pleasure? In married life, there is a fulness of joy in the exercise of passion incited by the love of offspring. There is much harm, and less happiness, in sexual indulgence for mere gratification. If, then, entire abstinence, as a sensual enjoyment, can do no injury, and may do much good, while, when reserved solely for offspring and higher growth, it confers infinite benefits, is it not the plain duty of husbands and wives to abstain from this expenditure of the vital force of their manhood and womanhood for mere sensual indulgence, and consecrate it to its true, ennobling purposes?

NINA! help me to solve this question, and let us record our reasonings upon this subject, that our offspring may know that their organization and happiness were objects of our deepest solicitude, and that we esteemed it the chief glory of our wedded life, to be THE HEALTHY PARENTS OF HEALTHY CHILDREN.

From the heart of thy husband,

ERNEST.

## ANSWER.

ERNEST:

THE point thou hast left for me to decide in our relations, is one that concerns equally every husband and every wife. There is no one question on which so much depends, as upon the rule of life which shall be adopted in respect to the personal relation. For thee, I cannot judge. Thou knowest the consequences to thine own body and soul of the exercise of animal passion. It is for the true man to abide by the results of his experience, and to use them in forming his ideas of right and wrong. According to thy statement of the consequences of undue excitement, the case is clear beyond a question. We all know that unbridled passion makes a total wreck of soul and body. This is not an attribute of man, as he was designed to be, nor yet of animals. It places him below the level of the brute, for there we never find it. The question becomes simply this: In man and woman, God has placed an instinct which has no natural activity till, through the action of the highest powers of the mind and heart, the two are led into the relation of marriage. Sympathy, respect, personal affection, and desire for perpetual companionship, are the true basis of this relation. The sexual magnetism slumbers, long after the heart and soul are thrilled with the rapture of mutual love. Passion is but the echo rendered by the flesh to the true marriage of the soul. The joy of personal intercourse is added, to fill up the measure of perfect oneness; yet it is but the effervescence, compared with the true nectar of love. Hence, its enjoyment will never be made the basis of the true relation. It belongs only to the hour of highest spiritual communion, when heart and soul are merged in the consciousness of but one existence, one life, one eternity. Then, the whole being may and must thrill in unison with such harmony. Passional intercourse is meant to be an ecstatic expression of the soul. Take from it that significance, and you rob it of every attraction. Such is the case when men degrade it from its high purpose, and subject the spirit to the flesh.

They tell of idol worship. Where will you find a more distorted perversion, than in the worship of the senses which society about us presents? The idol relics of olden time give us gigantic heads, and all the other members dwarfed. A symbol of the present day would give reversed proportions. It is for man to keep himself in the image in which he was made, with a power to grasp and control, for the welfare of the race, every element of his own nature and of the external world. Every husband, then, must decide whether he needs to restrain his natural propensities, in order to perfect his own spiritual and physical nature. If he finds in himself inordinate desires, yet he must consider, that what may contribute to his gratification may be unnatural to his wife. Her nature must not be outraged, any more than his. I have said, in a former letter, what I cannot too often repeat, that there are other endearments in married life, as potent to express love, more powerful to win and keep affection, than passional intercourse. The steady sweetness of temper in a husband, which leads the wife to fear no frowns nor fretful repulse, the eye which always rests upon her with joy and satisfaction, the assurance that, if she is but true to her womanly nature, she will be dear and lovely to her husband, the confidence and freedom from restraint which such assurance gives, are what the happiness of home is made of. Add to this, the certainty that no voice of passion or assumed authority will ever drown her gentlest intimations, that she is secure in the possession of him who loves her above all other created beings, and has consecrated himself to the full development of her being, in all its functions,—this is what will make a happy wife. Then, when, in the fulness of time, she meets the angel who shall whisper in her ear, "Blessed art thou among women," what a flood of joy rushes through her heart, to find that soul and body have harmoniously combined to give assurance of her love, which God alone could understand, and only he could fitly represent!

Is it certain that the office of reproduction in the mother does interfere with the development of the physical system? If it is true of the father, it is even more true of the mother. As now constituted, she must give up months to physical suffering and disability, and at last come back to life through the gates of death. If she is prostrated at the commencement, by a previous outrage of her nature, how can she hopefully enter upon this new responsibility? She must inflict upon her unborn child the consequences of previous wrong.

For woman, I can say, that married life would be a heaven, compared to what it is, if all passional expression were regulated according to the rules thou hast prescribed. Those are the only rules, an obedience to which, on the part of the husband, can elevate woman to the true equality with man which God intended. Here is the point wherein the movement for the rights of woman truly begins. Elevate her in this respect, save her from being victimized to sensuality in marriage, and her way is clear.

Ernest! thou hast appealed to my sense of right, to decide a most important question; and, so far as I am able to discern the truth, with all the energy of purpose with which I seek to follow the highest principles of action, by all the regard I feel for thy most perfect development in manhood, I will aid thee to fidelity to the convictions of thine own conscience. The love which has made us one for life and death, cannot be measured by common rules; nor shall its manifestations be copied from a common standard. If we stand alone in all the world, we will show what marriage, under its legitimate restrictions, may and should be, as a means of perfection to ourselves, and a great and glorious inheritance to those who are born under its happy auspices. The fond affections, the high resolves, the religious consecration of the elements of our whole being to one holy purpose, shall reäppear, to bless the earth with a new existence, whose heart and hand shall be strong to stem the tide of sin and suffering. Living to this end, we shall satisfy the utmost capacity of our natures for enjoyment here; and when at last we shall lie down to rest, no marble shall record the story of our life, for it shall be kept fresh in the loving hearts which will "rise up to call us blessed."

Thy loving wife,

NINA.

## LETTER XIV.

### GESTATION AND LACTATION.

TREATMENT OF THE WIFE BY THE HUSBAND DURING THESE PERIODS.

Nina:

My heart has never been thrilled by thy presence and thy love, as it has been during the past few months; not even when the consciousness of being loved by thee first dawned upon my being. I am a father, and thou, the mother of my child. In my bosom, at this moment, sweetly smiles and prattles the priceless treasure thy love hath bestowed upon me. Thou art no longer to me only a wife, but the mother of my child. Thou hast exalted me to the pride and glory, not only of being thy husband, but also of being the father of thy child. In the new relation in which thy love has placed me, the purest fragrance of heaven surrounds thee, all-concentrating influences enshrine thee. MOTHER OF MY CHILD! How can I but respect the function of thy nature that has placed this beauteous, innocent child of our love in my bosom, to call me FATHER and thee MOTHER! How does the memory of the act, in which this new immortal originated, now impress thee? How does the memory of thy husband, during the various periods through which thou hast passed in giving existence and nourishment to our child, now affect thee? If, in any respect, he has failed to embody thy ideal of a husband and a father, wilt thou frankly tell him? For, in this relation, no husband can, with safety to the happiness of his home, live for himself; for his wife and children he must live. His life, his honor, his heaven, will be in their true and perfect development and happiness.

To the true husband and father, where his wife and children are, there is his heaven. They are the true magnets to his heart. Other forces may turn his thoughts from them for a moment; but, as the needle turns by a natural attraction to the pole, so will his soul, when other forces are spent, as they must be, turn to these, its true treasures, and there find repose. Other attractions are transient and powerless, compared to the deep and permanent force that binds him to them.

Marriage (including the relations that grow out of it) is the central, vital relation of our being. From this result our deepest responsibilities, our most sacred duties, the holiest endearments and experiences of life, and the influences that are most potent in shaping our destiny. This should never be regarded as incidental to any other relation, political, religious, social, commercial, or literary; but all others should be measured and valued by their adaptation and their power to fit men and women for true marriage and parental relations, and to aid them to enter into, and to perform rightly and nobly, all the obligations and duties inherent in them; and thus to establish homes where nobler types of humanity may be prepared and developed. In their power over the organization, character and destiny of human beings, the Church is nothing, the State is nothing; religion, government, priests and politicians, are nothing, compared to marriage and parentage, to the husband and wife, the father and mother. Those who make marriage an appendage to commerce, to government or religion, to pecuniary or educational institutions, sacrifice the substance of life to the shadow.

Let this be one great end of government and religion, — to secure to each husband or wife the presence, care and sympathy of the loved one. Let all public and general institutions and arrangements of society have reference to this one end, to ensure to the wife the love, the tenderness and protection of the husband; and to the husband, the presence, the sympathy and counsel of the wife; and to parents, the affection and respect of their children; and to children, the tenderness, the care and companionship of their parents. Then would these arrangements and institutions be cherished for the good they do, rather than be feared for the evil they sanction. Then would they do much to perfect the organization, character and destiny of the race, and promote its progress.

In our correspondence, I have said much of the reproductive element, and the laws by which its expenditure should be governed. I have specified three, which seem to me to be natural and just, viz.: MUTUAL LOVE — THE CONDITIONS OF THE WIFE — and OFFSPRING. If reproduction were the sole object in the expenditure of this element, and its retention in the system sacredly cherished, except for this, it would greatly conduce to the health, beauty, strength and activity of the body, to the true development, nobleness and energy of the soul, to the freshness, life and refinement of social enjoyment, to the peace and elevating influence of home, and to the progress of the race in all that is true and noble.

Were the question asked — How can this element be rendered most conducive to enjoyment to body and soul, supposing a man is in pursuit of pleasure and wishes to make this power of his nature most perfectly to answer this end — will the object be gained by expending it or retaining it? — I believe Nature, and the history of mankind, would render this answer — RETAIN IT FOR PLEASURE; EXPEND IT ONLY FOR OFFSPRING, AND TRUE DEVELOPMENT. What would be said of him who was ever toiling for wealth, but who could derive no enjoyment from it, except by throwing it, fast as he earned it, into the fire or the sea? All would call him insane. Having, by severe toil, created wealth, his only pleasure in it consists in destroying it! But what would he differ from him, who, by the costly action of the vital forces, has elaborated and secreted this essential element of manhood, but who can derive no conscious, certain enjoyment from it, except in expending it? He that expends this life-principle of his manhood, for mere pleasure, whether in solitude or otherwise, will be sure to learn his mistake, when it will be too late to repair the injury. His pleasure will be like the spasmodic laugh of a maniac.

In addition to all I have said as to the conditions of the wife which should regulate the passional expression of her husband's love, I must add one thing more. There is a period in which she should resolutely resist all solicitations, come what may. I mean, *the period of gestation.* She has received into herself the elements of a new existence. From the moment of conception, the energies of her body and soul are put in requisition to develop and perfect the embryo. The one object of her life will be, if she understands her relation to her child, to give it a perfect organization. She should guard that tender being from harm, as she would her own soul. It is ever pleading, through her maternal instincts, for love and protection. She feels the call in every fibre of her being. Not for a moment should she yield to any thing that may injure herself, or the being she bears under her heart. God and all good spirits surround her, to shield her and her babe from harm. Who shall dare approach to outrage them?

Unaccountable as it may seem, the fact is undeniable, that the husband and the father is the first to demand that which she cannot grant without *injustice to herself and the being that looks to her for life and happiness.* Regardless of the health and feelings of his wife and child, he often insists on the gratification of his passion, and if the wife resists, he visits upon her and her child his indignation, to vex her soul and make her condition as uncomfortable as he can. Against such a disgrace to manhood, the condemnation of every decent man and woman should be directed. The only apology that can be offered for such abuses of marriage and parentage is ignorance. "They know not what they do;" therefore, let them be forgiven.

It is in vain to plead, for an excuse, that the wife, during this period, demands such expressions of his love..

She is in a diseased condition if she does. Could her nature, if in a true and healthy state, call for this indulgence? Would not the desire naturally cease from the time when her nature is directed to the purpose of perfecting her child? If she does demand it, no man will answer such a call, if he truly loves and respects his wife or child. Nature cries out against such a violation of all that is true, loving and wise. No man will excite his wife to desire such a manifestation of his love, if he be worthy of the name of husband or father. He will do all in his power to surround her with an influence so calm, so deep, so soothing, and so full of repose, that the entire energies of her body and soul may be left free to concentrate themselves upon his child, to beautify and perfect its organization.

How many might trace their diseased bodies and souls, their imbecility, idiocy and insanity, directly to the husband's treatment of his wife during the period of pregnancy! Against the ignorant or selfish demand of the husband, the wife pleads the injury to her nervous system, and thereby to the health of their child. He answers, that he cannot control himself so long, and tries to stimulate her passion. He succeeds, and thus her energies are diverted from their natural functions, to minister to the sensual gratification of the husband. The unnatural excitement deranges the action of the whole generative system, the pains and perils of childbirth are greatly aggravated, and the life of child and mother is oftentimes endangered. The action of sexual excitement on the nerves of the mother and the child is direct, powerful and destructive. When these consequences are fully understood, husbands will be appalled to behold the diseases of soul and body, the deep, enduring suffering, they have caused. That so many children die in infancy, may be traced directly, in good part, to the sexual abuse of the wife by the husband, during gestation.

As we would glorify and elevate the nature we bear; as we would secure to future generations a more perfect physical, intellectual and spiritual organization; as we would make home the source of our deepest, most intense, refined and enduring happiness, we should do what we can to call attention to this subject, and to urge on men the duty of controlling their passional nature, and of treating their wives naturally and nobly, during this most important and influential period in the life of woman.

What I have said of the period of Gestation, I should also say of Lactation. While the child receives its support from the mother, the food is injuriously affected by every great excitement, and especially by that of the sexual passion. This should be the law for the government of every husband, *never to have passional intercourse with his wife during Gestation or Lactation.* Nina! thou canst feel and speak on this subject as no man can. Must not every such indulgence be at the expense of both the mother and the child?

It is said that a man of strong nature and great vital energy cannot and will not control his passion for so long a time as Nature may require the mother's energies to perfect her child, during the periods of pregnancy and lactation, while he is living with her in daily intimacy; and that if he cannot find gratification with her, he will seek it among strangers. The apology is a libel upon manhood; and any true lover or husband will scorn to accept it for himself. Shame would forbid him to justify indulgence on such a ground. He knows that his passional nature can be subjected to his love; that the animal can be controlled by the spiritual, so long as the health, happiness and future destiny of his wife and child may require. There is ample scope for the action of the sexual element, without expending it in sensual indulgence. What does the wife demand of her husband at such times? Does she not call, in every fibre of her womanhood, for the expression of a love which may be accorded and received, not in wild, intense excitement, but as a soothing, sustaining, ever-present influence, which she may not be able to define, but which she feels as a life-giving presence? Is not the deep, longing desire of her soul to her husband and to the father of her child, for his encouraging smile, his sustaining sympathy, his gentle caress?—to be folded in his arms and sheltered in his bosom?—to receive from him every endearing expression, short of passional indulgence, while she is preparing to encircle his brow with a crown of glory, as the father of a living child? Is not this all she needs, or can healthfully receive? Is it not all the true husband should wish to impart? Here is room enough for the constant and healthy action of all the elements of man's nature, as a husband. To cherish and sustain thee, and aid thee in perfecting the organization and development of our child, for whose existence and destiny we must account to ourselves and our child, has afforded scope enough for all the strongest elements of my manhood.

As the omnipotent energies of God are under the control of his infinite love, so the energies of the husband, however deep and strong, may and should be governed by a love deeper and stronger still.

With emotions that cannot now find utterance, I subscribe myself,

Thy husband, and the happy father of thy child,

ERNEST.

## ANSWER.

Ernest:

As thou hast said to me, so I say to thee: my heart speaks to thee, as it never did before. I am a mother, and thou art the father of my child. How deep, how tender, how intense and sublime the relation of a mother, not only to her child, but also to him who has crowned her being with this happiness! Thou hast enshrined my brow with a diadem of beauty. I look back on my experience, from the time I received into myself the germ of this new life to the present hour, and an inexpressible tenderness, a concentrated, loving respect, and a deep, grateful yearning for the presence, protecting care, and manly love of my husband and the father of my babe, have filled my heart, and presided over my child's development, in every stage of its progress, before and since its birth. From its conception to the present time, the function of my nature which has given to us this pledge of our love and our happiness, has been a means of refinement and exaltation to my entire being.

It is the true office of love, to refine and exalt passion; and of passion, to intensify and ennoble the expressions of love. The memory of the act in which this new life originated is sacredly cherished. It was rendered delicate, and most acceptable, by the assurance that it was but the expression of your soul's deepest love. *In our passional relations, there is not a single memory or association which is not refined and noble.* I cannot conceive of the aversion some wives express in speaking of the animal passion of their husbands; it can never be associated in my mind with thee. I owe thee a deep debt of gratitude for this experience.

It is no slight responsibility which rests upon the man who first officiates as a husband at the Holy of Holies of woman's personal surrender of herself to the functions of maternity. He stands as the embodiment of an attribute of manhood, which, according as it is revealed in connection with love or without it, is for ever afterwards associated, in a wife's mind, with all that is true and noble, or mean, selfish and brutal. Thou, as my husband, in exalting me to the relation and dignity of a mother, hast been High Priest of this offering of my womanhood at the shrine of Love.

Robed in garments of consecration, thou hast performed thy rites with a pure heart. Thou hast left no stain upon the altar of our love. Thou hast sought to bestow on our child the priceless legacy of a deep, rich love-nature. Forevermore will thy wife feel that it is for thee to rule over her in the passional relation. She asks no protection but thy manly love, for she knows that an ever-watchful eye is open for her safety.

The Church may ordain bishops, the Pope may be acknowledged its head, but not even he has so holy, important and delicate a mission as the husband, who, for the first time, reveals the power of his manhood to his wife in this relation. All men will, ever after, be regarded by the wife in the light of this experience. I have heard women say, that, after this first experience with their husbands, they could not see a man, a stranger, passing in the street, without disgust at the thought of the animal passion accompanying his masculine nature. That was a revelation which I did not, at the time, comprehend; I can, now, deeply and fully, by contrast. When a husband, for the first time, thus urges upon his wife this expression of his love, for which her nature not only does not call, but which it positively and shrinkingly repels, her disgust can never be forgotten nor overcome. It is death to the sentiment of love in her heart, and to all the outgushings of her wifely affection.

The young wife comes to the husband with a heart full of confiding love. His animal passion is impetuous; he knows nothing of woman's nature; he is equally ignorant of the laws designed to govern his own sexual instinct, and he at once demands and takes from her what her nature shrinks from giving. From that hour, she dreads his passion. The doom of that home is sealed.

ERNEST! be this my highest tribute to thy manhood: *Thy wife fears not thy passion, for she has faith and knowledge, that love rules in your soul and body with an absolute control.* Man can exalt his sexual nature to no higher point, than to secure for it the grateful respect and perfect confidence of his wife. When it stands associated in her mind only with the holiest moments of her heart's desire for true manifestation, then the animal nature answers the highest object for which it was created. It serves not its own selfish ends; it waits on a Divinity whose service purifies and ennobles its own nature. It becomes a servant of the Most High.

Such ideas, such convictions and assurances, have been brought home to me, in my relation to thee as a wife. Thou hast, by thy self-control and considerate regard for the wishes and conditions of thy wife, inspired me with a deep and loving respect for thy passional nature, for the symbols of thy manhood, and for the deep, stern, but gentle heart, which, through them, has revealed its wealth.

*Can a husband help feeling proud and happy to receive such assurances from the heart of his wife?* They are due to thee, for they are true as eternal life. In thy person, manhood stands in its true dignity and nobleness before thy wife, and what higher office canst thou fulfil to her heart than this?

Could I but do justice to the emotions of my soul, in reading thy last letter, thou wouldst feel that through me thou hast reached the deepest chord of woman's heart. That letter has vividly recalled the experiences of the year when first the concentrated joy of a mother's heart came over me. My husband! thou hast lived out thy ideal in this relation. When I told thee that I could no longer assert exclusive right to thy affection, it was at that moment thy love assumed a more sustaining mode of expression. A more than mother's solicitude foresaw my wants, and gave to my physical weakness a manly support. No words can tell the susceptibility of a woman's nature, at these times, to external impressions of pleasure or pain. A word, a look, that at other times would pass unheeded, will bring the tears to her eyes. Mentally and bodily, she is most delicately attuned, and a passing breath will waken sweet or discordant music in her soul. If ever she needs a soothing love, it is while she bears a child under her heart. The nature of the child seems to shine through her, and claim the same tenderness which she will bestow after its birth. She cannot be trifled with, except at the risk of her own safety and that of her child. She does not ask for the passional element in her husband's love; she craves all other expressions of it, fully to perfect the new being; and just in proportion as she receives them, will a loving soul be infused into the strong and healthy frame of her child. A wife feels, from the moment she takes charge of the germ of a new being, in order to become a mother, that God is with her. She is set apart to fulfil the highest office of her being, and she can never willingly betray her trust. And when hope becomes reality, and the new being actually reposes by her side, or in her arms, and she offers it to him who has, with her, lent the highest energies of his soul and body to this personification of their love, she must, in her soul, say to every thought or word of passion, interfering with this new life, "*Stand off, for this is holy ground!*"

ERNEST! I have been true to my own soul, in the pictures I have drawn of the holy influence of married life. Thou hast a right to lay down rules for the benefit of the race, for thou hast tested their power by thine own experience; and I will add, that they have secured the happiness and growth of her whose progress thou hast made the chief object of thy care. It is from thy obedience to such rules of life, that I feel myself blessed in being thy wife, and twice blessed as the mother of thy child.

Thy wife,<br>NINA.

## LETTER XV.

#### HOME AND ITS INFLUENCE.

Nina:

Thou hast accomplished a mission to thy husband, for which he can never repay thee. Thou hast lifted the veil that hid from his spiritual eye the power and glory of his own manhood, and placed it in its true light before his mind. He was alone, — a bewildered wanderer by life's wayside, — a mystery to himself, with an ever-present call for a love and companionship not actualized; voiceless, but earnest, and often agonizing. From amid the throng that hurried past, came a voice, saying, "What wilt thou?" My heart answered, "I would see myself and thee." That voice replied, "Behold thyself and me!" I saw myself, a proud, stern, imperious, yet gentle, loving man; and by me one who said, "I am thy wife." It was the voice of God, saying to my bewildered heart, "Let there be light!" A new heaven and a new earth arose around me. From the hour in which our souls were made one by love, life has been a richer, nobler boon. Come what may to me or to thee, I must evermore feel a conscious pride that I am a man, and all thine own. I bless thee for the wreath thou hast twined around my brow. It is a garland of love, placed by the soul of deathless womanhood upon the brow of deathless manhood. My body and soul are dear to me, because they are dear to thee. Thou hast made them thine, and consecrated them to the perfection of thy nature and the fulfilment of thy destiny. For years, and without one moment's interruption, we have actualized the truth, that I am thine and thou art mine.

Beautiful has been the home of our love, the soul of each calmly and perfectly at rest in the bosom of the other. A power has been over us, to which submission has been our heaven. The feminine element of Nature, as incarnate in thee, has, during every hour of our united existence, been silently, but surely, moulding my character and shaping my destiny. The soul of the woman and the wife, speaking to me through the symbols and functions of thy physical organism, has daily breathed into me a more earnest longing for a truer and more manly life. I can never express to thee my gratitude for the ennobling influence thou hast exercised over me. That voiceless but ever-controlling agency has been to me what the sun and dew of heaven are to the earth; it has caused the wilderness of my life to bud and blossom like the rose."

HOME AND ITS INFLUENCE! With thanksgiving and the voice of melody for ever shall I have cause to sing of my home on earth, and its agency in my development and happiness. Compared with this, the school, the college, the church, the government, and general society, sink into insignificance, as means of spiritual life and growth. Indeed, they are of little use, except as they help to qualify men and women to make for themselves happy homes. They work evil, and only evil, when they serve but to entomb the natural and holy longing of the heart for such a home in the gloomy sepulchres of Ambition, Avarice, or Sensuality. In commercial, social, political or religious life, conscience becomes seared, reason obtuse, affection chilled, and the soul altogether bewildered by unnatural excitement in pursuit of that which, if obtained, can give no rest. Only in a true home can the soul attain its full development in all directions. Here, alone, can reason be made clear and vigorous, the conscience become a universe of light to guide the soul onward and upward, and affection be trained to delicacy, tenderness and fidelity. The pure in heart, who alone are so blessed as to see God, must be created and developed, not in the market, nor the school, nor the church, nor in halls of legislation, but in the true home of freedom and of rest, where all the elements and functions of soul and body can be called into healthful activity.

But what and where is that true home, — the home where children may be created in physical, intellectual and spiritual health and beauty, and developed into noble men and women, prepared by birth and education to enter into all natural relations, and to assume the responsibilities, and wisely to discharge the duties, growing out of such relations? Society must see and actually enjoy a nobler type of home, before it can hope to be blessed by the presence of nobler types of men and women. An ideal earthly home is ever present to the heart. Each man and woman has that ideal cherished deep in the soul, as the consummation of their present existence. How sad, that through bewildering ignorance, or impetuous passion, they should, by unnatural social, political and religious surroundings, render the actualization of their beautiful ideal impossible!

In all attempts to present an improved type of home, that home must first exist in the ideal, be examined and discussed in the ideal, before it can be made an actuality. The past is made illustrious by the names of those who have presented to the world model means to promote the refinement and elevation of man. Better had it been for the human family, had a larger portion of the talent, money and enterprise, which have been expended to furnish and administer model schools, churches and governments, been bestowed in giving to men and women the ideal of a true home on earth, and in helping them to actualize it. Those who help their fellow-beings to a nobler ideal of home, and show them how they can make it a living reality, are greater benefactors, and deserving of greater honor, than the founders of literary, ecclesiastical or governmental institutions.

It is unnatural, and therefore injurious, for man or woman, for any cause, to live in isolation from the other sex, thereby becoming unorganized fragments of humanity. Both, in so doing, violate the holiest instinct and highest law of their being. Man can always find wiser counsel, truer sympathy, in woman, than in man. No matter for what purpose he launches his bark on the ocean of life, without the loving presence and heroic devotion of woman, whether it be in pursuit of wealth, conquest, fame, philanthropy, or religion, he does it at the peril of his dearest interests. For the senseless titles, dignities and canonizations of the

Church, the equally senseless and clamorous plaudits of political parties, the eager aspirations after titles, station and wealth, and the roar and excitement of murderous battles, cannot give true rest and conscious self-respect. The time comes to all, when these would be gladly exchanged for the pure love and vitalizing sympathy of a wife at home. He who sacrifices the endearments and ennobling influences of home, *for any cause*, wrongs his own soul, and so far disqualifies himself to serve his fellow-beings, as he hinders, by so doing, his own true individual development. He most perfectly accomplishes his mission on earth, who presents to the world a specimen, in himself, of a most perfectly developed man. He is the most perfect man, who enters most truly into all natural relations, and performs most faithfully the duties that grow out of them.

He who is without a true home is without the means of the highest development. No matter for what he sacrifices home, he must suffer loss, for he has outraged the tenderest and most earnest instinct of his manhood,—that which ever calls for a place of rest for body and soul. "Foxes have holes, and the birds of the air have nests;" but how many sons and daughters of men are without a home on earth! They wander about from place to place with unappropriated hearts, that yearn to give out the wealth of their love to bless and to be blessed. Some of them having, for a brief time, experienced the blessings of a true home, live on "sweet memories" of the past. The loved ones who made their homes ever encircle them.

One sentiment ever fills and thrills their souls; a sentiment which can find expression only in such terms of endearment as rise spontaneously to the lips of conjugal and parental affection, and which are so welcome and significant in the sacred privacy of home.

The past has given to the present many records, delineating embodiments of truth and nobleness in domestic relations. Some of these are preserved in manuscript, never having been designed for the public eye and heart, and from this fact, being all the more truthful and reliable; for the husband and wife can speak to each other as they can to none others. One of these private histories is now before me, written by a husband for the eye and heart of his absent wife. It is entitled, "SWEET MEMORIES." What had been his material home, amid mountain scenery of unsurpassed wildness and beauty, is about to be exchanged for one in a distant land, to which his wife had gone. The husband had been left some days amid the scenes of their wedded bliss, and had kept a record of his interior and exterior life, as a memento of the home of their love, when they should be far away. He thus concludes: —

"I have entered the parlor to write my last word by the table and in the room of our home, where our hearts and our lives have so perfectly blended. What shall that last word be? Precious memories rush upon me. All the pet names, in which our united hearts have found expression, and which are so welcome and so appropriate, when every look, tone and act assures the loved one that they come from a heart all her own, crowd upon me, struggling for utterance. One sentiment is ever present in my heart, which can now find expression only in these words—'MY LOVE! MY DARLING!'

"This, as it seems to me, must ever be the one consecrating sentiment of the husband's life. This fathoms the depths of his being, and swallows up all other experiences. It consecrates all the elements and emblems of his manhood. It scatters the clouds of ignorance, drives away all mystery and bewilderment, makes the rough places plain, the crooked straight; levels the mountains and fills up the vallies of life, and casts up a highway of the Lord for his feet, and opens to him the kingdom of heaven.

"The sentiment these words alone can express is omnipotent for good and against evil. Amid the sacred associations and tender cares and joys of home, the husband's heart will ever be open to its redeeming influence. It consecrates and ennobles all the elements and functions of the wife's nature, surrounding them with hallowed beauty and delicacy. Whatever makes her a woman, and qualifies her to be his wife and the mother of his children, is sacred and lovely to him, as the emblem of truth and purity.

"As he looks over his wedded life, every thing he has done for the wife of his bosom, in the kitchen, the nursery, and parlor, will seem to him as acts of true worship. Nothing will seem like drudgery, nothing menial, or unbecoming the man or the husband. Nothing can seem unworthy his thoughts or hands, which can contribute to her health and happiness. The one abiding sentiment of his heart renders all he can do for her delicate and acceptable. However minute the service for one so loved, it seems refined and manly.

"The details of domestic economy can never be repulsive to the true husband. On the contrary, to relieve the wants and cares of the wife, in any way, and help her to bear the burdens of household labor, is not to serve as a menial, but to cherish her and sustain her as a husband; and there is no act by which he can secure her perfect trust and repose in his manhood, that is not made delicate and heroic by the consciousness that it is done for a loving, confiding wife.

"An expression of love can never seem coarse or menial to the loved one whose heart reciprocates the sentiment. In the Eden of their love, the tender respect with which each regards the physical elements and functions of the other will ensure the performance of all the nameless and constantly recurring services essential to the existence of a true and happy home, with conscious pride and satisfaction. Each rests without a fear in the bosom of the other. Man longs to be lovingly and tenderly cherished and caressed. He needs it to save him from a hard spirit, and from low, debasing influences. Man cannot caress himself; nor can man perform this delicate and beautiful mission to man. Woman alone can accomplish this most needful and endearing office of refinement for him; and that, too, most perfectly in the relation of a wife, in the vitalizing interchange of affection and helpful service in the consecrated privacy of home. From no other hand could a pure and noble man receive such a sacrament. Man needs these gentle, delicate offices, to develop and perfect his manhood. He will receive them only from a love that is undefiled.

"THE ACTION OF LOVE IS ALWAYS HEROIC. It ennobles and refines all its manifestations to the beloved. A truer and nobler sentiment was never uttered than the following, by a wife and a mother (Lady Mary Wortley Montague) : — '*The minutest details of domestic economy become elegant and refined, when they are ennobled by sentiment.*' Be this the ever-present, ever-controlling maxim of the kitchen, the bed-room and nursery, of every home — LOVE REFINES EVERY ACT TO WHICH IT PROMPTS. Drudgery, vulgarity, meanness, never characterize the labors of love in the true home. There, 'individual sovereignty' will be an unmeaning phrase; for the twain has led to oneness, each aspiring to no higher destiny, in their united life, than to be possessed and cared for by the other. To have ruled wisely, by love, over the soul of the other, in the enchanted circle of home, will be to each a more heroic and satisfactory achievement than the heads of earthly kingdoms ever accomplished.

"These musings are suggested by the memory of our blended hearts and lives in this dear home. The wife of my bosom, as the life-principle of my manhood, has consecrated all that surrounds me. This pleasant parlor, with its contents remaining as left by thee; the cottage, with the garlands of sweet flowers and evergreens with which Nature, aided by thy skill and care, has adorned it; these mountains, to which we have given names significant of our emotions as we have stood together on their tops; the amphitheatre of evergreens, where we have listened to the birds, the squirrels, the wind breathing through the branches, and to the *silence*, most eloquent and subduing of all, and whose retreats we have so fondly christened; — what so consecrates them? That one deep sentiment, that can find expression only in pet words and in corresponding deeds, has sanctified thee, and all connected with thee.

"What shall I say? *Silence* were, perhaps, the most expressive; but my heart throbs for utterance, and written words are now the only medium of communication. The day is bright, the air is filled with sweet odors, the mountains are defined in power and grandeur against the blue sky. Heaven above and earth beneath look bright and beautiful as the face of God; yet they utter but one sentiment, — a sentiment that ennobles our united past, and opens to our view a future of brightness and beauty.

"These mute witnesses of our love and joy speak now as they never did before. Though I leave them to go to thee, my heart is heavy, for it assures me I shall see them no more with thee. Come to me, then, in spirit; let us mingle our hearts once more amid these consecrated scenes. Then we will go forth, heart in heart and hand in hand, amid strange surroundings in other lands, to intertwine our 'sweet memories' of the past with our anticipations of a happy future."

Man may be surrounded with material beauty and elegance, and with kind and loving relatives and friends;

but if the wife be not there, home will seem desolate; the power is wanting which alone can meet the deepest want of his manly soul. Man can have no true home without a *wife*, nor can woman without a *husband*.

The *child*, also, is an essential element of a true home. Parentage is no less a law of our being than marriage. First, the wife and husband, then the child; and these, so far as the presence of human beings is concerned, are all that are essential to make a home. Though the occasional presence of those holding other and less intimate relations to us adds greatly to the pleasures and healthful influences of home, yet the husband, the wife and child, are all whose constant presence is essential; and the more intensely these concentrate their affection on one another, the more ennobling will be their united life. Only in the home that is created and consecrated by those intimate and endearing relations can marriage and parentage perform their perfect work in the regeneration and redemption of the race. In that hallowed retreat, and no where else, can men and women truly reveal the beauty and glory of their nature. In the wife, the husband sees the embodiment of a love for him, whose power and purity can never be estimated, in whose light he is proud to have his soul's most cherished secrets revealed, and whose highest aim is to call into activity whatever is manly and noble in her beloved. What soul does not yearn for a home in the bosom of a love which exists only to ennoble and to bless the loved one! — to live ever in the presence of one whose affection consecrates the entire being, and encircles it with the light and fragrance of heaven! Only such a love, in the sacred privacy of home, can truly interpret and meet the purest wants of our nature. Men and women can never truly comprehend and appreciate their manhood and womanhood, till they see themselves reflected in the mirror of a pure conjugal love.

The *isolated* home is the true home; and this necessarily results from the nature of marriage love, for such love is exclusive. The husband's soul naturally concentrates itself on the wife. Each seeks a peculiar personal manifestation of love from the other. There can be no community, no partnerships, in conjugal affection, except between the two. The child, the result and the embodiment of the love that made the twain one, may be added, and the harmony be maintained; for that comes but to call into activity a new element of life in that wedded pair, i. e., parental love, and not to share in that which made them one. But let a third party be admitted to share the treasures to which wedded love makes an exclusive claim, and such love will instantly repel the intruder, or die in the conflict. Conjugal love instinctively seeks retirement for its purest and most ennobling manifestations. To this end, it demands and it creates an isolated, exclusive home. In that holy of holies of human life, such love reveals the secret of its power, and introduces the blended pair, by its influence, into the kingdom of heaven.

It is said that exclusive love and an isolated home necessarily engender selfishness in the hearts of all its inmates. This is true, when ambition, avarice, vanity, or desire for sensual indulgence, creates and maintains that home. It is founded in selfishness, and can engender only that. But, in a home created by conjugal love, the single object of each is the happiness of the other, and every pulsation of such love, and every manifestation of it, expands the heart, and fills it with a more active sympathy with all of human kind. Through the medium of such exclusive love, and of the isolated home which it creates and in which it seeks a perfect manifestation and embodiment, the twain, made one, see human nature as they never did before. It appears more lovely, and capable of a higher growth and a more exalted destiny, and they are prepared to labor more wisely and efficiently to win men and women to a higher life. That such results are so seldom seen is not attributable to the fact that the home is *isolated*, or that the love that creates it is *exclusive;* but to the fact that it is the creation of sensual passion.

The man who regards the presence of the reproductive element in himself as a means of sensuous gratification, and marriage as a licensed mode of expending that element and of obtaining that gratification, can never hope to make for himself a pure and happy home. He regards the woman who has come to him as a wife, simply as a means to his passional indulgence. This is his highest ideal of a wife, and he thinks of his home mainly as a place where she can be made to minister to his sensuality, without public censure. He *demands* the surrender of her person to his passion, without regard to her wishes or her conditions of body or mind. He sacrifices her body and soul, and those of his children, on the altar of his sensuality. What motive has a woman to toil to make a happy home for a man who thus crushes her? She feels that she is dear to him only as a means of administering to his passion, and that he cares for his home, and comes to it, but for his sensual gratification. Then, by a constant expenditure of the vital element of his manhood, he enfeebles his reason, his conscience, his affection, and his power to love and appreciate his wife and child. He becomes repulsive, and incapable of forming true family relations. On our knowledge of the natural laws which should govern the expenditure of the reproductive element, and on our obedience to them, depend the question of a happy home. If man errs here, the element on which he must depend for the accomplishment of his desire will be a blight to his manhood; but if he seek a home for the health, comfort, purity and perfection of his wife and child, and finds his life in their true development and happiness, that element will be to him and to them a living fountain of joy and peace; it will make a heaven of his earthly home.

Man needs a home for the body, as well as for the soul. It is natural and right that a man and woman, living in the conjugal relation, should seek to surround themselves with material beauty and elegance, as well as comfort; for their own and for their children's sake, they should do this. I have no sympathy with that feeling which forbids men and women to seek and enjoy such elegancies, while others are destitute of the necessaries of life. I would help every husband and wife to a beautiful, elegant, healthful, material home. The best way to do this is to show them, by example, that such a home is possible, even to the poor, and how it can be attained. There are those who have great power to create material wealth, but none to make it conduce to their comfort and refinement. Others have no power to create it, but great skill to make what little they get contribute to their elevation and happiness. To know how to create it honestly, and to use it wisely, is a talent that should be and will be better cultivated and more highly appreciated, when men and women come more fully to understand the bearing of their material surroundings on the refining and ennobling influences of home.

Isolated from woman, man becomes stern, cold, hard and suspicious, low and coarse in his language, rough and repulsive in his habits. Purity and delicacy of speech and personal habits are essential to a true home of love. Love for a wife naturally tends to refine and elevate the husband, and prompts him to seek to make his inner and outer life pure and pleasing to her. To illustrate this power of the wife, I will again quote from "SWEET MEMORIES," a passage in which the husband records the influence of the wife in this particular : —

"The power of the wife over the husband! Yes, I know what it is. As I call to mind the gentle ways in which thou hast sought to perfect thy husband in his inner and outer life, my heart proudly acknowledges its indebtedness to thee. How instinctively man seeks to commend himself to the woman he loves! How joyfully he aims to be attractive in his personal habits and modes of manifestation, when he feels that, for this, he will be held more proudly to the heart of his beloved!

"Man needs some one to live for besides himself, and no one can so powerfully incite him to purity of heart and life as woman. His home, without a wife, would more resemble the lair of wild animals, than the home of human beings.

"Say what we may of self-respect and of the dignity and glory of human nature, — and too much cannot be said, if truly said, about it, — yet few have so deep and living a reverence for the nature they bear, and such an exalted view of their destiny, as to induce them, simply for the sake of that nature and that destiny, to study all ennobling habits in the regulation of their natural appetites, and the supply of their physical necessities. Only the living presence of the object of their love can stimulate them to persevere in a course of interior and exterior refinement, without which home becomes but another name for physical and spiritual debasement.

"I know that some men, without regard to external appliances, and from an innate sense of the dignity of their own nature, seek to form and maintain all pure and attractive habits. *This is what all should do;* but few do it. Men degenerate without an external influence. Man can never supply this to man. God will not supply it, except as he is present, embodied in the form of a loved one.

"What would men do to cultivate the beautiful, the graceful and orderly, if left alone? Some would do much; but, generally, they would do nothing. Woman, as a wife, a mother, a daughter, a sister, or friend, can alone supply to man the necessary power to enable him to resist all deteriorating tendencies. It is in the relation of wife that her power is most effective to refine and elevate. I know it is so. One year in thy presence, as thy husband, would do more to strengthen my aspirations after the pure and the beautiful, in the inner and outer life, than a life-time in the presence of men in isolation from women."

NINA! a man without a home is without a centre to his life. He may, like the earth, revolve upon his own axis; but his thoughts, affections, hopes, aims and aspirations, gather fondly and permanently around no fixed centre. They are all afloat, wandering and tempest-tossed, aimless and bewildered. With no wife, no child, no home, no rest, on earth, he looks to the spirit-land, and longs to be there, if, perchance, the desire of his soul for a pure home in the bosom of love may be fulfilled. To such a homeless wanderer, earth is robbed of its sweetest fragrance, its most attractive beauty, its highest glory, and its most refining and ennobling influence. To the true man, no flowers are so beautiful and so fragrant as those that bloom in the home of his love; no jewels so brilliant as the loved ones around whom his heart twines in his home; no crown of glory seems so resplendent as that which encircles the brow of his wife and his child; no smile is so eloquent, no voice so melodious, as those that meet and welcome him on the threshold of his home. There love finds free expression in all pet names and phrases, which it is bliss to give and receive; and in looks and acts still more expressive than words.

The following recollections of the husband of the most sacred penetralia of his conjugal life, will easily be appreciated by those who have lived in a true, harmonious relation. It is taken from "SWEET MEMORIES":—

"THE BRIDAL CHAMBER! What apartment of home so dear as this! Here we have communed most intimately with each other and with the Highest. Here we have bowed our souls and worshipped the power that made us one. How holy and how dear is this place!

"But how often it proves the place of secret assassination, where no mercy is shown to the helpless victim, appealing to the honor and pity of him who is bound to love and cherish her, and save her from all harm! These wails of wo that go up to the great Father will one day be heard and heeded.

"Could the most secret recesses of the homes of nations professedly civilized and Christian reveal their hidden depths, the story would appal the world! What crushed hearts, what trust betrayed, what indignation, what disgust! What a revelation of man to woman! Let the mysteries of prisons, camps, slave plantations, slave and pirate ships, and all places where *unlicensed* crime hides its shame, be revealed, and they would not surpass the corruption and ruin wrought under the sanction of what is called marriage. O for some moral Hercules to cleanse the fountains of human life and destiny, — to purify them of their appalling corruptions, — to fill them with perfect trust on the part of wives, of perfect self-control on the part of husbands, — to make them what they should and might be, the holy of holies of the great temple of Humanity!

"In these recesses of domestic life, where ignorance and passion so often work out their most fearful results, originate those who are to appear on earth in human form. Thence must issue the Adams and Eves who, in the future, are to possess and cultivate this Eden of God. Let that life be sacred to love, to wisdom, to purity, then would children of Love, sons and daughters of God, be born there."

But I forbear. I leave to thee the grateful task of giving, in detail, the spiritual elements of a true home. Thou art more competent to do justice to the subject than I am. Thou art the presiding genius of our home. I gratefully accept a home such as thy taste, thy firmness, thy judgment and thy love will make it. Breathe thy pure, heroic spirit into thy husband, to refine and ennoble his soul, and to make its external manifestations such as shall call out towards him thy deepest and tenderest love, and contribute to thy perfection, and to that of our child. Daily and hourly shall my manhood be consecrated to beautify and perfect our home. Thus will we live, each in and for the other; each, in all expressions of affection in the most secret and sacred intimacies of our domestic life, making the perfect development and happiness of the other the one great end of our existence, as husband

and wife, until our united aspirations, in regard to each other, shall be actualized, and our fondest hopes are lost in fruition.

Thy happy husband,

ERNEST.

## ANSWER.

Ernest:

A vision of beauty opens before us, in the future of our united life, and I gladly record my ideas of what our home must be, in order to realize our hopes.

A home, in the true sense, is the work of Nature. When two congenial hearts are united by love — that mighty experience of the soul, in which no gross element of worldly policy or personal ambition can mingle — marriage is the natural result. No sooner is marriage consummated in the heart, than its first demand is for a home; a spot consecrated to the most sacred emotions of the soul; a sanctum wherein the world has no right to intrude; where the heart may freely expand in every possible manifestation to which Nature prompts. Around that centre, every tender yearning clings; to secure it, the will bends its most persevering energies; and every personal sacrifice is willingly made for this great satisfaction of the heart. The *ideal* of home is always beautiful to those who love. If they fail to actualize their expectations, it is because, by ignorance or heedlessness, they do not develop into full and perfect fruit the exquisite bud of beauty which young love has opened in their hearts.

Among the many causes of disappointed hopes, *selfishness* seems more fruitful than any other of sad results. Where that is found, true love cannot exist; for the essence of love is self-forgetfulness. I cannot say *self-sacrifice*, for that implies a kind of martyrdom which true love never feels in consulting the happiness of the beloved. I mean that state of heart and mind, between those who love, which leads each to discover and prefer what is most suitable, comfortable and agreeable to the other; then it is no sacrifice to yield a particular point; then will spring up a generous rivalry as to which shall do most for the happiness of the other; and then, for once and for ever, the long-vexed question is settled as to who shall *rule*. The reign of Love removes the elements of conflict, and the voice of the heart, and the law of life, will be, "THY WILL, NOT MINE, BE DONE." Love must, Orpheus-like, subdue the Cerberus of selfishness, if it would gain entire possession of its beloved.

A generous self-forgetfulness in those who love will secure freedom of opinion, conscience and action, equal opportunities of improvement, and will promote that "life, liberty, and the pursuit of happiness," which are as essential elements in a happy home as in a secure government. That sort of power or influence is never useful which seeks to *manage* husband or wife. The soul instinctively rebels against it, however wise and judicious the influence may be. Freedom is the only atmosphere in which love can long exist. Even the poetic "silken cord" becomes a galling chain, when it demands the surrender of personal freedom; while generous love will soften even the severest experiences of life.

But the influence of unselfish love will not end here. It will regulate the social claims, assigning to all their due place and importance. Home will not be sacrificed to ambitious advancement, or ever be made to subserve such ends. The hospitality of the heart will be extended to all whose claims render them attractive, whatever be their rank; and as time wears on, that home will be the centre of such friends as fashion and conventional society can never command. If the inmates possess high mental and moral culture, they will attract their equals, and thus win, by their own merits, what pretension seeks in vain. A blessing for ever hovers over the home of Love, for its genial light shines out upon the coldness of this world like the cheer of an evening fire upon midnight darkness; and the traveller will bless the home wherein he has been welcomed, whether he be the elegant favorite of fortune, who finds in its unostentatious sincerity a charm he seeks elsewhere in vain, or the hunted wanderer, who receives comfort and protection for his houseless head. Wherever true love has made a home, it writes its story on the faces of all who dwell therein; it engraves words of peace and welcome on every door-post and threshold; it is fitly symbolized in the odors of sweet flowers, in the dancing shadows of the waving trees, and all day long the little birds sing of it in the boughs. Its foundations are broad and firm; no winds or storms can prevail against it, for it is based upon a rock; there is no need of sun by day or moon by night to give it light, for the brightness of heaven shines round about it. In such a noble, pure and lovely atmosphere does true love exist. The heart is right toward God and man, ever open in sympathy with distress, holding no fellowship with the mean and selfish, finding no charm in their society, but steadily fixed on those high and noble aims worthy of the nature of true manhood and womanhood.

To secure this home, love alone is requisite. Poverty and toil may be the daily portion of its members, yet the noble influences of home need not be sacrificed to gain. A comfortable supply for simple wants can be secured with moderate effort, still affording time for rest and cultivation of the mind, leaving the heart open to all genial influences, and thoughtful of the thousand daily attentions, which, springing from tender affection, render the simplest life elegant and full of happiness.

It is often questioned whether the husband or the wife gives the most decided character to the home. Undoubtedly, there are certain elements of domestic comfort, on which the happiness of home depends, for which we must look to the wife alone, such as neatness, order, regularity, without which a perfect home is impossible; yet, sometimes, the very precision of domestic arrangements becomes a tyranny which banishes all comfort. A wife needs strong, practical common sense, a thorough knowledge of the details of household labors, a clear judgment, and a well-governed temper, in order to regulate the domestic machinery, so that it may run smoothly, and without noise. But yet, these qualities should not so far predominate as to bury the spiritual element, and thus render her indifferent to the claims of the soul, which can alone save her from descending into the mere household drudge. Domestic care should not engross her whole time or thoughts.

When we consider that the true object of all this labor for external life is to clothe, feed, warm and protect the body, not for its own sake, but thereby to perfect and develop the immortal soul, and then observe how completely society substitutes the means for the end, or even overlooks the end entirely, how fatal seems the mistake, how monstrous the perversion! It is time for the women who cultivate a conscience to take a strong stand in this matter, to resist the senseless longing after fashionable display and the gratification of personal ambition, which make the influences of home a secondary or neglected consideration. Whatever be the whirl of fashion and folly in which a wise and loving wife and mother finds herself, she will be firm and independent in consulting the welfare of her family, at every cost. Her husband will not be goaded on to harassing perplexities in business, in order to gratify her desire for personal display; and only such society will be sought as makes no demands hostile to the true welfare of the loved ones at home.

The wife may do all this to diffuse a pure, hightoned, refined influence in her home. She may be mistress of all domestic accomplishments, with ready tact, a quick eye, and practised hand to smooth the rough places; and yet the husband may, by positive or negative defects, steal the very life and joy out of that home. His disposition may be fretful; he may scowl or take to sulky silence, or he may, even in attempting to contribute to domestic happiness, intermingle so much of himself as to spoil it all. Against such an influence, what avails all that the wife can do? It is impossible to decide which has the ruling influence in home. Either the husband or the wife can make of it a heaven or hell. Abiding happiness results only from the constant presence and omnipotent sway of a love that seeketh not its own, deeply rooted and sacredly cherished in the hearts of both.

In the true home, as I have thus endeavored to describe it, can childhood be reared with some prospect of a perfect development; for the same tender regard for the wife, which regulates the husband in every other manifestation, will consult her wishes as to the office of maternity. No rude indifference or fierce passion will cast the shadow of a painful association over her head, but the memory of her husband when absent, and the consciousness of his love and devotion to her health and perfection when present, will fill her soul with peace, and encircle her with light. No child will ever come except to bless that home, for, under the guidance of love, conscience and reason, none will ever come except in answer to the deep call of the heart of the wife. The following extract truly and beautifully expresses the feelings of a true wife, whose husband is worthy the trust reposed in him: —

"She knows that the love that encircles her is a mighty power, but no anxiety mingles with this assurance. Her wish will be a *law*. The strong arm on which she leans is a true emblem of the immovable trust, the child-like repose of heart, in which she confides soul and body to the keeping of her husband. He loves her with an impassioned, holy love; and though his physical nature vibrates with the powerful emotions of his soul, yet no fluttering of the heart, no dread of consequences, restrains her tenderness, for she knows that her happiness is dearer to him than his life. She is as calm in her security, as sure of his fidelity, as if God himself were pledged to keep her safe. And the husband *dares* to hold her thus, for he has proved the power of Love to conquer Passion, and compel it into subjection to the mighty ruler of his soul. Well do I say, that in such love as this, no sensuality is mingled, — for *that* acknowledges no sovereign; but Love ever controls its outward symbols. How all-powerful are they to express the emotions of the heart! When the interchange of thought and feeling becomes entire, when there remains but one heart, one will, one yearning desire for perfect union, when words fail to fathom the depths of the heart, then Nature takes up the web of Love, and interweaves it with tissues finer and more beautiful than thought can devise, uttering what could never be otherwise expressed, and leaving a "sweet memory," a holy consecration, that is of itself a sufficient credential of its heavenly origin. To seek a similar significance from passional expressions unprompted by pure love, were as vain as to listen for Æolian melodies without the breath of heaven." *

When the wife finds herself ready and willing to become a mother, then, if God will, a child will come, a messenger of joy and love, of which such parents will be worthy. The cares and responsibilities of watching over the frail being will be mutual; there will be no cold indifference, no impatience at the numerous demands of children, whose existence is an unwelcome burden; but each child will be royally received and entertained, as a messenger from the Most High. Childhood can meet no other appropriate welcome from earthly parents. The common mode of generating and receiving them is a perfect crucifixion of the true spirit of love. It is little enough that the most wise and tender parents can do for their child, but what can we hope for the young being that is created by passion, developed in aversion, and ushered into life by unloving hearts, to struggle through indifference and neglect?

There is a common idea among men, that the cares of infancy are the mother's business; that it is unnatural and effeminate to share these labors; and the husband who actually relieves the mother of this heavy responsibility is remarked among men as being "peculiar," and pointed out among women as a rare specimen of a husband. Why is this so? Is it not his *own*

---

* "The Mountain Home."

child that he holds in his arms, — as near to him as to the mother? And if, in the process of its development, her physical powers have been taxed to the utmost, so that long months, and sometimes years, are necessary to restore her vigor, is it natural or right, that, by day and night, in health or sickness, she should find no help in him whose powers are unexhausted, and whose relation to this little dependent one is as near and dear as hers? The husband who truly loves wife and child will never stop to question what his *duty* is; he will see what the mother's health and comfort require, and he will feel truly manly and dignified in doing whatever will promote them.

In the true home, childhood will thus spring from the heart of Love, and be ushered into an atmosphere of love in its earthly abode. The first action of the young heart is always the love of mother and father. By degrees, the opening mind will learn to respect what it loves, regarding those commands as law which are based upon a wise regard for the child's own welfare, and which are uniformly enforced with a patient firmness which leaves no alternative but obedience. From the foundation of a well-grounded love and respect for earthly parents, it is easy to carry the young thought to the highest conception of Love and Power. God will be to the child no abstract idea, afar off in the clouds, awfully great and severe; but a being of winning attractions, because he wears the aspect of a loving father — one of the dearest names on earth.

Parents must first be what they wish their children

to become; for the power of imitation is stronger than any other in youth. Gentle, unselfish, noble-minded parents, will fashion children after their own model, unless, by disregarding some law of Nature, they prevent her from executing her perfect work; as when a mother is overburdened by too rapid reproduction, and is obliged to confide to the ignorance of the nursery-maid, the care of those early days, in which the child receives an ineffaceable impression. She should never be compelled to that resort. Her body and mind require at least three years of rest after each birth. In that time, she can devote herself to the formation of those habits that will save her years of conflict in after life.

The difference between the best and worst domestic influences for childhood, consists in the aims which are presented to the young mind. Emulation, personal ambition, *self*, in some form or other, is, in most cases, the stimulus under which the best years of youth are wasted, and time and money lost. Instead of this, a constant reference to what is right, without regard to consequences, a reverential obedience to the voice of conscience in the smallest as in the greatest affairs of life, a generous acknowledgment of those who deserve distinction, a delicate regard for the welfare of others, — these are the qualities which will build up a character of moral greatness and of social attractiveness which the world needs, but too seldom shows.

Such training will give us young men firm and yet tender-hearted, whose taste instinctively shuns what is low and vulgar, and hence saves them from the temptations which might otherwise prove fatal; inflexible in integrity, heroic to oppose the wrong, and in whose inmost heart the dear affections of home will constitute the noblest, loveliest, most saving influences of this life. Or, if a daughter has been blessed with such domestic training, she will become the modest maiden, whose heart is full of womanly affection, whose intellect is trained to discern the realities from the shows of life, strong in her own self-respect, and holding a high-toned companionship with her brothers and their mates. If she be highly accomplished, as she may be with all this, by intercourse with books and the finest living minds of her time, and the refinements of music and art, her being will still be pervaded with a power, residing in her own uncorrupted nature, which will leave no room for the follies of self-conceit, and will assert itself in a native dignity, a wise sincerity, which will win the favor she neither seeks nor shuns.

Thus, with a rapid touch, I have defined the outlines of what I would have our home to be. I have written from a full heart, feeling that I have not penned a word which is beyond the possibility of being realized by us; for we already possess the all-important basis — a pure, imperishable love.

> " Home's not merely four square walls,
>     Though with pictures hung and gilded;
> Home is where affection calls,
>     Filled with shrines the heart hath builded!
> Home! — go watch the faithful dove,
>     Sailing in the heaven above us!
> Home is where there's one to love!
>     Home is where there's one to love us!

> "Home's not merely roof and room,
>   It needs something to endear it;
> Home is where the heart can bloom,
>   Where there's some kind lip to cheer it!
> What is home with none to meet,
>   None to welcome, none to greet us?
> Home is sweet, and only sweet,
>   Where there's one we love to meet us!"

Thus far, love has rendered our united life all we can ask or hope of happiness on earth. We have taken a deep draught of the living water, of which none who ever drinks can thirst again. Even if we meet uncongenial elements in life, we shall be fortified against them by these blessed realities; we will carry the sweet harmony of our own hearts into the harsh jargon of life's discord and sin.

O, blessed Love! — thrice blessed Home! If either of us be left to walk alone in the last dreary hours of life, your "sweet memories" will be our dearest earthly treasure, and the surest pledge of an eternal reunion, where death cannot come. If a kinder fate shall permit us to enter hand in hand upon the great realities of the future, we know that eternity can but consecrate and perfect the union now begun; and we will pray that the rich legacy of love which we leave to our child may be as sacredly preserved as it has been tenderly bestowed.

From the heart of love, thy

NINA.

# APPENDIX.

## THE SEXUAL ELEMENT.

### ITS NATURAL USE — ITS ABUSE.

THE following is an abstract of remarks, by L. DESLANDES, M.D., Member of the Royal Academy of Medicine at Paris, on Manhood. Speaking of the abuses of the sexual element, and of diseases and sufferings resulting from them, he says, in substance : —

"The bad effects of such abuses can be truly estimated only by a careful study of the reproductive system, in its relations with other organs, and considering the influence it exercises upon them. In this way, alone, can we arrive at a correct knowledge of the maladies and dangers of all kinds which attend the abuses of this element. What relation does it hold to the brain, the stomach, the liver, the lungs, &c.? Can its natural expenditure do much injury to the general system?

"The injury which results from the abuse of this element to the rest of the body, must be in an exact ratio with its influence when not abused. This element may be considered in two aspects: as it is *retained* in the system, and as it is *expended*.

"*Its influence when retained in the system.* This can be truly determined only by considering the conditions of those who, by any means, have been deprived of the power of secreting it. Men seldom understand how much of their power to enjoy life depends on the presence of this element in their physical organism. If they did, they could never expend it as they do. They would know that, as a mere source of permanent happiness, the retention of it in the system is of infinitely more importance than its expenditure.

"Consider the man who is born imbecile in this particular. His body and soul have been developed without the presence of the sexual element. Compare him with other men, and see in what he is deficient. His physical, intellectual and moral relations will all be deficient, so far as they depend on this element. By such a comparison, we may learn its powers, and the great difference between a man in whose development it has assisted, and one in whose growth it has taken no part. In the latter, the physical man is deficient in stature, in symmetry, in strength and activity. All the tissues are less developed; and some, not at all. This element, then, has a powerful effect on *nutrition;* for when it is wanting, the growth is always defective. The organism of the man who is deficient in the sexual element is necessarily imperfect. That which should have appeared at the period of puberty, not being seen, other parts of the system acquire but a partial growth. The study of these facts demonstrates the extent of the derangement that may result from sexual abuse; for that element which is abused by the libertine takes a most active part in the internal economy of all our tissues, and stamps them with the seal of vitality, of which those who are deprived of it ever remain destitute.

"Consider, also, the two in the various relations of life. Who would look to the man, destitute of the reproductive power, for thought, activity and sensibility? He is inactive, indifferent, apathetic, and liable to be excited to fear or anger by the least cause. He is pusillanimous; he cannot be gay, but is morose, and burdensome to himself and others. He is destitute of the feelings which attach man to man in unselfish friendships, and is incapable of love and devotion. He vegetates for himself; is an egotist; and if he has sentiments, they are generally those of envy, hatred and revenge, or, in some way, repulsive. He repels every body, and is repelled by all. The soul of him, who is destitute of this element, remains or becomes a dreary waste; incapable of vigorous and manly thoughts, and of generous, warm and noble sentiments. He cannot conceive nor execute any thing great.

"Such is the man destitute of the sexual element. His intellect, his heart, his whole soul, as well as his body, are mutilated. It is certain, then, that the development of the body and soul is essentially connected with this. Deprive a child of an arm or leg, and he will continue to develop in all other directions, as if no injury had been done him; but take away this element, and his entire nature must ever bear the marks of the injury. It is with this power that the sensualist, whether in legal marriage or out of it, by solitary indulgence or otherwise, trifles without hesitation or moderation. Can it be necessary to pursue this, to show that the abuse of this element is most dangerous to the entire man?

"To the influence of this element on the other parts of the system, the sexes owe their peculiar differences. Their organization, influenced by the difference in the sexual element, presents a different mode of existence, action and sensation. The sexual characteristics, but slightly marked at birth, become distinct as the sexual organs develop themselves. To mutilate the sexual nature of the male or female, prevents the regular development, and alters the special distinction of sex. We have seen that such an abuse renders man effeminate; we will add, that it renders the female more masculine, and gives her characteristics which naturally belong to the male.

"But it is especially before and during puberty that the sexual nature deserves most serious attention; for it is then it has most power over the general economy of life. This influence commences with the existence of this element, and increases as it does. Thus, the tastes, characters, inclinations, and generally, all which distinguishes the sexes in a moral and physical point of view, are marked from infancy. The influence of this element commences with life, but does not attain its fulness until puberty. At this period, which, in our climate, commences from 12 to 14 in females, and from 14 to 16 in males, this element has the most power over the general system. At this period, its development is more sudden, and its power more perceptible. At no period does the body grow so rapidly as during puberty. The body responds, in all its functions, like an echo, to all that takes place in the reproductive system.

"But the moral susceptibility is still more affected than that of the physical. The mind, directed and controlled by the most vivid, most varied and most transient impressions, takes up and lays aside the most opposite opinions, and adopts the wildest and most hazardous enterprises. This disposition has existed to so great a degree as even to constitute a kind of monomania. But the mental state, resulting from puberty, is characterized particularly by the readiness with which one shares the affections of others, partakes of their sympathies, and sympathises with them. This is the moment of generous ideas; it is the period of illusions. How much experience ought not the mind to gain, when passing through this passional tempest? It is not surprising to find cold hearts and weak minds among those in whom the sexual nature is abused. Being deprived of that element, which, at puberty, gave so marked an impulse to the body and soul, they do not feel its power: the most active and powerful of all moral excitants is wanting. Judge from this of its power; and yet it is this stimulant which the licensed, as well as the unlicensed sensualist, so abuses.

"We state, then, as a positive truth, that the reproductive element modifies extremely the action and sensation of the entire system, and modifies it in proportion as it is itself excited. This fact admitted, the question whether sexual abuse can or cannot do injury, is resolved. Life is so mysterious, and coition is so transient, that what takes place in the tissues during the excitement is concealed from view ; but we may be certain that something takes place in them ; that some disturbance occurs, and that the disturbance is greater during the act, than in the preceding states. This act exerts more influence than it appears to exert, as it deeply affects all parts of the organization. The retention of this element in the system, in a state of perfect repose, produces a powerful influence on the whole man. When excited and not expended, the effect is great, though not so injurious. The whole body feels the influence, and experiences a kind of febrile agitation. All the secretions undergo great modifications. The function of nutrition is strikingly modified.

"But the most striking fact connected with this state of excitement, is the development of a special, sexual sense. We shall not attempt to describe it. We may ask what it requires. As hunger impels to eat and thirst to drink, so this sense impels to sexual intercourse. It is the bond which brings the two sexes towards each other, which unites them, and which makes a perfect individual of the male and female. This sense may be only feebly excited, and then it has but a moderate power. But when it is excited, the chain with which it binds the will is of great power. The male dreams of the female, the latter of the male. One of the opposite sex is ever present to the imagination. Individuals and forms, which, at other times, appear by no means remarkable, now excite admiration. Riches and honor are no longer esteemed, and even life itself is considered not worth possessing, without the presence and companionship of one of the opposite sex. All necessities disappear before this one. Hunger and thirst are no longer felt. It is, in fact, a state of wild delirium. All the senses are concentrated in one ; it commands them, and receives from them all the illusions which they present to it. Such is the power of this element, when retained in the system. What, then, must result from its abuse, whether the unnatural expenditure be with one or more in legal marriage, or out of it, or whether it be in solitude ? "

# SEX, MARRIAGE AND SOCIETY

An Arno Press Collection

Abortion in Nineteenth-Century America. 1974

Aristotle, **The Works of Aristotle, The Famous Philosopher.** In Four Parts. With a New Introduction by Charles Rosenberg and Carroll Smith-Rosenberg. 1813

Beale, Lionel S., **Our Morality and the Moral Question:** Chiefly from the Medical Side. 1887

Bergeret, L. F. E., **The Preventive Obstacle,** Or Conjugal Onanism. 1870

**Birth Control and Family Planning in Nineteenth-Century America.** 1974

[Cooke, Nicholas Francis] **Satan in Society.** By a Physician. 1876

Duffey, E[liza] B., **The Relations of the Sexes.** 1876

Duffey, E[liza] B., **What Women Should Know:** A Woman's Book About Women; Containing Practical Information for Wives and Mothers. 1873

Ellis, Havelock, **Man and Woman:** A Study of Human Secondary Sexual Characters. 1904

Evans, Elizabeth Edson. **The Abuse of Maternity.** 1875

**Fertility Controlled!** The British Argument for Family Limitation. 1974

Gardner, Augustus K., **Conjugal Sins Against the Laws of Life and Health and Their Effects Upon the Father, Mother, and Child.** 1870

Graham, Sylvester, **A Lecture to Young Men.** 1834

Hammond, William A., **Sexual Impotence in the Male and Female.** 1887

Hersey, Thomas. **The Midwife's Practical Directory; Or, Woman's Confidential Friend.** 1836

Hollick, Frederick. **The Marriage Guide,** Or Natural History of Generation. 1850

Howe, Joseph W., **Excessive Venery, Masturbation and Continence.** 1887

Ingersoll, A. J., **In Health.** 1899

Jackson, James C., **The Sexual Organism, and Its Healthful Management.** 1861

Kellogg, J. H., **Plain Facts for Old and Young:** Embracing the Natural History and Hygiene of Organic Life. 1888

Lewis, Dio, **Chastity; Or, Our Secret Sins.** 1874

**The Male-Midwife and the Female Doctor:** The Gynecology Controversy in Nineteenth-Century America. 1974

Mauriceau, A. M., **The Married Woman's Private Medical Companion.** 1847

Miller, George N[oyes], **The Strike of a Sex and Zugassent's Discovery,** Or After the Sex Struck. [1905]

**A Proper Bostonian on Sex and Birth Control.** 1974

**The Prostitute and the Social Reformer:** Commercial Vice in the Progressive Era. 1974

Ryan, Michael, **The Philosophy of Marriage, in its Social, Moral, and Physical Relations.** 1839

**The Secret Vice Exposed!** Some Arguments Against Masturbation. 1974

**Sex and Science:** Phrenological Reflections on Sex and Marriage in Nineteenth-Century America. 1974

**Sex for the Common Man:** Nineteenth-Century Marriage Manuals. 1974

**Sexual Indulgence and Denial:** Variations on Continence. 1974

Storer, Horatio R. and Franklin Fiske Heard, **Criminal Abortion:** Its Nature, Its Evidence, and Its Law. 1868

Trall, R. T., **Sexual Physiology:** A Scientific and Popular Exposition of the Fundamental Problems in Sociology. 1881

Walling, William H. **Sexology.** 1904

Wright, Henry C., **Marriage and Parentage:** Or, the Reproductive Element in Man, As a Means to His Elevation and Happiness. 1855